WILLIAM PENN *the* POLITICIAN

His Relations with the English Government

William Penn at age fifty-two, as painted by Francis Place in 1696.
Reproduced by courtesy of the Historical Society of Pennsylvania.

WILLIAM PENN
the POLITICIAN

His Relations with the
English Government

JOSEPH E. ILLICK

CORNELL UNIVERSITY PRESS
Ithaca, New York

For Toni

Preface

THERE are many biographies of William Penn, all focusing primarily on his association with the Society of Friends and his prominent role in the cause of religious toleration. Even the founding of Pennsylvania has usually been viewed from this angle. But the Quaker's career as a politician has never received adequate notice. From this perspective, Penn assumes an equally important stature. His relations with the English government were of great significance to him, to Pennsylvania, and sometimes to the other proprietary and corporate colonies along the Atlantic seaboard in North America.

Penn's political career, though it involved many setbacks and ended in personal tragedy, was a success in terms of his initial intentions. He managed to establish a relatively autonomous proprietary colony when the home government's strategy was to gain a firmer control over the plantations. He was able to protect a province whose religious and political principles were strikingly different from those of Restoration England, and whose inhabitants acted independently of—and sometimes in opposition to—

the English government. It is my contention that Penn's success in establishing and protecting Pennsylvania was largely due to his influence with prominent statesmen.

To emphasize the importance of Penn's connections not only provides a fresh and useful approach to his career, but also goes a long way toward explaining the surprising ability of the private colonies to resist the centralizing tendencies of the home government, since Penn served as the leader of the group of proprietors and colonial agents who represented these colonies in England.

In his dealings with the government of Pennsylvania Penn showed less virtuosity as a politician, and the ironical relationship between provincial failure and imperial success is also treated in this book.

I began this study while on an Ames Fellowship at the University of Pennsylvania. I have since received money for research and typing costs from Kalamazoo College, Kalamazoo, Michigan; Lafayette College, Easton, Pennsylvania; and San Francisco State College, San Francisco, California. I am in grateful debt to all these institutions.

I should also like to express my thanks to the Trustees of the Albert Cook Myers Collection for granting me access to those papers, and particularly to Bart Anderson, who always added to the pleasure of my visits to the Chester County (Pa.) Historical Society where the Myers Collection is deposited. I appreciate the aid given me by the staff in the Manuscripts Division at the Historical Society of Pennsylvania.

I am grateful to Mary Maples Dunn of Bryn Mawr College and Leonidas Dodson of the University of Pennsylvania for commenting on my manuscript in its earlier stages. Richard S. Dunn, who suggested this project to me in the first place, and who was constantly available for consultation on its progress and alternately encouraged and discouraged me to my own best advantage, deserves considerable credit for the good features of this book. Finally, I wish to thank the editorial staff at Cornell University Press for their help and suggestions.

The book is dedicated to my wife, who, while never ceasing to be intellectually critical of my work, has had the good sense not to become emotionally entangled in it.

Throughout I have capitalized the names of institutions in England and used lower-case letters for comparable institutions in the plantations. The word "Council," for example, means the Privy Council of England, not the provincial council of Pennsylvania.

I have made a few minor changes in spelling when quoting from primary sources. But I have not attempted to redress the great liberties taken by some editors who have published primary material which I have quoted. This explains why Penn seems to express himself archaically at one point and in modern fashion at another.

I have used the following abbreviations:

ACM   Albert Cook Myers Collection of William Penn Papers

BTJ   *Board of Trade, Journals*

BTPG   *Board of Trade, Plantations General*

BTPr.   *Board of Trade, Proprietaries*

CSP   *Calendar of State Papers, Colonial Series, America and the West Indies*

DAB   *Dictionary of American Biography*

DNB   *Dictionary of National Biography*

HMC   Historical Manuscripts Commission

HSP   Historical Society of Pennsylvania

PMHB   *Pennsylvania Magazine of History and Biography*

JOSEPH E. ILLICK

San Francisco, California
April, 1965

Contents

CHAPTER I

Creative Statesman

(1644–1681)

IN the spring of 1665 Sir William Penn received an enthusiastic note from his son:

At my arrival at Harwich...I took post for London....I hasted to Whitehall, where, not finding the King up, I presented myself to my Lord of Arlington and Colonel Ashburnham. At his majesty's knocking, he was informed there was an express from the Duke; at which, earnestly skipping out of his bed, he came only in his gown and slippers; who, when he saw me, said, "Oh, is't you? How is Sir William?"[1]

Young William Penn's intimacy with Charles II, his brother James, Duke of York, and the courtiers gathered around the Stuart throne was to prove extremely useful to him in the future. For Admiral Penn's son became the leader of a despised sect in a nation supercharged with

[1]WP to Sir William Penn, 6 May 1665, in Samuel M. Janney, *The Life of William Penn* (6th ed., rev.; Philadelphia, 1882), p. 26. My account of Penn's early life is based on *ibid.*, pp. 1–107, and on Catherine O. Peare, *William Penn* (Philadelphia and New York, 1957), pp. 1–147.

1

religious animosities, and he gained renown as a liberal political theorist during a reign which aimed to restore the royal prerogative of the past. He might have hoped at best for a grudging tolerance by the Crown, especially with regard to his political activities; he could have expected permanent jailing or execution. Instead, Penn was able to use his court connections to relieve Quakers from persecution in England and to further their interests in New Jersey. At the same time he was an active figure in the newly formed Whig party, whose hostility to royal power was undisguised. Immediately thereafter he successfully prevailed upon the Crown for a large grant of land and power in America, where he intended to put into effect his dual theories of religious and political liberty—theories which were strikingly different from Stuart principle and practice. Furthermore, Penn did not do this at a time when the Crown was known for its largess in colonial affairs. On the contrary, the years of his initial activity in America were also years of increasing economic and political supervision of the colonies by the home government.

Under these circumstances, Penn's achievement was remarkable. But while the nature of his success is apparent, the means have remained obscure. To examine not only the nature of Penn's success but also the means by which he achieved it is the purpose of this book.

Although Penn was born into the Anglican royalist tradition, he rejected both its religious philosophy and its political theory. The repudiation of Anglicanism came first. At the age of ten he had a religious experience in a moment of solitude. Two years later he listened to Thomas Loe, one of the first Quaker itinerants, and was moved to tears. At Oxford, which he entered at the age of fifteen,

Penn was influenced by Dr. John Owen, former dean of Christ Church and a well-known Puritan preacher. Consequently, he and others like him refused to wear the surplice and made a point of missing chapel. The result, even for the son of Sir William Penn, was expulsion. His angered father sent him abroad in an attempt to divert him from his religious foolishness by immersing him in the manners and mores of the Continent. But young William thwarted this effort, forsaking the gaiety of Paris for the piety of the Huguenot south country.

The lad returned to England unreformed, and so his father put him about worldly pursuits. Reading law at Lincoln's Inn was cut short by the London plague. Soon, however, Penn was off to Ireland to attend his father's estates. Shortly thereafter he received recognition in England for the part he played in helping to quell a mutiny of troops near Dublin, and for a time the future Quaker thought he would like to be a soldier.[2] In fact, this was the prelude to a period of religious militancy. Penn again heard Thomas Loe preach; he stood up, wept, but found he could not utter a word. From this deeply felt experience stemmed his association with the Society of Friends, a group reviled by its contemporaries. At this time it was composed of humble folk; the young aristocrat was easily identifiable among them.

His attendance at Quaker meetings led to imprisonment and gave him his first taste of martyrdom. It also brought a letter from his father commanding him to return to England. Young William's sense of filial responsibility was sufficient to make him obey; indeed, the ties to his father

[2]Surprisingly enough, Sir William Penn was not favorable to this plan. "I wish your youthful desires mayn't outrun your discretion," he wrote to his son (17 July 1666, in Peare, *Penn,* p. 54).

3

and the world the admiral represented were too strong ever to be severed.[3] He did not forsake the Quaker cause, however, but tried to use the connections he had gained through his father's position to obtain relief for persecuted Friends. Twice in 1668 he visited Whitehall, once speaking with the Duke of Buckingham and another time with Sir Henry Berwick, a secretary of state.[4] It was common knowledge in court circles that young William Penn was a Quaker.

In November, 1668, Penn published the first of his many exegetic pamphlets. *The Sandy Foundation Shaken,* although aimed at the Presbyterians, was anathema to the Church of England as well. By broadcasting his unorthodox opinions to the British public, the young Quaker could only offend a government whose spiritual authority rested in a national church. Within the month a warrant was issued for his arrest, and he was banished to the Tower. The cause for his imprisonment and not the custody itself—Sir William had twice been in the Tower—was the source of social stigma. Yet such was his father's influence with the Crown that Charles II proffered young William release if he would renounce what he had written. From the King's point of view this was a munificent offer. It reflected the high regard in which Sir William Penn was held. It is likely, too, that Charles II had not forgotten the eulogy young William had written while at Oxford.

[3]The Quaker whom Penn asked to accompany him to England in order to give him strength to meet his father was Josiah Coale, whose family background was every bit as respectable as Penn's. George Fox, the founder of the Society of Friends, had simply turned his back on his family when it attempted to interfere with his mission.

[4]"Fragments of an Apology for Himself," in HSP, *Memoirs* (14 vols.; Philadelphia, 1826–1895), III, pt. 2, 238.

It was dedicated to the Duke of Gloucester, the second of the King's brothers, who had died suddenly of smallpox.[5]

Penn refused the King's offer, an audacious act. Nor would he give in to Dr. Stillingfleet, later Bishop of Worcester, who as the King's messenger tried to change the young Quaker's mind. But Penn—and this was one of the secrets of his success—was never so zealous as to refuse compromise. Although unwilling to change his position, he was anxious to explain it carefully—for he honestly felt he had been misunderstood. He sent his explanation to the Earl of Arlington, principal secretary of state, and he published it as *Innocency with Her Open Face. Presented by way of Apology for the Book Entitled, The Sandy Foundation Shaken.* That such action won him his freedom is a further commentary on the value of his connections.

Again young William was sent by his father to Ireland, and again this failed to remove him from religious—and, inevitably, political—controversy. It was merely the exchange of one scene of conflict for another. As the son of a great landowner, Penn was able to use his influence for the release of persecuted Friends. In August, 1670, he returned to England. Here he found that a second Conventicle Act, more stringent than the first, had been passed in his absence. The new restraint upon religious meetings was taken as the signal for a more intensive campaign against the sects. Penn took up the challenge and preached publicly in London, although he knew that in so doing he was inviting arrest. As was foreseen, he and one of his colleagues, William Mead, were taken into custody and brought before the Lord Mayor for trial.

[5]This eulogy is reprinted in Thomas Clarkson, *Memoirs of the Private and Public Life of William Penn* (2 vols.; London, 1813), I, 9.

In English history this trial has great legal significance, because after the jury was fined and imprisoned for delivering a verdict favorable to Penn and contrary to the command of the Mayor, the Chief Justice declared such action highly illegal. This verdict has been viewed as a major step toward the freedom of the jury. In the career of William Penn the trial had a different significance. The young Quaker had already spoken against the principle of religious uniformity. "What if I differ from some religious apprehensions?" he had written to the Earl of Arlington while he was in the Tower. "Am I therefore incompatible with human societies? Shall it not be remembered with what success kingdoms and commonwealths have lived under the balance of divers parties?"[6] But the religious policy of the realm *was* uniformity, a principle which Penn had challenged not only by word but by deed. At his trial, he dwelled on the theme that the fundamental rights of Englishmen were broken by such measures as were responsible for his being hauled into court.[7]

This emphasis recalled the rallying cry of Hampden and Pym, and surely Charles II must have shuddered at the memory. Penn's dangerous religious beliefs were leading him further and further into the equally hazardous region of political debate.[8]

He was, of course, imprisoned again. But his father was allowed to bail him out privately. Not only was the young Quaker treated leniently, but the admiral, now on his deathbed, was able to obtain a promise from the

[6] Janney, *Penn,* p. 58.

[7] A record of this trial is in *ibid.,* pp. 67–81.

[8] This is not to say that Penn's religious principles formed the sole base of his political philosophy. For the sources of the latter see Mary Maples, "William Penn, Classical Republican," *PMHB,* LXXXI (1957), 138–156.

Stuart brothers that they would continue to bestow their favor upon his wayward son. The Duke of York was of the Roman persuasion, and Charles II may well have been a crypto-Catholic, but these facts do not necessarily explain the favor shown Penn, a fellow sufferer at the hands of Anglicanism. Penn's *A Seasonable Caveat against Popery* (written in 1670, the year of his father's death), while not calculated to incense public opinion against Catholics, was not friendly to them either. The more probable explanation of the Stuarts' promise to Admiral Penn was their inability to deny the request of a dying man; the remarkable fact about this promise was that it was faithfully honored.

But Penn felt no obligation to change his ways as a result of the Stuart vow to his father. Soon after the admiral's death he was again imprisoned for public preaching, this time for six months. During this period he was able to complete six tracts, all on the same subject. The most famous of them was *The Great Case of Liberty of Conscience Once More Briefly Debated and Defended by the Authority of Reason, Scripture, and Antiquity.* Again he crossed the thin line which divided religious from political debate in seventeenth-century England, and again his nonconformist, republican point of view was at odds with the Anglican, royalist tradition.[9]

Released from prison in 1671, Penn embarked with other Quakers on a missionary sojourn to the Continent. He returned to marry Gulielma Springett in April, 1672. Marriage itself may be a maturing experience; the tribulation that followed in the wake of Penn's union certainly was. Of the four children born to Guli Penn in these years,

[9] *The Select Works of William Penn* (3rd ed., 5 vols.; London, 1782), III, 1–51.

only one lived past infancy. Richard Penn, younger brother of the Quaker leader, died in 1673 at the age of eighteen. During this period William Penn was in semiretirement. The first five years of his marriage were, as one of his biographers has put it, "a kind of interim between his service as a young martyr and his role as a politico-religious leader in creating Quaker colonies in America."[10] His youthful exuberance gave way to a more disciplined zeal. Although he remained a staunch defender of religious toleration, he no longer embarrassed his royal friends by publicly violating the law in order to challenge its validity.

Penn did not completely abdicate his role as militant Quaker during the early years of his marriage, however. When George Fox was imprisoned in 1673—"the cause worshipping God after another manner than that of the Church of England"—Penn again traveled to Whitehall, where he had not been in five years. There is no record that young Penn and James Stuart had met any other time than in the admiral's presence in 1665, although they were well known to each other by reputation. In 1673 they were reunited, and a close friendship began. This relationship was primarily responsible for the Stuarts' fidelity to their vow to the admiral concerning his son. No proof survives of intimacy between Charles II and William Penn, but the fact that James exerted considerable influence over his brother after 1669 made it unnecessary for Penn to be near to the King.[11]

The mutual attraction between the Duke of York and William Penn, who was eleven years the Duke's junior, is not easily explained. The two men had dissimilar backgrounds and tastes, although they had in common a strong

[10]Peare, *Penn,* p. 148.
[11]F. C. Turner, *James II* (New York, 1948), pp. 91–94.

8

feeling for religion. Like Penn, James had had a conversion experience; at the same time, and even more rapidly than Penn had emerged as a Quaker leader, he gained public prominence. The result—"an entire change...in the character of James"—came in 1668, the year in which Penn was first imprisoned. James became more serious in outlook, more aware of his political responsibilities, and less licentious in his private life.[12] But while the turn of affairs in 1668 lent a new gravity to both men's lives, and while Penn was noticeably sobered by events in the early 1670's, in other ways they remained unalike. Politically, James was entirely opposed to the existence of Parliament concurrently with the monarchy; Penn at this time was a strong supporter of the legislative power.[13] James' moderation in his private life simply meant that he was temporarily content with one mistress; Penn's chastity before marriage and his fidelity and devotion to his wife afterward have never been questioned.

Yet the issue of religion was sufficiently powerful to draw the Catholic duke and the Quaker leader together. James, who had recently lost control of the Admiralty as a result of the Test Act of March, 1673, assured Penn that "he was against all Persecution for the sake of Religion." As Penn recalled the scene, the Duke "was pleased to take a very particular notice of me, both for the relation my Father

[12]*Ibid.*, p. 87.
[13]*Ibid.*, pp. 122, 127. Penn had written concerning his trial with William Mead in September, 1670: "All the various kinds or models of government that are in the world, stand either upon will and power, or condition and contract; the first rule by men; the second, by laws. It is our happiness to be born under such a constitution, as is most abhorrent in itself of all arbitrary government; and which is, and ever has been, most choice and careful of her laws, by which all right is preserved" (*Works of WP*, I, 112).

had had to his service in the Navy, and the care he had promised him to show in my regard upon all occasions. That he wondered I had not been with him, and that whenever I had any business thither, he would order that I should have access."[14] Over the course of the next decade and a half, the relationship with James Stuart would prove most fruitful to William Penn. James' connection with New Jersey, formerly an appendage of New York, and his apparent ownership of the territory which was to become Pennsylvania were factors of the greatest value to the Quaker leader in his colonial ventures. When the younger Stuart became king, he was in an excellent position not only to protect Penn's possessions in the New World, but also to give relief to the Quakers in England. Ultimately, this friendship worked to Penn's disadvantage. He became identified with the reign of James II and, temporarily, suffered the same unhappy fate. But for the present the alliance was useful.

Even at the earliest stage of their relationship, however, Penn was taking James' pronouncements on toleration too literally, failing to compare them to Stuart practice. The problem of religious persecution always weighed heavily on Penn. He, like most of his fellow Quakers, had been persecuted for his beliefs. Without forsaking these beliefs, he rejected martyrdom for two reasons: his tribulations in the early 1670's and the realization that he could use his court connections to further his religious cause. Undoubtedly, Penn played a major part in convincing Quakers of the wisdom of resisting, rather than accepting, affliction. In 1675 the Society of Friends decided that it was ethical to combat persecution by laying detailed accounts of their

[14]HSP, *Memoirs*, III, pt. 2, 240–242.

10

suffering before the King and Parliament and to seek redress through "such means as consist with the unity of Friends and their own peace and satisfaction." The Meeting for Sufferings was instituted, to be attended by Quakers who would and could act as effectively as possible within these limits. Until 1681, when he left for Pennsylvania, Penn directed the Meeting's parliamentary activity. It was usually he who drafted addresses to the King and Council and who led delegations of Quakers to wait on the monarch.[15]

While the Stuarts at least gave the appearance of being sympathetic to the young Quaker's battle against religious persecution, they had not the slightest fondness for his political principles. Party platforms, if not organized parties themselves, were being molded in the heat of political controversy which marked the late 1670's, and William Penn had cast his lot with the Whigs. In 1679 he published a pamphlet, *England's Great Interest in the Choice of This New Parliament,* which has been called "one of the first clear statements of party doctrine put before the English electorate."[16] Penn was not satisfied merely to define the issues. He worked diligently for the candidacy of Algernon Sidney, who had already sat in the Long Parliament and, having returned to England after a forced exile in the early years of the Restoration, was

[15]Arnold Lloyd, *Quaker Social History, 1669–1738* (New York, 1950), pp. 11–12, 89–90. Penn's activities from 1677 to 1681 are briefly outlined in this book.

[16]David Ogg, *England in the Reign of Charles II* (2 vols.; Oxford, 1955–1956), II, 586. The French ambassador, Barillon, informed Louis XIV that Penn was one of the leaders of a political party which had its strength in London. The letter, dated 5 December 1680, appears in John Dalrymple, *Memoirs of Great Britain and Ireland* (3 vols.; London, 1790), III, 287.

anxious to get back into politics. Sidney had not only taken up arms against Charles II but had also served as one of the commissioners in that unfortunate monarch's trial. His election to Parliament was strongly opposed by the Court in 1679, and his victory after several questionable defeats was declared void. Yet in the face of this hostility, Penn openly endorsed Sidney and, after the first defeat, offered to use his influence with highly placed men "in reversing this business."[17] In theory Penn, who advocated limited monarchy, was not as radical as Sidney, who believed a republic to be the ideal form of government.[18] But they agreed on many political principles, and in any case, Penn's open league with Sidney was the most striking feature of their relationship. He had entered politics in the same way that he had embraced religion: with an enthusiasm which took little heed of the official point of view.[19]

William Penn's efforts in the late 1670's were not sufficient to secure either religious toleration or the acceptance of Whig policies in England. Perhaps it would not have occurred to him to attempt the establishment of these principles elsewhere had his attention not been forced on affairs in America. It was fortunate and not entirely fortuitous that Penn became involved in an area in which the Duke of York had a stake.

In 1664, James had been granted a charter for the region then occupied by the Dutch in North America, but soon

[17]*DNB,* XVIII, 202–210; Janney, *Penn,* pp. 153–156.
[18]Maples, "William Penn," p. 151.
[19]Penn did not follow his fellow Whigs in demanding a Protestant succession, an indication that he knew the value of his association with James Stuart (*ibid.,* p. 149).

to be captured by the English. It was specified that all land from the west side of the Connecticut River to the east side of Delaware Bay would be part of the projected ducal proprietary.[20] A few months after he got this territory, James transferred the region between the Hudson and Delaware Rivers—soon to be named New Jersey—to John, Lord Berkeley, and Sir George Carteret. Only the land, and not the powers of government, was released, although Berkeley and Carteret were not fully aware of this limitation.[21]

New York was reconquered by the Dutch in 1673 and returned to England at the end of the war, obliging the Duke to give Berkeley and Carteret another deed for New Jersey. Before this was done, however, Berkeley sold his proprietary rights to two Quakers, Edward Byllinge and John Fenwick.[22] Because of this complication, the Duke released only the upper half of the area (East New Jersey to Carteret, under the same terms as previously) and took no action regarding the lower half. It was at this point that William Penn appeared on the scene.

Penn was not called in to settle matters with the Duke of York. Rather, a quarrel had arisen between Fenwick and Byllinge; in order to settle the dispute out of court, as Friends were wont to do, Penn was asked to arbitrate.

[20]F. N. Thorpe, *The Federal and State Constitutions, Colonial Charters, and Other Organic Laws* (7 vols.; Washington, D. C., 1909), 1637–1640. The wording of the charter of 1674 was virtually the same as that of 1664 with respect to boundaries.

[21]C. M. Andrews, *The Colonial Period of American History* (4 vols.; New Haven, 1934–1938), III, 138–140.

[22]*Ibid.*, p. 151. Fenwick was actually Byllinge's agent. Both got involved in the New Jersey venture with the hope of quick financial returns (J. E. Pomfret, *The Province of West New Jersey, 1609–1702* [Princeton, 1956], p. 66).

Furthermore, Byllinge went into bankruptcy, and Penn joined two of his creditors as a trustee for him in West New Jersey.[23] Once involved in the affairs of West New Jersey, Penn again proved the value of his connection with the Duke. His first move was to obtain a formal division of territory between East and West New Jersey. This was accomplished, according to Penn, "after no little labor, trouble, and cost."[24] He and Robert Barclay, the noted Scottish Friend and apologist, convinced James that such a division was necessary to West New Jersey's security.[25]

Little evidence survives surrounding this transaction between the Duke of York and William Penn. One thing is certain, however: Penn made no promises which would bind West New Jersey to the authoritarian political institutions which ruled New York. On the contrary, the plan of government for West New Jersey drawn up by Penn and Byllinge—the "Laws, Concessions, and Agreements" of March 3, 1676/77—has been characterized as broad and liberal, yet appropriate and practical. "This noteworthy document provided for entire liberty of conscience, security from illegal arrest, trial by jury, legal guaranty of indi-

[23]Gawen Lawrie and Nicholas Lucas were the other two trustees (*ibid.,* pp. 67–69). Fenwick came into possession of one-tenth of West Jersey before the dispute was settled, thus intensifying the chaotic state of affairs in that colony.

[24]*Ibid.,* pp. 73–74; Andrews, *Colonial Period,* III, 153.

[25]Soon after the deed was issued, Barclay wrote to Penn from London: "I have been constantly following my business since [I last saw thee] and have had occassione to be twice with the Duke since thou art gone. I have found him generous in keeping his bond and I am like to effectuate something by his means. Thy friend Ashtone [an old acquaintance of Penn's whose friendship was renewed simultaneously with James' in 1673] proved wonderful serviceable to me for which I expect thou wilt thank him: being at present in great haist I have not time to enlarge" (20 July 1676, in HSP, Penn-Forbes collection, II, 15. On Ashton see *DNB, I,* 649–650).

vidual rights, complete control of taxation by the...
voters...and above all else the calling of a general assembly, the members of which were to be either proprietors or
freeholders, and the voters, balloting secretly, were to consist of the entire body of proprietors, freeholders, and inhabitants residing in the province."[26] While liberty of
conscience was guaranteed to persons of any religion in
New York as well as West New Jersey, politically the two
colonies were poles apart. The Duke of York could rule
his province without a popular assembly. He controlled all
appointments, made all laws and ordinances, and determined all judicial matters, except in cases of appeal. His
control over economic matters in the colony was virtually
absolute. He had considerable latitude in the exercise of
his military prerogatives and, by implication in the New
York charter, had a voice in practically all matters affect-
ing the inhabitants.[27] All this contrasted vividly with
Penn's liberal political ideas, which were now institutionalized in a neighboring colony and sure to cause discontent
in New York.

But Penn and his colleagues were by no means in com-

[26]Andrews, *Colonial Period,* III, 166–167. See also Pomfret, *West
New Jersey,* pp. 92–101, which gives more credit to Byllinge than to
Penn for the framing of this plan of government.

[27]Andrews, *Colonial Period,* III, 97–99. Andrews qualifies the
effect of these institutions: "Though literally interpreted the duke's
charter contains the most extreme expression of proprietary authority
to be found in any of the feudal grants of soil and government in
English America,... it may be doubted whether the powers actually
exercised by James and his appointees were anywhere near as
absolute as were those of the Maryland proprietors at the same time."
Assuming Andrews is correct, this situation existed because of James'
inability to administer his affairs in the New World as closely as he
would have liked. For the powers he was given in New York were
in complete accord with his political principles.

plete control of the political situation. While West New Jersey was legally separated from East New Jersey and had its own frame of government, the proprietors' rights to the soil and to the powers of government remained unconfirmed. Nor was the Duke, possibly regretting his largess of earlier years, inclined to surrender any more of his authority in New Jersey. As early as August, 1676—only a month after the formal division of the Jerseys—the lieutenant governor of New York, Sir Edmund Andros, was informed of this fact.[28]

The issue did not come to a head for several years. When it did, the subject in dispute was Andros' order that customs on all goods imported into New Jersey be paid to New York. Resistance to this measure increased until the Duke of York's secretary, Sir John Werden, finally inquired: "Are Sir G. Carteret and the Quakers by the grant of the soil empowered to erect different Governments and Commonwealths within their respective lands, or are they not like all other people in the territory subject to the laws enforced in New York?"[29]

James was in no position to turn his full attention to this issue, however. In 1679, the tide of anti-Catholicism was at its height, and he had had to leave England in March, returning only briefly in October and then departing for Scotland, where he remained until February, 1679/80.[30] For his part, Penn was aware of the crucial nature of the customs issue, but he could not keep up with the peripatetic Duke. He therefore prevailed upon Robert

[28]Pomfret, *West New Jersey,* p. 83.

[29]Werden to Lords of Trade, 19 September 1679, in *CSP, 1677–80,* sec. 1123. This query is preceded by a history of New York's relationship to New Jersey (in terms of taxes) through the seventeenth century.

[30]*DNB,* X, 623.

Barclay to go to Edinburgh, where he would have ready access to James through the Earl of Perth, Barclay's kinsman and an influential Scottish privy councilor. Although Barclay agreed to consult with the Duke, he was pessimistic about the outcome, partly because he believed West New Jersey had been mismanaged from the start.[31]

Barclay's apprehensions regarding a consultation were justified, but not as a result of the province's internal affairs. Rather, James believed that New York's right to tax New Jersey had been upheld by the Attorney General, Sir William Jones.[32] Informing Penn of this, Barclay pointed out that the Duke was on his way to London, where the Quaker leader might deal with the problem as he saw fit. But, warned Barclay,

he [James] took notice of that expression of thy letter wherein thou sayes thou had lost thy reputation by thy attendance at St. James & therefore said he had not seen thee in these times of his troubles. I perceave some has not been wanting to possesse him with no good opinion of thee and as one who is not his friend, which conceit perhaps has no good influence in this matter.[33]

[31]Pomfret, *West New Jersey*, p. 111; R. Barclay to George Fox, 31 December 1679, in ACM, LVII, 207. Fox agreed with Barclay's prognosis but encouraged him to try nonetheless (Fox to Barclay, 18 January 1679/80, ACM, LVII, 208).

[32]Jones, according to Barclay, discussed the matter with Sir Leoline Jenkins, a courtier and diplomat soon to be appointed a privy councillor and secretary of state. Barclay does not give the date of this meeting.

[33]R. Barclay to WP, 31 January 1679/80, in HSP, Penn-Forbes Collection, II, 15. Barclay warned Penn: "Whoever be employed to represent things to him [the Duke] or treat with him at London E. B. [Edward Byllinge] will not be fit for he has ane ill opinion of him but speaks very advantageously of G. L. [Gawen Lawrie, one of Penn's fellow trustees] as a Discreet wise man." Penn doubtlessly followed this advice, much to the consternation of certain suspicious

Given Penn's affinity for the younger Stuart, his reputation undoubtedly did suffer as a result of the hysteria aroused by the Popish Plot. But Penn was not the sort to desert his friends in time of trouble, as was demonstrated by his refusal to support the Whig demand for a Protestant succession. Barclay was probably correct in suspecting the Quaker's enemies of poisoning James' mind, in which case the Duke's secretary would have played a prominent role. Penn did not bother to disguise his dislike for Sir John Werden, who always asserted the ducal prerogative strongly and sometimes even more vigorously than James himself approved. Ironically, Werden deserted his master at the crucial moment in 1688, while Penn remained loyal.[34]

It was clear that Penn would have to win the Duke's favor again if the independent status of New Jersey was to be defended. The Quaker's stakes in the procurement of a deed from James to assure this independent status had risen; he was now a proprietor, as well as a trustee, of West New Jersey. Furthermore, Sir George Carteret died on January 14, 1679/80, and Penn became a prospective purchaser of East New Jersey. Fortunately, he had a way of bringing men to his point of view; he prevailed upon the Duke to reconsider the question of the right of New York to tax New Jersey. More than persuasive powers and personal friendship were involved, however, for James could hope that a conciliatory attitude in this matter would

---

West New Jersey trustees, who accused Lawrie of pursuing a "sinister self end, and private Interest than a real Public charge as was pretended," and noted that Penn was "concerned therein also" (M. Foster, T. Atherton, and T. Starkey to A. Sharp, 16 May 1680, in ACM, LVII, 220–221).

[34]On Werden, see *DNB*, XX, 1206. It is interesting that Werden's father deserted both Charles I and James II at the last moment (*ibid.*, p. 296).

win him Quaker support in England during his time of troubles. But this was secondary. Samuel Jennings, deputy governor of New Jersey and Penn's agent there, stated that Penn's "interest was the great means of obtaining the Grant of the Duke."[35]

The taxation issue was put before Sir William Jones again, although Jones was no longer Attorney General and had even joined the Court's opposition. When he

[35]Samuel Jennings, *Truth Rescued from Forgery and Falsehood* (Philadelphia, 1699), p. 45. Duke of York to R. Barclay, 27 June 1680, in ACM, LVII, 246. See also E. B. O'Callaghan and Berthold Fernow, eds., *Documents Relative to the Colonial History of the State of New York* (15 vols.; Albany, 1856–1887), III, 284; *CSP, 1677–80,* sec. 1497. The scarcity of records concerning the events which brought the matter before Sir William Jones has given rise to several theories. C. M. Andrews states that a protest from Edward Byllinge reached the Lords of Trade, who sent it on to Attorney General Jones (*Colonial Period,* III, 168). But Jones no longer held that post (*DNB,* X, 1060–1061), and it is questionable whether the Lords of Trade would have assumed jurisdiction over a protest against the Duke of York. In *The Province of East New Jersey, 1609–1702* (Princeton, 1962), pp. 120–121, J. E. Pomfret claims that the Duke submitted the matter to Jones precisely because he knew Jones, unfriendly to him, would deliver a decision against him. This would gain James the support of Quakers and other Dissenters and consequently strengthen his cause. But Pomfret's undocumented assertion is also difficult to accept. It is not explained why the Duke did not simply release the government of West Jersey to the proprietors without consulting Jones; this surely would have cast him in a more favorable light before the Dissenters. On the other hand, no attention is paid to the fact that James might have expected a favorable decision from Jones. Barclay's letter of 31 January 1679/80, already cited, would lead one to believe this, as would Samuel Jennings' claim that the Duke "much relied" on Jones' opinion (*Truth Rescued,* pp. 45–46). No one, to my knowledge, has considered the possibility of there having been a decision by Jones previous to that delivered in July, 1680. In 1700 Penn mentioned a meeting between Jones and Sir Leoline Jenkins as having occurred in 1678 (WP to C. Lawton, 21 December 1700, in HSP, WP Letter Book [1699–1701],

handed down his opinion on July 28, 1680, it was in the Quaker's favor. The Duke, according to Jones, had no right to demand that the inhabitants of New Jersey pay customs to the New York government. The decision was not, of course, legally binding on James. But, as Barclay put it, "because of his word he having said he would submit to Sr. Will. Jones judgment in the case, [he did so,] and yet Warden [Werden], and others I perceave reckne he was trapaned in it."[36] On August 6, 1680, the Duke issued a deed of release to the proprietors of West New Jersey. In November, Werden informed Lieutenant Governor Andros that the Duke did "confirm and release to the proprietors of both moytys [East and West] of New Jersey, all theirs and his right to any thing (besides the rent reserved) wch heeretofore may have been doubtful, whether as to governmt or publique dutyes in or from the places within their graunts."[37] William Penn had won the day.

When James recognized that the right of government in West New Jersey went with the soil, he issued a paper investing this right solely in the chief proprietor, Edward Byllinge (who did, however, take Penn's advice on the

---

pp. 74–81), which, in view of Barclay's mentioning it on 31 January 1679/80, was not a case of Penn's sometimes-faulty memory placing the decision two years before it occurred. (Jenkins did spend most of the time from December, 1675, to August, 1679, outside of England. Penn could have meant 1679 instead of 1678. See *DNB*, X, 739–742.) The above information has structured my own interpretation.

[36]R. Barclay to WP, 23 September 1681, in HSP, Gratz Collection.

[37]*CSP, 1677–80*, secs. 1479, 1500, 1579; J. Werden to E. Andros, 6 November 1680, in O'Callaghan and Fernow, *N.Y. Colonial Docs.*, III, 285–286. Charles II did not give his sanction to the deed of release for West New Jersey until 1683 (Andrews, *Colonial Period*, III, 168 n.). For the deeds to both East and West New Jersey see W. A. Whitehead *et al.*, eds., *Archives of the State of New Jersey, 1631–1800* (30 vols.; Newark, etc., 1880–1906), ser. 1, I, 323–345.

choice of governor). Penn relinquished his trusteeship in June, 1681, but he remained a proprietor of West New Jersey, acquiring more land and engaging in other activities.[38] Furthermore, his purchase of East New Jersey with eleven other men was confirmed by deeds in February, 1681/82, and he therefore became a proprietor of that colony as well.[39]

Penn never severed his affiliation with New Jersey, but he was well aware of the difficulties regarding that project. There was dissension within the proprietary group, and in 1680 it was by no means clear that the bickering had ended. Because of the uncertainty of the New Jersey grant, there had been trouble with New York. Perhaps this was not terminated either. Penn had begun to dream of a settlement where he could be the sole proprietor, controlling the land for his own financial gain and granting the settlers self-government and religious liberty. But to accomplish this he would need from the Crown an absolute title, in terms of both political power and land ownership, to an unsettled area in America. Just across the Delaware from New Jersey there was such an area, presumably a part of James Stuart's New York grant.

On June 1, 1680, William Penn petitioned Charles II for "a grant of a tract of land in America lying north of Maryland, on the east bounded with Delaware River, on

[38]Pomfret, *West New Jersey*, pp. 127–128, 135, 137; J. E. Pomfret, "The Proprietors of West New Jersey, 1674–1702," *PMHB*, LXV (1951), 138; Samuel Hazard *et al.*, eds., *Pennsylvania Archives* (9 ser., 138 vols.; Philadelphia and Harrisburg, 1852–1949), ser. 1, I, 58–62.

[39]Penn sat on the East New Jersey council in March, 1683, where he was able to exercise an ameliorating influence on criminal law being codified at that time (Andrews, *Colonial Period*, III, 153–154; Pomfret, *East New Jersey*, pp. 130, 173).

the West limited as Maryland is, and northward to extend as far as plantable, which is altogether Indian."[40] Within two weeks the petition was considered by the Lords of Trade and Plantations, before whom Penn agreed that his projected grant should extend 3° northward from Maryland, the other bounds to remain as he had named them. Copies of the petition were then sent to the Duke of York and Lord Baltimore. Before the end of the month, the agents of both these men had replied to the petition. Sir John Werden objected: "By all that I can observe of the boundaries mentioned in Mr. Penn's petition they agree well enough with that Colony which has hitherto (since the conquest of New York...) been held as an appendix and part of the Government of New York by the name of Delaware Colony, or more particularly Newcastle Colony....But what are its proper boundaries (those of latitude and longitude being so very little known...) I am unable to say. If this be what Mr. Penn would have, I presume the Lords of Trade and Plantations will not encourage his pretentions to it." The principal concern of Baltimore's agents was to ensure that the southern boundary of Penn's grant be specifically set at the latitude

---

[40]CSP, 1677–80, sec. 1373. The process of granting the charter for Pennsylvania can be followed in a number of books. The best source is Hazard et al., Pa. Archives, ser. 2, XVI, 345–358. This volume contains full reports of the meetings of the Lords of Trade and the names of all the attendants. W. H. Browne et al., eds., Archives of Maryland (65 vols.; Baltimore, 1883–1952), V, 271–274, also reports the meetings in full when they concern the boundary questions (to be discussed later). Samuel Hazard, Annals of Pennsylvania, from the Discovery of Delaware, 1609–1682 (Philadelphia, 1850), pp. 474–488, is a narrative account of the process. CSP, 1677–80 and CSP, 1681–85, although apt to abbreviate reports of the meetings, is cited most often here because it is the most generally accessible printed source.

passing through Susquehanna Fort, and that "Lord Baltimore's Council be allowed a sight of the grant before it be passed."[41] Officially, the project was neglected until October, 1680.

In the interim Penn convinced the Duke of York to put the New York–New Jersey controversy before Sir William Jones again. The Lords of Trade's instruction that Penn should apply to the Duke for clearance from Werden's objection to the grant of "Delaware Colony" was superfluous.[42] The Quaker had already discussed the project with his royal friend. Five days before James departed again for Scotland, Werden informed the Lords:

Since our previous correspondence respecting Mr. William Penn's petition he has represented to the Duke his case and circumstances (in relation to the reasons he has to expect the King's favour therein) to be such that the Duke commands me to acquaint you...that he is very willing that Mr. Penn's request may meet with success, that is, that he may have a grant of the land that lies on the north of Newcastle Colony and on the west side of Delaware River, beginning at the 40th degree of latitude, and extending as far as the King pleaseth, under such regulations as their Lordships may think fit.[43]

Having received this message, the Lords of Trade did not debate whether Penn should receive a tract of land in America; his ownership was considered a *fait accompli*.

But the question to be raised is why the Duke of York— and Charles II also, for he must have shared in the decision—acceded to Penn's desire for this valuable grant of land. The background of friendship between the Stuarts and the Penns, beginning with Sir William's early adher-

[41]*CSP, 1677–80*, secs. 1390, 1402–1404.
[42]*BTJ*, II (1679–1682), 178–179.
[43]16 October 1680, in *CSP, 1677–80*, sec. 1544.

ence to the cause of a restoration of the monarchy and cul-
minating in the Stuarts' promise to look after his son, was
an important factor in the decision. The hoariest explanation of the grant to Penn gives this relationship a monetary
twist: the Crown owed £16,000 to Sir William and gave
his son a tract of land in America in lieu of this debt.[44]
This explanation is given credence by the wording of
Penn's petition to the King, as well as by the urgent financial situation of the Crown at the moment, which would
certainly have precluded payment in cash.[45] Yet the very
enormity of the royal debt leads one to doubt that the
£16,000 owed to Penn was of grave concern to the Stuarts.
The obligation they felt toward the Quaker was more the
result of a personal than a financial debt owed to his
deceased father.

It has also been argued that Charles II favored the
grant to Penn on the grounds that it would get him out
of England, along with the Quakers and other Whiggish
Dissenters who might be expected to oppose the Court
party.[46] This interpretation has been challenged on two
counts: there is no written evidence to support it; and there
is good reason to believe that few Dissenters had the franchise.[47] It is difficult to reject this theory totally, however,
in view of Penn's promotion of Algernon Sidney's candidacy in 1679 and his political writings of that period.
Furthermore, such a policy on the Crown's part would have

[44]See, for example, John Oldmixon, *The British Empire in America* (2 vols.; London, 1708), I, 296–297.

[45]Edward Hughes, *Studies in Administration and Finance, 1558–
1825* (Manchester, 1934), p. 153.

[46]Fulmer Mood, "William Penn and English Politics, 1680–81,"
Journal of the Friends Historical Society, XXXII (1934), 1–19.

[47]Andrews, *Colonial Period*, III, 279n.

been consistent with the tactic of appeasing the Nonconformists in England.

The Duke of York had another reason, American rather than English in origin, for disposing of the land west of the Delaware and north of Maryland. His main interest in New York had been material and financial, but he was not gaining any revenue from his property. To the contrary, the cost of defense was a great and continuous burden.[48] The decision that New York could not levy duties on New Jersey augmented this load and, therefore, inclined James to agree to Penn's request for the region south of New York.

The foregoing explanation, while it brings out some of the reasons for granting the land to Penn, does not account for the political nature of the charter he received. The Maryland charter, issued in 1632, was evidence that the early Stuarts were not much interested in colonizing America at their own expense. George Calvert, like William Penn, saw the New World as a haven for his persecuted coreligionists, and he had the Court connections necessary to get a land grant. The virtually absolute powers his son had received as proprietor of Maryland allowed him to govern as he wished.

But conditions changed during the next half century. The English government became increasingly interested in the colonies. This new interest was first manifested in economic affairs. In response to the maritime rivalry with Holland, an act to regulate colonial trade and navigation was passed in 1651, passed again in 1660, and supplemented in succeeding years with other acts having the same general purpose—to ensure that England would derive the maximum benefit from her colonies.

[48]*Ibid.,* 99–104, 119–122; O'Callaghan and Fernow, *N.Y. Colonial Docs.,* III, 304.

These regulations did not rule out new grants of proprietary charters, however. In 1663, just such a patent was issued to eight men, most of whom were intimate with the newly restored monarch. The Carolina charter was really a reward for services rendered, the proprietors expecting considerable financial return from the venture. But the increasing interest of the home government was also apparent in this grant; the military value of a colony on the southern frontier was recognized. The motive behind the issue of the New York charter in the following year was even more strategic: this proprietary patent was granted while the Dutch still controlled New Netherland.

With consideration being given to the economic and strategic value of the American colonies, it was inevitable that political affairs would also come into the purview of the home government. Conditions in England accelerated this development. As Charles II strengthened the monarchy in the face of the Whig challenge, he took a stronger stand with respect to the colonies. The year 1675 marked the turning point in plantation affairs. The creation of the Lords of Trade, an arm of the executive branch, was symbolic of the new vigor. The primary duty of this body was to ensure rigid adherence to the acts of trade and navigation, but the closer commercial control soon led to interference in the governments of private colonies. From this time until the Glorious Revolution, attempts were made to increase the Crown's hold on the plantations, as witnessed by the reduction of the Bermuda and Massachusetts charters and the establishment of the Dominion of New England.[49]

[49]Andrews, *Colonial Period*, IV, chaps. i–vi, describes England's Colonial policy up to 1696. Michael G. Hall, *Edward Randolph and the American Colonies, 1676–1701* (Chapel Hill, 1960), chaps. ii–v,

It was during this period that Penn's interest was aroused and his project launched in America. A more inauspicious time for such a venture could not have been found, since the Crown was revoking charters, not granting them. Yet Penn not only got a large tract of land in America, he was also given a "true and absolute proprietary."[50] To explain this anomaly, it has been argued that Penn's charter "was couched in the only form known to the lawyers and officials of the day, that of a proprietary possession."[51] There is surely truth in this argument, but to accept it completely is to believe that the Stuarts were incapable of innovation, which was certainly not the case.

One might also say that the grant to Penn was, in reality, less in the form of an outright gift from the Crown than a transfer from one proprietor to another. This would place the burden on James and suggest that Charles acquiesced in his younger brother's desire. Such an assumption is not without grounds; a few years earlier Charles claimed that James was "the only person in England in whom I can have entire confidence."[52] On the other hand, New York was not an ordinary proprietary, since it would become a royal colony at its owner's accession. Therefore, the notion of Penn's grant as simply a proprietary transfer must also be qualified.

---

portrays the years 1676 to 1689 through the eyes of one of the major participants. Philip S. Haffenden, "The Crown and the Colonial Charters, 1675–1688," *William and Mary Quarterly*, XV (1958), 297–311, 452–466, contains new and interesting insights into that period.

[50]The Charter for Pennsylvania, issued on 4 March 1680/81, is in Thorpe, *Federal and State Constitutions*, 3035–3044. It has more recently been printed in David C. Douglas, ed., *English Historical Documents* (7 vols. [series incomplete]; London and New York, 1953–1959), IX, 93–101.

[51]Andrews, *Colonial Period*, III, 281.

[52]Turner, *James II*, p. 126.

A third explanation may be made from a different vantage point: compared to the contemporaneous exclusion controversy, the processing of the Pennsylvania patent was insignificant business and unworthy of lengthy consideration. Hence a charter conforming to Penn's desire might travel through official channels without serious scrutiny and consequent alteration.[53] But this reasoning is based on the assumption that the patent for Pennsylvania did not receive serious attention and that, as a result, Penn was granted liberal terms which important government officials would have opposed had they not been absorbed in other matters. These assumptions need to be examined if the proprietary grant to William Penn is to be understood.

Compared to the four days required to process the grant of New York to the Duke of York, the nine-month gestation of the Pennsylvania patent has seemed long indeed to some historians. It should be remembered, however, that the Connecticut charter of 1662 was reviewed for four months, the Rhode Island charter of 1663 for six. Action on the Carolina charter is thought to have been initiated as early as 1660.[54] In fact, the patent for Pennsylvania

[53]In a more comprehensive study of this particular possibility, the following conclusion was reached. "More was attempted in these years (1675–1688) than at any other period until the 1760's, but the absorbing constitutional struggle which was raging in England exacted a telling tribute in the time and attention that could be devoted to the colonies. In addition, events conspired to remove the higher administrative officials from office with such frequency as to render seemingly impossible the natural development of any plan" (Haffenden, "Crown and Colonial Charters," p. 299). See also W. T. Root, "The Lords of Trade and Plantations, 1675–1696," *American Historical Review*, XXIII (1917–1918), 24.

[54]Andrews, *Colonial Period*, II, 42–46, 134–135; III, 187.

was under official consideration for only four months, from October, 1680, to February, 1680/81.[55]

In this short time, however, the patent which Penn had submitted not only was studied by the Lords of Trade in committee but received particular attention from Sir Francis North, Chief Justice of Common Pleas; Creswell Levinz, Attorney General; and Henry Compton, Bishop of London.[56] All these observers had remarks and recommendations to make concerning the patent, thus introducing many of the restrictive features into the Pennsylvania charter. The assumption that Penn's draft was not given serious attention must be discarded.

Some historians have attempted to justify the proprietary nature of the grant to Penn by emphasizing the restrictive features introduced into his charter; they claim that if the hand of the home government was not strengthened by this grant, neither was it weakened.[57] Doubtless the intent of the officials who examined the patent was to restrain Penn. But an examination of the seven "restrictive" clauses in the Pennsylvania charter shows that this effort was not successful.[58]

[55]The process can be followed in *CSP, 1677–80,* secs. 1565, 1566, 1574, 1580, 1583, 1584, 1592–1595, 1599, 1603, 1609, 1618, 1619; *CSP, 1681–85,* secs. 6, 8, 29, 30, 32. See also *BTJ,* II (1679–1682), 224, 228–229, 233, 243, 248–249, 253.

[56]The agents of Lord Baltimore also saw a draft of the patent, and the Duke of York's agent was allowed to make recommendations concerning the boundary provisions.

[57]See W. T. Root, *The Relations of Pennsylvania with the British Government, 1696–1765* (New York, 1912), pp. 1–5; Andrews, *Colonial Period,* III, 281–285.

[58]A clause-by-clause comparison of the Pennsylvania charter with other proprietary charters may be found in H. L. Carson, *The Genesis of the Charter of Pennsylvania* (Philadelphia, 1919), esp. pp. 1–48. Carson's work appears in abbreviated form in *PMHB,* XLIII (1919), 289–331. His method of approach, as well as some

Three of these clauses dealt directly with the enforcement of the acts of trade and navigation. The first explicitly demanded obedience to "the Acts of Navigation, and other laws on that behalf made," a stipulation contained in no other charter. The second stated that all royal officials must be admitted to those areas of the province where they might be needed for enforcement purposes. The third called for the presence of an agent representing Pennsylvania in London, to be answerable for violations of the said acts.

The novelty of the first clause has led to an exaggeration of its stringency. After all, the acts of trade and navigation were to be universally applied. As to the second restriction, the admittance of royal officials to the colonies was not a serious colonial problem before or after 1680. The third clause was not strictly enforced. Penn himself looked on the placement of an agent at Court as an act of deference and loyalty to the King, not as a duty dictated by his charter.

A fourth restrictive clause in the charter stipulated that a transcript of every law passed in the colony must be sent to the Privy Council for confirmation or annulment. No other proprietary or corporate colony had such a charter provision. In both Carolina and Maryland, however, the proprietors controlled the governor, and therefore his veto, in order to check legislation. New York had no popular assembly before 1683, at which time it was specified that all laws passed could be vetoed by the Duke of York. Connecticut and Rhode Island were not re-

---

of his conclusions, differs from mine, which may be found in J. E. Illick, "The Pennsylvania Grant: A Re-evaluation," *PMHB*, LXXXIV (1961), 380–390. My argument concerning the charter restrictions appears in shortened form in the next several paragraphs of text; footnotes may be gotten from the article in *PMHB*.

quired to transmit their laws but did so infrequently. Thus, the stipulation in the Pennsylvania charter did not create a situation unique to that colony.

Furthermore, the effectiveness of this provision was hindered by its very nature. Pennsylvania was permitted five years to transmit a law after its passage. Thus, many acts of a temporary nature had expired before the Privy Council could render a verdict. As to permanent laws, the Council had to take action on a piece of legislation six months after it reached England or it would be automatically confirmed. Hence, the clause calling for royal disallowance was undermined at the start.

In the Pennsylvania charter the right of receiving, hearing, and determining all appeals from the colony's courts was also reserved to the King, who could reverse any judgment of the provincial judiciary. In the earlier colonial settlements the whole administration of justice was covered by a general statement in the charter. But the wording became more and more definite until, in 1664, the patent to the Duke of York specifically mentioned appeal to the King in Council. This clause was copied into Penn's charter almost verbatim. Although the charter issued to the Bahamas in 1670 contained no appeals provision, the New Hampshire commission of 1680 is explicit in its demand that appellate jurisdiction should be the Crown's privilege. The Pennsylvania charter was in the New York–New Hampshire tradition.

Another clause in Penn's charter—one stating that the King would impose no taxes on the colony "unless the same be with the consent of the proprietary, or chief governor, or assembly, or by act of Parliament"—has been the cause of debate among historians. Was Parliament, or was it not, given the power of taxation? The clause was apparently in the draft of a patent submitted by Penn to the Lords of Trade, though probably without the phrase "or by act of Parliament," and was brought to the Lords' attention by the Attorney General. But the official records do not disclose the intent of the framers. It has been suggested that the clause came as a direct result of the recent West New Jersey decision, and that it was therefore intended to shield Pennsylvania from the arbitrary taxation of a neighboring colony. Actually, it is not necessary to decide whether the clause should be interpreted in its positive or negative sense, since Parliament did not exercise what may have been its taxing prerogative until 1763. Then it was exercised without regard for particular colonial charters.

The final restrictive clause in the Pennsylvania charter called upon the colony to accept clergymen of the Church of England if its inhabitants desired them. This was not a new requirement. In 1662, Charles II directed Massachusetts to guarantee religious freedom to Anglicans. The Carolina charter of 1663 allowed the proprietors to give "indulgencies and dispensations" to those inhabitants who could not conform to the Church of England, the implication being that the majority of settlers would conform. The commission to New Hampshire in 1680 called for "liberty of conscience...unto all protestants; and that especially as shall be conformable to the rites of the Church of England, shall be particularly countenanced & encouraged." It was a short step indeed to the clause calling for free admittance of Anglican clergy, a provision inserted in Penn's charter by Henry Compton, Bishop of London. Nevertheless, the Quaker proprietor's well-publicized ideas on religious freedom made this restriction superfluous in his own time.

The absence of a clause guaranteeing Penn the rights enjoyed by the bishops of Durham has been interpreted as restrictive, since the proprietary charters of Maryland, Maine, and Carolina contain such a clause. But the patent to New York, which of all the colonial charters conferred on its grantee the widest powers, was also devoid of such a clause. Nor is it likely that Penn included such a provision in the draft he submitted, for no one who examined the patent remarked on its presence.

The proprietary nature of the Pennsylvania charter cannot be explained by pointing to its restrictive features. With the exception of the Durham clause and the limitations already discussed, the provisions of Penns' patent were the same as those of the proprietary charters of Maine, Maryland, and Carolina. Yet a number of these so-called limitations were already established in practice, and were now merely set down explicitly. And the clause which might have been most restrictive of all—that demanding that all laws be transmitted to England for possible disallowance by the King in Council—was crippled by the disparity between the five years the law was allowed to remain in Pennsylvania after passage and the six months which the King in Council had to consider it.

The blame for this disparity cannot be laid to the architect of the clause, Chief Justice North. In his recommendation that it be included, he left blank the time to be allowed between passage and confirmation or nullification. The official records do not reveal who made the "five years–six months" decision, but a letter written by Penn in 1686 suggests how it was accomplished. Fearing that the Lords of Trade were about to take action against the laws of Pennsylvania, he wrote to Thomas Lloyd, president of the provincial council: "We may use the advantages the Pening of my charter gave us (& by Sr. Wm. Jones, was intended to me & the colony) with what Success we are able, Know, that if once in five years, ours are presented to the said Commtt [Lords of Trade] or the King rather, it is as much as we are obliged to."[59] This was the same Sir William Jones who had decided the West New Jersey customs case in Penn's favor. Formerly Solicitor General and, immediately afterward, Attorney General of England, he had given up this royal employment and entered the House of Commons in 1680 with "the fame of being the greatest lawyer in England and a very wise man."[60] With the legal counsel of such an able adviser, it is no wonder that Penn's draft could survive official scrutiny without being seriously restrictive. This fact, thus far overlooked by historians who have treated the subject, is of major significance.

But what was the nature of the official scrutiny which Penn's draft had to survive? It has been argued that Charles II's advisers opposed their monarch's desire to grant Penn a charter.[61] This undocumented assertion needs to be more closely examined. The central figures in the Privy Council, which was reorganized just before the Pennsylvania charter came under official consideration in October, 1680, were Robert Spencer, Earl of Sunderland; Lawrence Hyde, soon to be Earl of Rochester; and Sidney Godolphin, later Earl of Godolphin. Temporarily below

[59]WP to Thomas Lloyd, 21 and 22 September 1686, in ACM, XXVIII, 280–308. Reprinted in *PMHB,* LXXX (1956), 239–245. For a fuller explanation of Penn's strategy here, see Chapter II.

[60]Auchitell Grey, *Debates of the House of Commons* (London, 1763), p. 451, quoted in *DNB,* X, 1060.

[61]Haffenden, "Crown and Colonial Charters," p. 309; Andrews, *Colonial Period,* IV, 371. No footnotes support these statements. Neither *CSP* nor *BTJ* betray any signs of opposition to Charles II.

these men, but perennially in the King's Council, was George Savile, Marquis of Halifax.[62]

Robert Spencer and William Penn first met at Oxford, where they struck up a close friendship. In 1661, Spencer was apparently expelled with Penn from the University for reasons of religion.[63] Spencer's other early companions included his uncle, Henry Sidney; his brother-in-law, Harry (Henry) Savile; Sidney Godolphin; William Trumbull, later a secretary of state; and Henry Compton, later Bishop of London. Penn was in correspondence with all these men at one time or another.[64]

In 1643, Spencer had succeeded to the family title of Earl of Sunderland. He was appointed a secretary of state in 1679; in May, 1680, he took charge of the more important southern department.[65] Bigger things than Penn's patent were on Sunderland's mind in the autumn of 1680.

[62]Ogg, *Charles II*, pp. 592–593. On Sunderland see J. P. Kenyon, *Robert Spencer, Earl of Sunderland, 1641–1702* (London, New York, and Toronto, 1958). On Hyde see John Biggs-Davison, *Tory Lives* (London, 1952), chap. ii. Sir Tresham Lever's *Godolphin, His Life and Times* (London, 1952) is the most recent biography of that man. H. C. Foxcroft's *A Character of the Trimmer* (Cambridge, England, 1946) is a first-rate account of the life and times of Halifax.

[63]Clarkson, *Penn*, I, 8, 11.

[64]Robert Spencer's mother was Dorothy Sidney, sister of Algernon and Henry. His sister, also Dorothy, was married to George Savile, first Marquis of Halifax. Halifax's father was a brother-in-law of the Earl of Shaftesbury. Robert Spencer also had a strong Whig connection; one of his cousins was William, Lord Russell.

[65]At this time there were two secretaries, and until 1706, the senior secretary held the southern department, and the junior held the northern department, with few exceptions. The American colonies lay in the southern department, but it was not unusual for a secretary to transact business, which according to the rule, should have been his colleague's duty (M. A. Thomson, *The Secretaries of State, 1681–1782* [Oxford, 1932], pp. 2–3).

He became secretly, but inextricably, involved in the exclusion controversy. In the House of Lords in November, he had to vote in favor of barring James from the succession or else be impeached. His dismissal from the Privy Council was thereby inevitable, but he was kept on until January 1680/81, because he favored William of Orange rather than Monmouth. In these circumstances it may be hard to believe that Sunderland would or could do a great deal for Penn. Yet some years later the Quaker proprietor wrote to the agile statesman, recently returned to power: "my noble Benefactors, of which the Ld. Sunderland was one of the first, in the business of my American Country."[66]

While Penn's relationship with Sunderland had roots extending to their days at Oxford, there is no record of friendship or even acquaintanceship between Penn and either Lawrence Hyde or Sidney Godolphin before 1680. The absence of evidence, of course, may not tell the true story. Concerning Godolphin, this is of little import; he, like Sunderland, went into the exclusionist camp, leaving Hyde as the King's only close adviser in late 1680 and early 1681.[67] If Hyde had no earlier contact with Penn, he was nevertheless helpful to him at this time. Less than six months after the Pennsylvania charter was issued, Robert Barclay wrote to Penn: "My advice to thee as to that is to deal with the L. Hide who is thy friend." Soon thereafter Penn thanked Hyde for "the many favours I am indebted to thee," and found occasion to ask for more of the same.[68] To Halifax, whom Penn had known before

[66]WP to Lord Sunderland, 28 July 1683, HSP, *Memoirs,* II, 244.
[67]Godfrey Davies, "Council and Cabinet, 1679–88," *English Historical Review,* XXXVII (1922), 49.
[68]R. Barclay to WP, 23 September 1681, in HSP, Society Collection; WP to Lord Hyde, 5 February 1682/3, in Janney, *Penn,* p. 226; WP

he applied for his grant, he later wrote: "The country I enjoy by the King's goodness and bounty, came not to my hands without the marks and prints of thy singular favour."[69]

Furthermore, it is unlikely that many, if any, of the lesser privy counselors attending the Lords of Trade would have challenged the grant to Penn. Only Viscount Fauconberg and the Earls of Essex and Bridgewater had a history of prolonged opposition to the Court.[70] But opposition might be expected from another quarter. The conscientious civil servant, though of lesser status than the privy counselor, was frequently in a position to influence the judgment of his superiors.[71]

William Blathwayt, secretary to the Lords of Trade, was such a man in such a situation.[72] And he was not

to Earl of Rochester, 14 June and 24 July 1683, in ACM, XXV, 86–88, 149–151.

[69]WP to Marquis of Halifax, 24 July 1683, in ACM, XXV, 142–143.

[70]A list of the privy counselors from October, 1680, to March, 1680/81, accompanied by the number of times each attended the Lords of Trade when the Pennsylvania grant was under consideration, is in the Appendix to Illick, "The Pennsylvania Grant." The Lords of Trade was actually a standing committee of the Privy Council (R. P. Bieber, *The Lords of Trade, 1675–96* [Allentown, 1919]). On Fauconberg, Essex, and Bridgewater see *DNB*, II, 142; III, 921; VI, 574–575.

[71]Hall's recent biography of Edward Randolph, already cited, provides an excellent illustration of this point.

[72]In September, 1675, Blathwayt became assistant to Sir Robert Southwell, secretary to the Lords of Trade. Southwell was very interested in colonial affairs, but in 1679 he sold his office to one Francis Gwyn, a move which "left Blathwayt virtually in sole charge of the plantation office" (G. A. Jacobsen, *William Blathwayt* [New Haven, 1932], pp. 86–95. This biography must be used with care since, in her anxiety to make her subject seem more important and wise than he was, Miss Jacobsen is sometimes unreliable).

friendly to Penn's project, for he stood squarely behind the policy of assault upon the proprietary and corporate colonies. But a powerful secretary of state with views opposed to Blathwayt's would, of course, considerably diminish his influence. In 1680, the two secretaries were Sir Leoline Jenkins and the Earl of Sunderland. The former did not interfere in matters relating to the colonies. But Sunderland, who completely overawed Blathwayt, doubtlessly informed the secretary to the Lords of Trade of his views on the grant to Penn. It was Blathwayt who, in his official capacity, drew the final draft of the Pennsylvania charter. As his biographer has said of this incident, "he was only the docile tool of agents more powerful than himself."[73] There is every reason to believe this assertion, and to believe that the "powerful agents" included the King's advisers, as well as the monarch and his brother.

In summary, the assumption that the Pennsylvania patent did not receive serious attention, and that as a result of this oversight Penn was granted liberal terms which important government officials would have opposed had they not been absorbed in other matters, is not acceptable. The charter was scrutinized by important officials, but their recommendations did not represent a serious

[73]*Ibid.*, pp. 105–106, 118–119. Miss Jacobsen maintains that Penn paid special tribute to Secretary of State Jenkins for securing the grant, but the letter she cites as evidence does not support her argument. On the other hand, she is unaware of Sunderland's aid to Penn. She also claims, hoping to clear her subject of any complicity in Penn's charter, that Blathwayt never received any mark of gratitude from Penn. Unfortunately, she overlooked a letter Penn wrote to Gwyn and Blathwayt on November 21, 1682: "I ware your favours about me which will not let me forget you" (HSP, Photostat from Friends House Library in London).

break with the past (although they could hardly be considered liberal). Penn's success in this regard was partially due, of course, to the craftiness of his legal counsel. Finally, those highly placed statesmen who were absorbed in more crucial matters than the processing of the Pennsylvania charter were not opposed to the grant; indeed, it appears as though they contributed to its success.

There was, in fact, good reason for these men to support the grant to Penn. The prospective colony had great potential as a trade depot. That Pennsylvania was called upon specifically to obey the acts of trade and navigation indicates that this potential was immediately noticed. Part of the impetus behind England's increasingly active colonial policy was commercial. Penn himself recognized this when, in 1680, he published a tract entitled *The Benefit of Plantations or Colonies* in which he listed four reasons to show that colonies "inriched and strengthened" England, and six reasons why England's apparent loss of population was due to causes other than emigration to America.[74] Furthermore, Pennsylvania had great appeal because of its strategic value. The area was a sparsely populated gap in the string of colonies along the Atlantic seaboard, possibly open to French or Dutch attack. Ironically, the desire to bolster the defenses of English America probably played a part in the founding of a refuge for the Society of Friends.

This much may finally be said about the grant to Penn. Charles II and the Duke of York were willing that the Quaker leader get the land for personal, political, and economic reasons. Mercantilists and royalists alike could unite on the desirability of the bequest on commercial and strategic grounds. But the attitude of the home govern-

[74]Andrews, *Colonial Period,* IV, 337 n., enumerates these reasons.

ment was becoming increasingly antiproprietary, and so efforts were made to include a number of restrictions in the charter. The severity of these restraints has been overrated. Penn's success in this whole matter can be attributed to the fact that he was a vigorous man with important connections who made his bid for favors at an advantageous moment. Yet the difficulties he encountered should not be forgotten. A letter he wrote to a close friend shortly after the charter was issued is a reminder of this fact, and it also serves as an excellent illustration of the way in which Penn combined faith and worldliness:

And as to my Country it is the effect of much patience & faith as well as cost & charges: for in no outward thing have I known a greater exercise & my minde more inwardly resigned, to feele the Lds hand to bring it to pass, & truly I owne it their. & so it came to me their as great opposition of envious grt men, & since I have been maid to look to the Ld. & believe in him, as to the obtaining of it, more than ever as to any outward substance, it comforts me, & I am firme in my faith that the Ld will prosper it, if I & they that are & may be ingaged, do not greeve him by an unworthy use of it.[75]

The new proprietor might attribute his success to supernatural aid when writing to Friends, but historians must emphasize the contribution of important statesmen.

William Penn now turned to the "use of it," for in Pennsylvania he had a laboratory where he could embody his political and religious ideas in a framework for a community: "There may be room there, though not here, *for such an holy experiment.*"[76] To several Friends who

[75]WP to T. Janney, 21 August 1681, in *PMHB*, XXXII (1908), 501–502.

[76]WP to J. Harrison, 25 August 1681, in Janney, *Penn,* p. 175. Penn,

had been associated with him in West New Jersey he wrote: "As my understanding and inclination have been much directed to observe and reprove mischiefs in government, so it is now put into my power to settle one. For the matters of liberty and privilege, I propose that which is extraordinary, and to leave *myself and successors no power of doing mischief,* that *the will of one man may not hinder the good of an whole country.* But," Penn added, in that tone of moderation he had lately acquired, "to publish these things now, and here, as matters stand, would not be wise; and I am advised to reserve that till I come there."[77]

The reason for Penn's circumspection is quite clear. He was placing the conception of the divine right of government over against the Stuart conception of the divine right of kings.[78] The contrast between Penn's plan for his colony and the contemporary political scene in England was striking.[The first Frame of Government for Pennsylvania, published on April 25, 1682, and supplemented by the Laws Agreed Upon in England, May 5, 1682, specified that the colony have a governor (the proprietor or his deputy) who would have a treble vote in the provincial council, a body of seventy-two members, one-third of whom were to be elected each year. There was also an assembly, two hundred in number elected annually. The franchise was to be extended to a free person who owned one hundred acres, a free servant who owned fifty, or any man who would pay the requisite taxes. The governor and council were to initiate legislation, see to its execution, superintend

---

like the Puritans before him, was conscious of his colony as an example to the Old World.

[77]WP to R. Turner, A. Sharp, and R. Roberts, 12 April 1681, in Janney, *Penn,* p. 172.

[78]William I. Hull, *William Penn. A Topical Biography* (London, New York, Toronto, 1937), p. 227.

41

judicial business, choose officers, and, in general, do the important work of the colony. The assembly was to meet yearly to pass bills into law and to impeach criminals.[79]

While in Pennsylvania all officials but the governor were to be elected, or chosen by those already elected, the situation in England was quite the opposite. Charles II had dismissed Parliament on March 28, 1681, three weeks after Penn received his charter. In the remaining years of his reign he never again summoned the legislature. The judicial bench was subservient to him.[80] The King could now rule unhampered. It appeared as though Penn were rendering a judgment on the English political scene when he proclaimed in the preface to his first Frame of Government: "If men be bad, let the government be never so good, they will endeavour to warp and spoil it to their turn." Penn had consulted with Algernon Sidney on the framework for his government. Symbolically, soon after Penn departed for his colony, Sidney was executed as an enemy of the state.

[79]Staughton George *et al.*, eds., *Charter to William Penn, and Laws of the Province of Pennsylvania, Passed Between the Years 1682 and 1700 Preceded by the Duke of York's Laws...* (Harrisburg, 1879), contains these early documents concerning the government. The best summary of the framing of these instruments and their consequent alteration is in W. R. Shepherd, *History of Proprietary Government in Pennsylvania* (New York, 1896), pt. 2, chap. iv. The minutes of the provincial council are in *Colonial Records of Pennsylvania, 1683–1790* (16 vols.; Philadelphia, 1852–1853). The preface to Vol. I contains the frames of government and the first laws, as does the preface to the minutes of the assembly (which also has the minutes of the meetings of the Lords of Trade concerning the granting of the Pennsylvania charter). See *Votes and Proceedings of the House of Representatives of the Province of Pennsylvania. 1682–1776* (6 vols.; Philadelphia, 1752–1756), reprinted in Hazard *et al.*, *Pa. Archives*, ser. 8.

[80]Ogg, *Charles II*, II, 620.

The contrast between Penn's political principles and those of his royal benefactors could hardly have been greater. This was true with regard to religion as well. In England, conformity to the national church was enforced by law. James Stuart, though he paid homage to toleration and apparently furthered this cause by royal decree several years later, was in actuality planning to effect his own "holy experiment": the Roman Catholic domination of England. In contrast, the Frame of Government for Pennsylvania required only that the colonists believe in God and that freemen and officials be Christians. Although this was less liberal than the "Laws, Concessions, and Agreements" of West New Jersey, which guaranteed complete religious freedom, the important fact is that Penn maintained principles which he knew were opposed to the official viewpoint.

He did not, however, create an issue out of these differences, as he might earlier have done. As he said, "to publish these things now, and here, would not be wise." In a pamphlet entitled *Some Account of the Province of Pennsilvania in America,* brought out in 1681, he simply noted that the colonists would have "the rights and freedoms of England." His real emphasis was on the material bounty of the place, its excellent situation ("600 miles nearer the sun than England"), and the prosperity that settlers could expect if they removed to Pennsylvania.[81] The Quaker proprietor was himself anxious to leave England, and without creating a stir, in order to see the "holy experiment" at work in his wilderness laboratory.

In 1668, William Penn joined the Society of Friends and began to work actively in the Quaker cause. Soon after-

[81]Douglas, ed., *English Historical Docs.,* IX, 122–128.

ward, his interest in politics became apparent. By 1682, he had translated his religious and political ideas into the framework for an actual community. That he was able to accomplish so much in so short a time may be attributed partly to a creative and purposeful energy, partly to a sense of the possible. Penn began his religious career as a martyr, but, realizing both the futility of this course and his ability to ameliorate conditions through official channels, he abandoned this role in order to combat persecution by legal means. Simultaneously, he shed his radicalism. Penn was first a political theorist and Whig supporter, but, perceiving the unlikelihood of governmental reform in England and even despairing of gaining relief for Quakers, he resolved to build society anew in America.

Besides his vigor and his practicality, Penn had his royal benefactors to thank for his success. And he was eminently successful. At the age of thirty-eight he had accomplished more than most men do in a lifetime. He was now going to Pennsylvania to enjoy the fruits of his labor.

CHAPTER II

Aggressive Proprietor

(1682–1685)

ON August 30, 1682, the 300-ton *Welcome* set sail for America with William Penn aboard. In addition to the royal charter for Pennsylvania, the Quaker proprietor carried with him the instruments to be used in the creation of his "holy experiment": the first Frame of Government and the forty Laws Agreed Upon in England.[1] More than this, he brought four patents he had received from the Duke of York barely a week before the *Welcome* sailed. These included a ten-thousand-year lease and an absolute deed for the area within a twelve-mile radius of New Castle, as well as two similar transfers for the area south of the twelve-mile circle down to Cape Henlopen, including the islands in the Delaware. For New Castle Penn was to pay a token fee; for the rest he was to pass on to the Duke one-half of all rents or profits.[2] Although the deeds

[1] Penn had, as well, "Certain Conditions or Concessions" made to the original purchasers of land in the province. See *Colonial Recs.*, I, 26–29.

[2] Hazard *et al.*, *Pa. Archives*, ser. 2, XVI, 364–367. As a precaution-

made no express grant of political authority, it soon became obvious that Penn was going to exercise such powers along the west bank of the lower Delaware, a region known as the Three Lower Counties.

In late October the *Welcome* landed in New Castle. There to meet Penn was his cousin, William Markham, who had been acting as deputy governor of Pennsylvania in the proprietor's absence.[3] Also waiting him were two of the Duke's attorneys, who gave him "one turf with a twigg upon it a porringer with River water and soyle in part of all what was specified in the sd Indenture or deed of Infeoffment from his Royal Highness," signifying Penn's possession of the town and county of New Castle. Several days later Markham received Kent and Sussex counties in a similar ceremony.[4] Penn received pledges of fidelity and obedience from the New Castle magistrates, whose commissions he renewed, and a declaration of loyalty from the people. For his part, Penn promised the inhabitants of this area the same privileges to be enjoyed by the Pennsylvanians, including the right to make their own laws, for

---

ary measure, Penn also had the Duke convey to him any jurisdiction New York might have had over Pennsylvania (*ibid.*, pp. 363–364).

[3]Markham's mother was Sir William Penn's sister. The deputy governor was a member of the Church of England (*DAB*, XII, 285–286). He had received his commission from Penn in April, 1681, and left England almost immediately, accompanied by Penn's land commissioners (Peare, *Penn*, p. 222). Markham's enthusiasm rivaled that of his eminent cousin. He wrote home to his wife from the new colony: "Here people live to be above a hundred years of age. Provisions of all sorts are indifferent plentiful, venison especially... wild fowl of all sorts; partridges I am cloyed with...here are abundance of wild turkeys...duck, mallard, geese, and swans in abundance...fish are in great plenty" (*ibid.*, p. 248).

[4]*PMHB*, LIV (1930), 214–216; see also Hazard *et al.*, *Pa. Archives*, ser. 2, XVI, 371–373. Kent and Sussex were at that time called Jones and New Deal.

which purpose an assembly would be called.[5] Having been under the jurisdiction of New York, the residents of the Three Lower Counties had not previously experienced representative government.

Penn had now committed himself to an extension of the "holy experiment" into a region where his political authority was dubious. In order to strengthen his hold on the Three Lower Counties, he traveled to New York and presented his deeds from the Duke to Anthony Brockholls, temporary governor of that province. Brockholls then wrote to the Duke's attorneys at New Castle: "We being fully satisfied (after seeing the indentures) of the said William Penn's right to the possession and enjoyment of the premises...give you our thanks for your good services done in your several offices and stations, during the time you remained under His Royal Highness's government, expecting no further account than that you readily submit and yield all due obedience and conformity to the powers granted to the said William Penn."[6] Again, there was no mention of political power.

To Penn, this limitation was more theoretical than real. When he issued writs for the election of the first provincial assembly, the delegates were to be chosen not only from each of the three counties of Pennsylvania, but also from each of the Three Lower Counties.[7] Neither the first Frame of Government nor the Laws Agreed Upon in England were intended to apply to the latter region; certainly the inhabitants of that area had had no hand in

[5]Peare, *Penn,* p. 247; Janney, *Penn,* pp. 205–206. Janney states: "There can be no doubt it was understood he [Penn] was to be governor of the territory on behalf of the duke." In view of the circumstances, it is unlikely that Penn felt so restrained.

[6]Peare, *Penn,* p. 252.

[7]George *et al., Charter to William Penn,* pp. 472–473.

the drafting of these instruments. But now its representatives were to constitute one-half the membership of the assembly merely because the proprietor wished it so. Furthermore, it was probably Penn who planted in the minds of the delegates from the Three Lower Counties the idea of joining with Pennsylvania. This became an accomplished fact on December 6, two days after the assembly convened. Penn could then claim: "I have annexed the *Lower Counties* (lately obtained) to the province."[8]

Up to this point, the proprietor had met no opposition. Not only had he successfully concluded the business of the Three Lower Counties, but he was pleased to find that his land commissioners had selected an excellent site for Philadelphia and had begun to lay out the city according to his grid plan. Furthermore, he had a long and fruitful conference with the local Indians. Then he encountered the provincial assembly. No sooner had that body met than it organized several committees, one of which was a "Committee of Foresight, for the Preparation of Provincial Bills." Later, in a debate on the rules which would govern the legislature, it was proposed and voted in the affirmative "That any Member may offer any Bill, publick or private, tending to the publick Good, except in the Case of levying Taxes."[9] Both actions were contrary to the first Frame of Government, which denied the assembly the right to initiate legislation. Nor was the assembly successful in this

[8]WP to ?, 29 December 1682, in Robert Proud, *History of Pennsylvania from...1681, till after the Year 1742* (2 vols.; Philadelphia, 1797–1798), II, 209. Hazard *et al., Pa. Archives,* ser. 8, I, 5.

[9]*Ibid.,* pp. 2, 5. See also H. Frank Eshleman, "The Struggle and Rise of Popular Power in Pennsylvania's First Two Decades (1682–1701)," *PMHB,* XXXIV (1910), 129–161, and Edwin B. Bronner, *William Penn's "Holy Experiment." The Founding of Pennsylvania, 1681–1701* (New York and London, 1962).

early bid for power. But it stood up to the proprietor where it could do so. To the forty Laws Agreed Upon in England, Penn had added fifty more. Nineteen of these were rejected by the assembly.[10]

The aggressiveness of the assembly, and particularly of a small Quaker clique which came to control it, was to be one of the hallmarks of Pennsylvania's colonial history and a source of vexation to the proprietor. But in 1682 the lower house was more cooperative than contrary. The laws it enacted at Chester in December, 1682, gave Penn the tools necessary to shape his experiment. And the proprietor showed no fear of meeting the legislature soon again, for in February, 1682/83, general elections were held, this time to choose delegates to the first provincial council as well as to the second assembly.

When the legislature met in Philadelphia in March, 1683, two major objections were raised to the first Frame of Government. One was that it called for the election of an unwieldy number of representatives in both houses, a difficulty which the proprietor had already recognized and was willing to remedy. He took less kindly to the other objection, that the rights of the assembly were too limited. The lower house itself was split between those who wanted "the Privilege of proposing to them [the governor and council] such Things as might tend to the Benefit of the Province..." and those who opposed not only this increased privilege but the more modest proposal that the assembly be allowed to discuss bills at length. The second faction would have restored to the proprietor "that Privi-

[10]George *et al.*, *Charter to William Penn*, pp. 107–123, 472–481 This should be supplemented with new information on the subject to be found in Marvin W. Schlegel, "The Text of the Great Law of 1682," *Pennsylvania History*, XI (1944), 276–283.

49

lege [which] in his too great Bounty he had conferred upon them, *viz.* Of having the Power of giving a negative Voice, &c. to the Bills proposed unto them by himself, and Provincial Council, than to endeavor to diminish his Power." Although the lower house was not unified in its desire, there was no doubt where the majority sentiment lay. It rejected the proposal, already accepted by the council, that "the Governor shall have an over-ruling Voice in the Provincial Council, and in the Assembly."[11]

At the end of the session, a second Frame of Government, sometimes referred to as the Charter of Liberties, was agreed to by proprietor, council, and assembly. The major change was to reduce the number of councilors and assemblymen. The lower house was not given the right to initiate legislation. Penn argued that should such a privilege be extended, the assembly might pass laws contrary to the royal charter, thus putting the existence of the colony in danger.[12] A third feature of the new document should also be noted. Under the terms of the first Frame, Penn was allowed to appoint the initial group of provincial officials—judges, sheriffs, justices, coroners—after which

[11]George *et al., Charter to William Penn,* pp. 155–161, 483–491; Hazard *et al., Pa. Archives,* ser. 8, I, 14–15, 19. It has been suggested that Quakers favored returning power to the proprietor, lest the non-Quaker delegates from the Three Lower Counties control the government through the assembly. (See Shepherd, *Proprietary Government,* pp. 248–249.) There is no evidence, however, that the Pennsylvania Quakers feared a loss of power in the assembly. Note, for example, that the contest for the speakership in 1684 was between two Philadelphians.

[12]A proviso was added to the council's right of initiating bills, stating that none should be inconsistent with the royal patent (*ibid.,* pp. 245–246; *Colonial Recs.,* I, 59).

This Charter of Liberties should not be confused with the more famous 1701 document of the same title.

time the people could fill these offices by election. In the second Frame, the proprietor was granted the right to appoint these officials during his lifetime.

Penn's obvious desire was to tighten his grip on the province. But to explain this apparent change of heart simply by noting that he "feared the rising power of the people" is to neglect a major motive for his action.[13] Penn realized that the manner in which the Pennsylvania government operated would affect his relations with the Crown, especially in the early 1680's, when the home government was increasing its control over the plantations. Regardless of his political principles, Penn had to take this situation into account. It must be conceded, however, that he was no democrat. Liberal by English standards, in America he was a conservative. Perhaps it was the change in his circumstances: Penn clearly enjoyed the exercise of his proprietary privilege.

How far the proprietor intended to go in strengthening his hold on provincial affairs can only be guessed. On March 26, 1684, he went so far as to suggest that a bill be drawn up which would allow him to choose the members of the council.[14] But his relations were smooth with the two assemblies that met after the second Frame was approved and before he left the province for England.[15] And, rather than appoint a deputy governor to rule in his absence, he commissioned the provincial council to take over the executive functions of the colony.[16] Theo-

[13]This is the contention of H. Frank Eshleman, "Struggle and Rise of Popular Power," p. 137.

[14]*Colonial Recs.,* I, 98.

[15]These were held in Philadelphia (October, 1683) and New Castle (May, 1684). (See George *et al., Charter to William Penn,* pp. 491–496, and Hazard *et al., Pa. Archives,* ser. 8, I, 43–58.)

[16]*Colonial Recs.,* I, 119.

retically, this meant that the executive office was elective. Furthermore, he appointed the speaker of the most recent assembly as chief justice of Pennsylvania.[17] He then sailed home, having acted as governor of his proprietary for less than two years.

Had the "holy experiment" been institutionalized in this brief period? That more than 150 laws had been passed suggests that this question should be answered positively. But it should be said, by way of qualification, that a number of these laws grew out of the peculiar beliefs of Friends and represented, therefore, simply an institutionalization of Quaker mores.[18] More important, the Pennsylvania assembly did not have all the rights possessed by the English House of Commons. The reason for this limitation lay primarily in Penn's desire to restrain the colonists lest they act in a manner which would endanger the royal charter. In order to maintain good relations with the home government, Penn was willing to compromise the "holy experiment."

Penn was now leaving the colony, but not because Pennsylvania was being threatened with royal control. Rather, the proprietor feared that he might lose the Three Lower Counties to Maryland. To forestall this possibility he was returning to London, where, four years earlier, the seeds of this controversy with his southern neighbor had been inadvertently sown.

When Penn applied for his grant in June, 1680, the agents of Lord Baltimore asked that the southern boundary of the proposed colony pass through a landmark known

[17]Shepherd, *Proprietary Government*, p. 253.

[18]A concise discussion of the nature of these laws is in Bronner, *Holy Experiment*, pp. 35–39.

as Susquehanna Fort, and that Baltimore's lawyer be allowed to see the patent before it was finally approved. Sir John Werden, the Duke of York's agent, opposed the grant altogether, but he had to retreat from this position after Penn conferred with the Duke. This about-face was the signal for the business of the patent to be resumed. Nevertheless, when Secretary Blathwayt passed Werden's revised opinion on to the Lords of Trade, he cautioned: "There are several Dutch and Swedish plantations which have been long under the English Government, that lie scattered on the westward of Delaware River, and some... perhaps within the bounds of Mr. Penn's petition, and have for a long time either acknowledged the protection of the Duke of York or of Lord Baltimore, near whose borders they are settled."[19] The fate of these settlements was not considered important enough to be discussed at this time, although their origins would later figure prominently in the boundary controversy. It is surprising, however, that Blathwayt's ambiguity about the allegiance of these settlements did not arouse the curiosity of the Lords of Trade.

The Maryland charter of 1632 conferred on Cecilius Calvert the land west of the Delaware River "which lieth under the fortieth degree of north latitude...." The New York charters of 1664 and 1674 designated the Delaware as the western boundary of that province. Theoretically, the Delaware peninsula—the land between the Delaware and Chesapeake Rivers—below 40° and above 38° belonged to Maryland. Between 1632 and 1664, however, Dutch colonies had been settled at New Castle, Whorekill (now Lewes) and St. Jones (near what is now Dover). When New Amsterdam was captured by the English, the Dutch colonies on the lower Delaware, which had been under the

[19]*CSP, 1677–80,* sec. 1565.

aegis of the Dutch on the Hudson, were presumed to be a part of New York. Lord Baltimore was in no position to quarrel with the King's brother about this, even if he had a mind to. On the other hand, the Duke had no written, legal title to the area, a defect Werden was aware of but never mentioned to the Lords of Trade.[20]

He did, however, inform the Lords of James' opinion on Penn's draft of a patent: "The Duke's intention is that Mr. Penn's grant be bounded on the east side by Delaware River, and that his south limit be twenty or thirty miles beyond New Castle, which extent northward of New Castle we guess may reach as far as the beginning of the 40th degree of latitude."[21] Three days later, on November 23, 1680, Werden wrote again to the Lords of Trade:

Mr. Penn having fallen into discourse with me of his concerns in America since I wrote to you on Saturday, I have told him of the substance of what I wrote, and he seems to fear that if his south limits be strictly set at twenty or thirty miles north from New Castle town, he shall have so little of the river left as very much to prevent the hopes he hath of improving the rest within his patent; but on the other side he is willing that twelve English miles north of Newcastle be his boundary, and believes that the distance will fall under the beginning of the 40th degree of latitude. I have already signified to you all that I know the Duke's mind herein, which is in general to keep some convenient distance from Newcastle northward for a boundary to the colony; but I confess I do not understand

[20]Sir John Werden to Sir Edmund Andros, governor of New York, 31 August 1676 and 7 May 1677, in O'Callaghan and Fernow, *N. Y. Colonial Docs.*, III, 238, 246.

[21]*CSP, 1677–80* sec. 1599. Both Werden and Baltimore's agents were shown the boundary provisions of Penn's draft, but only Werden responded (*ibid.*, secs. 1594–1595). Although Penn's draft is not extant, it may be presumed that he stipulated 40° as the southern boundary.

why 'tis precisely necessary to insist on just such a number of miles more or less in a country of which we know so little, and when all the benefits are intended to the patentee that others enjoy, so I submit this point to their Lordship's consideration, and do not think it material to add more at present.[22]

The settlement of the boundaries finally devolved on Chief Justice North, whose ignorance of the American terrain was comparable to that of his colleagues. His draft, which in phraseology closely resembled the final charter, contained the words "12 Miles Distance Northwards of Newcastle Town" and "fortieth Degree of Northern Latitude."[23] No mention was made of Susquehanna Fort, although Penn had agreed to the request of Baltimore's agents in this regard. In Penn's defense it can be said that both Werden and Baltimore's agents were invited to comment on the draft at a meeting of the Lords of Trade, but there is no record that they did so.[24] As a result, the clauses in the Pennsylvania charter appeared substantially as North had drawn them:

the said lands to be bounded...on the south, by a circle drawn at twelve miles, distance from New Castle Northwards, and Westwards unto the beginning of the fortieth degree of Northerne Latitude; and then by a streight line Westwards.

It is no wonder that the Quaker proprietor later wrote to

[22]*Ibid.,* sec. 1603.

[23]*Ibid.,* sec. 1609; Hazard *et al., Pa. Archives,* ser. 2, XVI, 353–354.

[24]*CSP, 1677–80,* secs. 1618, 1619; *CSP, 1681–5,* sec. 6. It is certainly hard to see why the Maryland interests did not protest. Penn wrote that the agents of both New York and Maryland acquiesced on the boundaries ([WP] to Mr. Lewen, [16] December 1680, in Edward B. Mathews *et al., Report on the Resurvey of the Maryland–Pennsylvania Boundary Part of the Mason and Dixon Line* [Harrisburg, 1909], p. 237).

the Chief Justice, "I determined to render my most humble thanks for the many favors I received at the Lord North's hand, in the passing and great dispatch of my patent."[25] What North did not know, of course, was that 40° latitude is well over twelve miles north of New Castle.

Though Penn had met with success in obtaining favorable boundaries for his colony, he was not satisfied. Fearing that Pennsylvania did not provide a convenient outlet to the Atlantic, he began a campaign to obtain the area on the west bank of the lower Delaware, which was under the control of New York. Robert Barclay served as Penn's liaison man in Scotland with the Duke of York, as he had during the New Jersey business, and again Barclay reported an initial failure. Both Werden and the Duke thought it was "improper for him [James] to give a graunt of what he has not a patent for himself other objections they have also against it." Barclay felt, however, that their attitude might be changed, and "having occasione to see the Lady Lockhart I thought it not improper to desire her recommendation to [Attorney General] Levinz which she readily gave."[26]

But when Penn continued to press the issue, he received an extremely cold reply from Werden: "As to your fresh proposition...repeated in this last letter vizt that his Royal Highness would conferr on you the rest of what he possesseth in and about New Castle...I told your friends [Barclay and George Keith, another Quaker in Scotland], what I now repeat to you, that the Duke was not pleased to come to any resolution as yet in that particular"[27] By

[25]WP to Sir Francis North, 24 July 1683, in HSP, *Memoirs*, I, 439–440.

[26]R. Barclay to WP, 15 April 1681, in HSP, Dreer Collection, Letters of WP, p. 61.

[27]Sir John Werden to WP, 16 July 1681, in O'Callaghan and

the late summer of 1681 Barclay concluded that Penn's project was being blocked by the Duke's secretary alone. He traced Werden's animus to a belief that Penn had trapped James into accepting Sir William Jones' decision regarding the New Jersey customs issue.[28] Penn later concurred with Barclay's explanation of the source of his trouble: "Sir J. Warden. . . I hear is too Spanish, and as he told me they call him in Spain, Don Juan del Ablo, for my agent can hardly make him understand the duke's commands, without a more powerful interpreter."[29] But Barclay was not altogether correct in his diagnosis of Werden's motivation, which was partly economic. To Governor Dongan of New York, Werden wrote: "you should use great care to hinder Mr. Pen and the inhabitants of both Jerseys from obstructing the Peltry trade of New York and that in order to this you should prevent all you can the uniteing of any part of either Jersey with Mr. Pen (who as you observe) is very intent on his owne interest in those parts."[30]

Fernow, *N. Y. Colonial Docs.*, III, 290; an abbreviated version appears in *CSP, 1681–5,* sec. 179.

[28]R. Barclay to WP, 19 August 1681, in HSP, William Fisher Logan Collection; Barclay to WP, 23 September 1681, in HSP, Gratz Collection, Colonial Governors (also in Society Collection). It was in the second letter that Barclay advised Penn to "deal with the L. Hide [Lawrence Hyde] who is thy friend to call for the governor [Sir Edmund Andros] now at London and after he [Hyde] has fully informed himself from him [Andros] to gett him [Hyde] then to writt to the Duke and use his influence to persuade him [the Duke] to it."

[29]WP to Lord Hyde, 5 February 1682/83, in Janney, *Penn,* p. 226. Penn may have been punning here, "del Ablo" being a weak disguise for diablo, or devil. Or, "Ablo" could be his way of spelling "Hablo" (pronounced "ablo"), the first person singular of the verb "talk."

[30]Werden to Dongan, 10 March 1683/84, in O'Callaghan and Fernow, *N.Y. Colonial Docs.,* III, 341. See also Werden to Dongan, 27

Fortunately for Penn, he did not have to deal with the Duke through Werden for long. The altered political climate in England allowed James to come to London in the spring of 1682. The two men could now discuss Penn's project personally. The deeds for the Three Lower Counties issued to the Quaker proprietor on August 21 and 24, 1682, were the direct result of this meeting. It was not until March 22, 1682/83, however, that Charles II formally granted this area to his brother, thus casting doubt on the validity of James' transfer to Penn.[31]

Meanwhile, the first attempts were being made in America to arrive at a satisfactory demarcation line between Pennsylvania and Maryland. In April, 1681, Charles II had written to Baltimore, announcing the grant of the new colony, noting its boundary provisions and requesting the Maryland proprietor to assist in establishing these boundaries. Simultaneously, Penn informed Baltimore of the appointment of William Markham as deputy governor of the province and his own desire for a speedy agreement on their mutual border.[32]

Markham called on Baltimore in August, 1681, but fell

August 1684, in *ibid.*, p. 350. Both letters appear in abbreviated form in *CSP, 1681–5*, secs. 1583, 1848. Penn had also asked for the islands in the Delaware around New Castle (see n. 27, above), a grant which Werden definitely opposed. See Werden to Andros, 12 May 1681, in O'Callaghan and Fernow, *N. Y. Colonial Docs.*, III, 286; abbreviated in *CSP, 1681–5*, sec. 103.

[31]Hazard *et al., Pa. Archives.*, ser. 2, XVI, 378–379. James Logan later said that Penn often claimed to have paid for this patent on the promise of its conveyance to him. *PMHB*, LIV (1930), 217. Penn's anxiety about this patent is evident in a letter to Lawrence Hyde, 5 February 1682/83, in Janney, *Penn*, p. 226.

[32]Charles II to Lord Baltimore, 2 April 1681, in Hazard *et al., Pa. Archives*, ser. 2, XVI, 426; WP to Baltimore, 10 April 1681, in Hazard, *Annals*, pp. 503–505.

ill on arrival; thus a satisfactory discussion could not take place. Markham's illness was a portent of future relations between the two colonies. The continued delay of negotiation created suspicion on both sides, and an undiplomatic gesture by Penn turned this into mutual hostility. In September, 1681, he wrote a letter to influential citizens of Cecil and Baltimore counties in Maryland, assuring them that they were no longer liable to pay taxes to the Maryland government.[33] Penn was later to justify this action by claiming that he thought these counties fell within his patent, conveniently forgetting that he had originally requested a grant of land *north* of Maryland. In fact, the proprietor was now making an uncharacteristically brazen attempt to get more land.

Nevertheless, Markham and Baltimore eventually had another meeting, this time in Upland (now Chester, Pennsylvania) in September, 1682. With a surveying instrument they shot the latitude of Upland at approximately 39° 46′ (the true latitude is 39° 51′). Both men apparently agreed that Upland was below 40°, and thereafter Markham adhered strictly to the idea that an arc of the twelve-mile circle described around New Castle was Pennsylvania's southeastern boundary.[34]

One month after this conference at Upland, Penn landed at New Castle armed with the deed giving him possession of the Three Lower Counties. The Quaker proprietor assumed political control of this region immediately. Within six weeks the area was united to Pennsylvania by an act of the provincial assembly. In theory, however, the Three

[33]Hazard *et al.*, *Pa. Archives*, ser. 1, I, 38–39.

[34]Notes on the conferences between Markham and Baltimore and their respective opinions appear in Browne *et al.*, *Md. Archives*, V, 374–379, as well as in *PMHB*, VI (1882), 412–434.

Lower Counties remained part of Maryland by the terms of its royal charter.

Early in December, 1682, Penn had his first conference with Lord Baltimore. Not surprisingly, he refused to discuss the Three Lower Counties in this or later conversations with his southern neighbor; he was willing to talk only about the location of the border between Maryland and Pennsylvania west of New Castle. Although this aspect of the boundary controversy between the two colonies was never to be seriously considered in England during the lifetimes of the two proprietors, Penn could not foresee this. Consequently, he vigorously pursued his policy of attempting to gain the maximum amount of territory to the south, relying on his royal connections as much as possible. His motivation was economic—he wanted both land and water. The former would produce revenue through sales and quitrents; the latter would give the province a more lucrative commerce.

At the outset of the December conference, Penn relied on a letter from Charles II to Baltimore in which the King stated that the northern boundary of Maryland should be determined by measuring 2° from the southern boundary (the latitude of Watkins Point) at sixty miles per degree.[35] Since this was contrary to his charter, Baltimore refused to consider it, and Penn agreed to waive the letter and begin measurement at a latitude established by tradition: 37° 15′ at Cape Charles. This differed from the King's proposal only in that it would have entailed measuring a longer distance over forest, swamp, and water. Baltimore favored direct measurement by instrument of 40° as the simplest and most accurate method, and one which con-

[35]Charles II to Baltimore, 19 August 1682, Browne *et al.,* *Md. Archives,* V, 371–372.

formed to his charter. The conference adjourned with the problem unresolved.[36]

The two proprietors met again in May, 1683. Penn tried to make use of Charles II's letter again, although he had earlier agreed to waive it. He candidly admitted that by taking an observation at Watkins Point and measuring north from there he expected (incorrectly, however) to gain six or seven miles and thus the headwaters of the Chesapeake. Baltimore again refused this method and asked why measurement could not as well be taken at 40° as at Watkins Point. Penn apparently consented to this (the text is not clear) on the condition that Baltimore sell him enough land to allow Pennsylvania an outlet to the Chesapeake. The Maryland proprietor refused.

During the course of the conference, as reported by Baltimore, much heat was generated when at one point Penn said "he would procure it [an outlet to the Chesapeake] from his Majestie to which I answered that if he Could impose his dictates upon the King and Council it would be in vaine for me to hope to have Justice don me but I was not (as I told him) of opinion that he could impose in that kind."[37] The impasse between Penn and Baltimore made it virtually imperative that the problem be transferred to England. If Baltimore had been aware of his adversary's previous success with the Stuarts and their advisers, he would certainly have spoken with less assurance.

[36]Penn's account of this conference is in Janney, *Penn*, pp. 222–223; Baltimore's account is in Browne *et al.*, *Md. Archives*, V, 379–390.

[37]Baltimore recorded the conference in *ibid.*, pp. 397–400. Penn gave an account of both the December and May conferences in a letter to the Lords of Trade, 6 August 1683, in *CSP, 1681–5*, sec. 1179.

That aspect of the Pennsylvania-Maryland conflict involving the Three Lower Counties was already under discussion in England. The patent given by Charles II to his brother in March, 1682/83, covered only the New Castle area. James immediately petitioned for a more beneficial grant, probably at Penn's request. This was to include the eastern half of the Delaware peninsula as far south as Cape Henlopen, that is, to the settlement at Lewes in Sussex county (38° 45′). James' application was sent to the Marquis of Halifax, then Lord Privy Seal, on April 13, 1683. Almost simultaneously Halifax received a letter from Baltimore, pleading his case against Penn. On April 17, both documents were introduced to the Lords of Trade, who recommended that Sir Francis North "have a view of the several Boundarys of the Patents granted to the Lord Baltemore and Mr. Penn as also to His Royal Highness of New Castle...and in the mean time that application be made to His Royal Highness that he would please not to pass any conveyance to Mr. Penn of those parts until the bounds between Lord Baltemore and him be settled." By the end of May the King had endorsed this position.[38]

On May 31, the Lords of Trade heard both sides of the

[38]Browne et al., Md. Archives, V, 391–394. W. R. Shepherd is of the opinion that the Duke's second patent was in the "course of preparation when it was stopped by a counter petition from the agents of Baltimore" (Proprietary Government, p. 120). Rather, Richard Burk, Baltimore's agent, was summoned to the Lords of Trade and told when he appeared (27 April) that he could present a petition of complaint against Penn to the King. This Burk did, asking that the processing of the new patent for the Three Lower Counties wait upon the determination of boundaries. The King agreed and referred the matter of boundaries to the Lords of Trade for further investigation on 31 May (Browne et al., Md. Archives, V, 394, 396). Therefore, it was really Baltimore's letter to Halifax that turned the tide.

controversy concerning the Three Lower Counties. Richard Burk, Baltimore's agent, maintained that the land in question was included in the Maryland charter. Philip Ford and Solicitor General Sir Edward Herbert, representing William Penn and the Duke of York respectively, argued that since the west bank of the lower Delaware was inhabited by Dutch and Swedes before 1632, it could not have been granted to Maryland because the charter of 1632 prohibited the granting of land already occupied by Christians.[39] Furthermore, Ford and Herbert argued, the Duke had held this region since 1664; why should Baltimore suddenly find alien possession a hardship after two decades?[40] Baltimore, when he was later informed of this point, answered: "My father in life time and since his decease I have petitioned His Royal Highness for a hearing of that matter; but His Highness his greater affairs did not afford time for it whilst I was in England."[41] As to

[39]The Maryland charter contained the phrase "in a country hitherto uncultivated." Note, however, that the Pennsylvania charter specified: "in the parts of America not yet cultivated and planted." Penn certainly did not intend to forfeit the already inhabited areas of Pennsylvania.

[40]*Ibid.*, p. 396. There had been abortive attempts by the Dutch to settle along the west bank of the Delaware before the Maryland charter was issued. In 1632 the area granted to Baltimore was inhabited only by Indians. In 1638 Swedes established the first permanent non-English settlement in the area. This was later absorbed by the Dutch. The fact that England denied the right of the Dutch to settle anywhere between Cape Fear and Nova Scotia was no real deterrent to New Amsterdam. But the presence of Dutch colonies along the west bank of the Delaware may well have been the reason why Baltimore asked, and was granted, that his patent to Maryland be reconfirmed in 1661 (A. C. Myers, ed., *Narratives of Early Pennsylvania, West New Jersey, and Delaware* [New York, 1912], p. 62; Hazard, *Annals*, pp. 21–28, 327).

[41]Baltimore to W. Blathwayt, 7 December 1683, in O'Callaghan and Fernow, *N. Y. Colonial Docs.*, III, 339–340.

the argument regarding Dutch and Swedish settlements, Ford and Herbert were implying that England had recognized the right of foreign settlement in this area before 1664, which was not true. Nevertheless, the ownership of the Three Lower Counties came to revolve about this question of whether or not the area was settled by Europeans before 1632. At least, this was the ostensible issue. A brief discussion among the disputants on June 12, 1683, left the question unresolved. Philip Ford set about to get the documents which would prove Penn's case.[42]

Theoretically, Baltimore's case for ownership was the better one. But Penn was in control of the area by means of a transfer from the Duke of York, a point of equal importance. Neither proprietor was confident of his position. In June, 1683, just when word that the Lords of Trade had decided to review the various patents should have arrived in America, both Penn and Baltimore initiated correspondence with important figures in the British government, thus implicitly admitting that the force of personalities, not the merits of the points at issue, would determine the outcome of the controversy.

The Maryland proprietor wrote to the secretary of the Lords of Trade, William Blathwayt; a privy councilor, the Marquis of Halifax; and Sir Leoline Jenkins, a secretary of state. He requested that no final decision on the question be made until he could be heard personally, which would be in May or June of 1684.[43] William Penn was able to select a wider range of correspondents. He also played more

[42]Browne *et al., Md. Archives,* V, 401–402. The problem was not considered again for a year, later delays coming as a result of the impending arrival of the proprietors in England (*ibid.,* pp. 404–405).

[43]These letters, which were written on 11 and 12 June 1683, are in *ibid.,* pp. 397, 400–401. Baltimore wrote again to Blathwayt and Jenkins in December (*ibid.,* pp. 402–404).

carefully on the apparent prejudices of each recipient and spread his communications over a somewhat longer period.

Penn's letters all conformed to the same general pattern: a castigation of Baltimore was followed by a plea for aid against him. Often the proprietor went on to laud the virtues of his own province, emphasizing its contribution to British trade. These letters were sent to high-placed civil servants, William Blathwayt and William Bridgman; to minor statesmen, Henry Savile and Henry Sidney; to privy councilors, the Earls of Dartmouth, Rochester, and Sunderland, the Marquis of Halifax and Sir Francis North; and to the Duke of York and Charles II. It was to Rochester and Sunderland that Penn most plaintively poured out his story, although he notified only the Duke of York of his plan to follow Baltimore to England. These letters were delivered personally by William Markham, who had been sent to England for the purpose of guarding the colony's interests against Maryland.[44]

Unfortunately for Baltimore, he had placed his confi-

<hr />

[44]WP to Blathwayt, 30 July 1683, in ACM, XXV, 219–220; WP to W. Bridgman, 1 August 1683, in *CSP, 1681–5,* sec. 1171; WP to H. Savile, 30 July 1683, in Hazard *et al., Pa. Archives,* ser. 1, I, 68; WP to H. Sidney, 24 July 1683, in Janney, *Penn,* pp. 231–232; WP to Dartmouth, 28 July 1683, in ACM, XXV, 134–185; WP to Rochester, 14 June 1683, in ACM, XXV, 86–88; WP to Rochester, 24 July 1683, in ACM, XXV, 149–151; WP to Rochester, 2 February 1683/84, in HSP, *Memoirs,* I, 442–446; WP to Sunderland, 14 June 1683, in HSP, Photostats; WP to Sunderland, 28 July 1683, in HSP, *Memoirs,* II, 243–247; WP to Halifax, 24 July 1683, in ACM, XXV, 142–143; WP to Halifax, 9 February 1683/84, in HSP, *Memoirs,* I, 418–422; WP to North, 24 July 1683, in *ibid.,* pp. 446–449; WP to Duke of York, 8 June 1684, in Janney, *Penn,* p. 253; WP to Charles II, 13 August 1683, in HSP, *Memoirs,* II, 241–243. Two other letters were written to persons who, though unidentified, were apparently influential (WP to ?, 24 July 1683, in ACM, XXV, 175–177; WP to ?, 30 July 1683, in *PMHB,* XXXIX [1915], 233).

dence in the wrong men in England. His Quaker adversary had not. Both Halifax and Jenkins were out of favor with the French Court, while Sunderland had its confidence; and the French wielded much influence with Charles II at this time. Sunderland had weathered the exclusion controversy and was readmitted to the privy council in October, 1682. He was appointed a secretary of state three months later. Rochester was responsible for the reconciliation between Sunderland and the Duke of York, or so said Halifax, Rochester's major rival.[45] For a moment it appeared that the Halifax faction might triumph over the group that had crystallized around Rochester. In August, 1684, Rochester was moved from his influential treasury post to the unimportant position of Lord President of the Council, possibly as a prelude to a ministerial revolution which would have put Halifax at the pinnacle of power. This possibility was nipped in the bud with the death of Charles II in February, 1684/85. The accession of James signalized the downfall of Halifax, who was removed from the Council in October, 1685. Rochester was reappointed Lord Treasurer.[46]

While the changing structure of British politics would favor Penn, other developments were to hurt Baltimore's cause still further. Sir Leoline Jenkins resigned in 1684 and was to die soon afterward.[47] William Blathwayt, who received letters from both proprietors but was acknowledged to be a close friend of Baltimore's, would in the

[45]H. C. Foxcroft, *The Life and Letters of George Savile, First Marquis of Halifax* (2 vols.; London, New York, 1898), I, 373–375, 379–380. For the rivalry between Halifax and Sunderland see Andrew Browning, ed., *Memoirs of Sir John Reresby* (Glasgow, 1936), p. 295. Reresby notes that Dartmouth (another Penn correspondent), as well as Rochester, was one of "the Duke's [of York] cheife favourits."

[46]Foxcroft, *Halifax*, I, 420–435.   [47]*DNB*, X, 741.

crucial years 1684 and 1685 be too interested and involved in the subjugation of New England to give other matters much attention.[48] Sir Francis North, who had drawn the boundary terms for Penn's charter and was later directed to examine the patents of Maryland, Pennsylvania, and New York in this regard, was to retire after the coronation of James II and die in September, 1685.[49] North's value to Baltimore was not that the Chief Justice would favor Maryland, but rather that his experience in this affair would have tempered the Stuart favoritism toward Penn.

Neither proprietor in America could know, however, that affairs would move in this direction. Both felt the necessity to go to the scene where the momentous decision would be made. Again Baltimore was at a disadvantage. Although his return to England was motivated primarily by the boundary controversy, he also wanted to dispel the bad favor with which his colony was regarded by the home government. As a result of infringement of the navigation acts, he had even been threatened with *quo warranto* proceedings.[50] The relationship between Baltimore and the Crown was further impaired when news reached England that the royal customs collector in Maryland had been murdered by the proprietor's nephew.[51]

---

[48]Jacobsen, *Blathwayt*, pp. 116–119. For example, on 2 September 1685, Edward Randolph sent a memorial to the Lords of Trade: "I humbly intreat That the Commission prepared by Mr. Blathwayt may be read before yr Lordsps enter upon the matters in difference betwixt the Ld. Baltimore & Mr. Penn." R. N. Toppan and A. T. S. Goodrick, *Edward Randolph: Including His Letters and Official Papers...1676–1703* (7 vols.; Boston, 1898–1909), IV, 43.

[49]*DNB*, XIV, 602.

[50]Andrews, *Colonial Period*, II, 333; W. L. Grant and James Munro, eds., *Acts of the Privy Council of England: Colonial Series* (6 vols.; London, 1912–1923), II, sec. 64.

[51]Edward Randolph wrote to Sir Robert Southwell about the

Unlike Baltimore, Penn had only one reason for leaving his province and one cause to fight for in England—the enlargement of Pennsylvania. And although he had heard reports that the liberal nature of certain Pennsylvania laws made him "a butt for the arrows of mallise to be shot at," he was not under attack by the home government[52] On reaching England, however, he found a situation very different from the one he had left two years earlier. The Whig cause was in complete collapse and the campaign against Dissenters at high pitch. Penn described the new scene:

I arrived from America the 6th of October, '84... [The King and the Duke of York] received me very graciously, as did the ministers very civilly. Yet I found things in general with another face than I left them: sour and stern, and resolved to hold the reins of power with a stiffer hand than heretofore, especially over...state or church dissenters....

This made it hard for me, a professed dissenter, to turn myself—for that party having been my acquaintance, my inclination, and my interest too: to shift them I would not, to

murder: "This busines falls out unluckily for my Lord Baltamore who had sett up this Talbott to confront & disturb Mr. Penns people from planting in the lands under dispute.... Its thought his Majestie will appoint a Govr in Maryland in a little tyme" (29 January 1684/85, in Toppan and Goodrick, *Randolph*, IV, 4–5). Randolph was also referring to one of two other actions in which the nephew in question, George Talbott, was detrimental to Baltimore's cause. He carelessly ran a line at some distance south of 40°, which was construed by the Penns (and some residents of Maryland) to be Baltimore's idea of his northern boundary; he later made a trip to Penn's home and demanded that the proprietor deliver the Delaware territory to his uncle.

[52]George Hutcheson to WP, 18 March 1682/83, in HSP, Penn papers from Friends House, London. A news letter of 13 January 1682/83 reported Penn deceased, having died a papist (HMC, *The Manuscripts of the Earl of Egmont* [2 vols.; Dublin, 1909], p. 126).

serve them I saw I could not, and to keep fair with a dis-
pleased and resolved government, that had weathered its point
upon them, humbled and mortified them, and was daily
improving all advantages against them, was a difficult task to
perform.

Finding myself narrowed in this manner, that one day
I was received well at court as proprietor and governor of a
province of the crown, and the next taken up at a meeting by
Hilton and Collingwood, and the third smoakt and informed
of for meeting with the men of the whig stamp; after informing myself of the state of things, I cast about in mind
what way I might be helpful to the public, and as little hurtful
to my concerns as I could, for I had then a cause depending
about bounds of land in America with the Lord Baltimore,
before the council, that was of importance to me.[53]

Even as "proprietor and governor" Penn did not find
his lot an altogether easy one. Soon after he arrived in
London, he was called upon by the Treasury to pay a fine
of £53 for violation of the acts of trade. But, unlike

[53] Janney, *Penn,* pp. 261–262. The knowledge that Baltimore
planned to attend the Lords of Trade in person was the cause for
the delay of a hearing on the boundary controversy until the summer
of 1684, when Solicitor General Herbert informed Blathwayt that
the Duke of York was disturbed at the committee's lack of action.
The Lords, in turn, requested the agents of Penn and Baltimore to
attend on July 23. On that day Baltimore himself showed up, but
Philip Ford asked for a further delay since Herbert was unable to
attend. This was granted until late September. In the interim it was
learned that Penn would soon be on his way to England. Herbert
now reversed his field and requested that the business be put off
until December, when it was hoped Penn would bring the committee his evidence of Dutch occupancy of Delaware before 1637.
Hazard *et al., Pa. Archives,* ser. 2, XVI, 400–401; Browne *et al., Md.
Archives,* V, 417–419. For an abbreviated account of these meetings
see *CSP, 1681–5,* secs. 1781, 1788, 1807, 1811, 1878.

Baltimore, Penn received no threat of *quo warranto* proceedings.[54] As a Quaker, he continued to serve in the cause of toleration. He was able, for example, to secure the Duke of York's aid in obtaining pardon for a Dissenter. Yet in reality he was pursuing a more moderate course in this regard than previously. Specifically, he left unpublished a pamphlet in which he argued that the kingdom would benefit economically, and the King politically, if the government's policy were more moderate toward nonconformists. "The times," Penn wrote, were "too set and rough for print."[55] As far as politics is concerned, there is no evidence that he participated under the Whig banner at this time. Penn now had a vested interest to protect and a case concerning it pending before the government. Where his early radicalism had been moderated by circumstances in the late 1670's, his concerns in the mid-1680's were turning to a conservative course.

Penn's arrival in England should have meant that the Lords of Trade, whose meeting had been delayed until December, 1684, in expectation of his presence, could convene to discuss the question of Delaware in earnest. Yet the business was simply "put off to another Time."[56] The unstated explanation for this delay was that Penn's secretary had carelessly left in Pennsylvania the supposed proofs that the Dutch had occupied the Delaware area before 1632.[57] That the business could be postponed so easily was indicative of the favor in which Penn was held. Yet in January, before the documents could be gotten, it

[54] William A. Shaw, ed., *Calendar of Treasury Books* (27 vols. [1660–1718]; London, 1904–1957), VII, 1455; VIII, 212–213, 1009.

[55] Janney, *Penn*, pp. 262–263.

[56] Hazard *et al.*, *Pa. Archives*, ser. 2, XVI, 401–402.

[57] WP to T. Lloyd, 7 October 1684, in ACM, XXVII, 21.

was rumored that the King had considered the Pennsyl-vania-Maryland controversy and decided to "revoke their patents and allow no more such independent Govern-ments," a move that would certainly have conformed to the general policy of the Crown.[58]

Then, on February 6, 1684/85, Charles II died. The accession of his brother was not a signal for the reversal of government policy concerning private charters; rather, the attacks increased. But so far as Penn was concerned, James had always been the friendlier of the two Stuarts. Even if they differed on political principles and religious beliefs, James Stuart and William Penn were much alike in temperament—serious, purposeful, industrious. Charles Stuart had been quite different. He was lazy and disliked routine. He made no claim to moral courage and self-sacri-fice. He held no strong religious convictions. More posi-tively, he had a sense of humor, an insight into human nature, and a sound political sense complemented by flexibility.[59] This not to say that Charles II and Penn were too unlike to have been personal friends, though there survives no record that they were. It should be clear, however, that while James would espouse the Quaker's cause as a matter of conviction and dedication, Charles would do so as a matter of political expediency. He would not—and, indeed, did not intend to—except Penn's cause from his government's policy.

Not only was James Stuart friendlier to Penn than Charles was, but he had a special interest in the issue of the Three Lower Counties. Meanwhile Baltimore was

[58]Edward Randolph to Sir Robert Southwell, 29 January 1684/85, in Toppan and Goodrick, *Randolph*, IV, 4–5.

[59]Ogg, *Charles II*, I, 148–149. Ogg notes: "As a man and as a Stuart he [Charles] was a remarkable exception."

forced overnight into the embarrassing position of arguing that the King, when he was Duke of York, claimed land which he did not actually own. These factors more than offset any gains that Baltimore might have expected by virtue of his Catholicism.

Discussion of the issue began in August, 1685, when Penn himself confidently initiated proceedings.[60] Baltimore was now more reluctant than ever to go before the Lords of Trade; only a month earlier the Crown had instituted the threatened *quo warranto* proceedings against him.[61] It was probably this fact which moved Penn to action. When he requested that the business of the Three Lower Counties be transacted promptly, he carefully pointed out that the question was one of land, not power. Therefore, the decision of the Lords of Trade would not affect or interfere with the *quo warranto* proceedings. While it cannot be said with certainty that Penn was trying to facilitate these proceedings, he was definitely trying to get all the benefit he could out of Baltimore's awkward position.

At a meeting of the Lords of Trade on September 2, Penn introduced his proofs of Swedish and Dutch occupancy of the west bank of the lower Delaware before the granting of Maryland's charter.[62] One month later, Balti-

[60]*CSP, 1685–8,* sec. 320.

[61]Grant and Munro, *Acts of Privy Council, Colonial,* II, secs. 193–194.

[62]Hazard *et al., Pa. Archives,* ser. 2, XVI, 403. Baltimore had been sent copies of these proofs a year earlier, but apparently offered no defense against them. Nicholas Bayard to WP, 16 April 1684: HSP, T. Cadwalader Collection, Penn vs. Baltimore. The evidence regarding the Dutch is discussed in W. A. Powell, "Fight of a Century Between the Penns and the Calverts...," *Maryland Historical Maga-*

more presented his evidence to the contrary. He also produced a copy of a report by the commissioners of foreign plantations given on April 4, 1638, approving Maryland's ownership of the Isle of Kent, north of 39°. This paper was introduced because Penn had claimed that the phrase in his charter of 1680/81—"beginning of the fortieth degree"—referred to the entire area between the thirty-ninth and fortieth parallels. But the Maryland proprietor was unable to produce an attested record of the 1638 commissioners' report.[63]

On October 17, 1685, the Lords of Trade handed down their opinion: "The Tract of Land, now in Dispute, does not belong to my Lord Baltimore; but, in as much as it yet remains doubtful, what are the true Boundaries of the Land called Delaware [the Three Lower Counties], which their Lordships now adjudge to belong to his Majesty, their Lordships will meet again for the Settlement of those Boundaries between his Majesty, and the Lord Baltimore."[64]

Penn was jubilant. The decision was a real victory for him. "We have, after much patience cost & paines, cap the Lord Balt. & indeed, the Lords did show much Kindness as well as Justice, commending my cause as well as my management," he wrote to a Friend in Pennsylvania.[65] Unfortunately, no account book was kept to inform future historians where costs were incurred. But it is clear from

zine, XXIX (1934), pp. 83–101, and answered in N. B. Wainwright, "The Missing Evidence. Penn v. Baltimore," PMHB, LXXX (1956), 227–235.

[63]Shepherd, Proprietary Government, p. 126; Hazard et al., Pa. Archives, ser. 2, XVI, 403–404.

[64]Ibid., 404.

[65]WP to Phineas Pemberton, 26 October 1685, in ACM, XVIII, 15–18.

Penn's earlier correspondence where he placed his confidence.

When they met again, the Lords of Trade proposed that "the whole Peninsula, or Tract of Land, called Delaware, from East to West, as far as Cape Hinlopen Southward, may be divided into two equal Parts, between his Majesty and my Lord Baltimore." What the Lords had done was to use as a guide to the division of the Delaware peninsula the application for a more beneficial grant made by the Duke of York in March, 1682/83. Disheartened, Baltimore offered no objections, and the proposal was sent to the King, the very man who had initially requested this demarcation![66] On November 13, 1685, James II approved the proposal as it had been sent to him: "Whereof the said Lord Baltimore and William Penn Esq; together with their respective Officers, and all others whom it may concern, are to take Notice, and give due and ready Obedience thereunto."[67]

The west bank of the lower Delaware was indisputably in James' hands, and Penn had no reason to doubt that the King intended it for him. The Quaker proprietor had triumphed over his southern neighbor, whose case was undoubtedly the stronger. But in order to gain this victory, Penn had succumbed to sophistry, using arguments against Baltimore that he himself could not have accepted. He had made his bid for the Delaware territory at the very time when Baltimore was most vulnerable, least able to retali-

[66] The document set the upper boundary at "the 40th Degree of Northern Latitude," a phrase as vague as that in Penn's charter. No lessons regarding language, apparently, had been learned from this controversy.

[67] Hazard et al., Pa. Archives, ser. 2, XVI, 404–406.

ate. More important to his success, if less enhancing to his reputation, was his dependence on well-cultivated connections, the most useful of whom was the King, to sustain his weak cause. As Penn himself said, the territory was obtained at great cost.

CHAPTER III

Indiscreet Courtier

(1686–1688)

BY the time the controversy between Penn and Baltimore had been resolved, the reign of James II was already nine months old. This period of gestation, and not Mary of Modena's, was the real cause of the monarch's downfall. Ten days after his accession, James appointed the Earl of Rochester, a strong royalist and churchman, to the key position of Lord Treasurer. Rochester's brother, the Earl of Clarendon, was given the privy seal. But before the year was out, this apparent orientation toward the Church of England was ended. The appointment of the Earl of Sunderland to the Lord Presidency of the Council on December 4, 1685, threw Rochester on the defensive and marked the initiation of the King's real policy, the conversion of England to Roman Catholicism.[1] It was partly because of his absorption in the business of the boundary that Penn did not realize the coloration the reign was taking.

[1]Kenyon, *Sunderland,* pp. 113–126; Turner, *James II,* pp. 238, 248–250.

At the time of his accession, James labeled the Anglicans "le parti royal," who had "showed themselves so eminently loyal in the worst of times." The Dissenters, on the other hand, he characterized as "de vrais républicains."[2] Nine months later the support of the latter group was necessary if James was to survive the enmity of the former. Yet this support would not be easy to obtain. For the Dissenters felt that the King should worship in private, as they were compelled to do.[3] More important, nowhere in England was a greater stigma attached to Roman Catholicism than among the sects. Nevertheless, Catholics and Dissenters had one plight in common: both were subject to persecution as a result of their refusal to conform to the Church of England. It was by using the ploy of religious toleration that James could hope to make his alliance.

There were several causes for which Quakers could be fined, imprisoned, or dispossessed under acts which went as far back as the fifth year of Elizabeth's reign. Anyone in England who refused to take the oath of supremacy and allegiance was subject to praemunire, an unfortunate circumstance for Quakers who abjured swearing. Members of the Society of Friends were also convicted under the laws condemning recusancy. In fact, shortly after Penn got his charter for Pennsylvania, Lawrence Hyde directed the Court of Exchequer to discharge him from a fine of £20 a month "for as much as we are very well satified that he is not or ever was a Popish recusant."[4] Finally, Quakers were threatened with fines, imprisonment, or both under the Conventicle Acts, which prohibited unlawful convocation (over five persons in religious meeting whose prac-

---

[2]Kenyon, *Sunderland*, p. 112.
[3]Turner, *James II,* p. 247.
[4]Lloyd, *Quaker Social History*, p. 99.

tices contradicted the Church of England), and a related act, dating from the sixteenth century, which prohibited assembly "in violent and tumultuous manner." Penn judged that there were 1,400 Quakers in prison in England and Wales when James II came to the throne.[5]

Before he left for America, Penn had actively sought relief for Dissenters from persecution, especially through the Quaker Meeting for Sufferings. When he returned to England, he resumed this work. He saw his relationship with the new King as a means of gaining the complete and permanent religious toleration which he was unable to obtain under Charles II. James, in turn, realized that he might use Penn to cement a royal friendship with the sects. Thus King and Quaker saw each other as an instrument for the achievement of their respective ends. The crucial difference was that the leader of the Society of Friends had a goal which was attainable, if not altogether probable, under the circumstances; the aim of the Catholic monarch could not be fulfilled. But because Penn was unaware of James' real intent, was unwilling to recognize it, or did not think it should be taken seriously (his writings do not make his position clear), he allowed himself to be led to ruin with his ruler.[6]

At the beginning of the reign, the Quaker leader thought that the implementation of religious toleration was simply

[5]Janney, *Penn,* p. 267.

[6]In a recent attempt to re-evaluate the relationship between the two men in the period 1685–1688, the problem has been stated in these terms: "Penn's enemies argue: 'Penn was loyal to James II, which makes him either a fool or a knave.' Penn's admirers argue: 'Penn was loyal to James II, but there were extenuating circumstances [Penn's quest for religious freedom].'. . . Yet all this implicitly sets aside a third alternative that, if viable, would make the friendship less extraordinary and by no means inexplicable. The alternative

a matter of time. "I was with the King, he was very kind and familiar as formerly, standing as usually, among his nobles, and afterwards took me into his closet. I perceave he will do little for the dissenters till the Coronation."[7] Several weeks later, in a letter to the president of Pennsylvania's provincial council, he appeared even more hopeful.

The king is dead: and the duke succeeds peaceably.... Be careful no indecent speeches pass against the government, for the king, going with his queen publicly to mass at Whitehall, gives occasion. He declared he concealed himself to obey his brother, and that now he would be above-board; which we like the better on many accounts. I was with him, and told him so; but, withal, hoped we should come in for a share. He smiled, and said he desired not that peaceable people should be disturbed for their religion. And till his coronation, ... no hopes of release; and, till the parliament [to meet 19 May 1685], no hopes of any fixed liberty.... Though he [James II] has not his brother's abilities, he has great discipline and industry.[8]

---

is to argue: 'Penn was loyal to James II, and he was right'" Vincent Buranelli, "William Penn and James II," *Proceedings of the American Philosophical Society,* CIV [1960], 36).

There is more novelty than substance in this point of view. It is puerile to argue that personal loyalty is more comprehensible if based on "right"; human relationships cannot be measured by rational standards alone. Many of Penn's sorrows stemmed from the fact that he was a poor judge of men, an irrational trait. The greatest of these sorrows began with the Glorious Revolution. To accept Buranelli's alternative, however, involves more than squaring morality with friendship. It connotes acceptance of the idea that James II was right; right, that is, in Penn's terms. Buranelli mistakenly believes that James II genuinely desired religious toleration.

[7]WP to Stephen Crisp, 28 February 1684/85, in ACM, XVIII, 104–107.

[8]WP to Thomas Lloyd, 16 March 1684/85, in Janney, *Penn,* pp. 263–265. Penn also bade Lloyd to proclaim James II immediately and

Penn's optimism was unwarranted. James II made no immediate proclamation to release those imprisoned for religious reasons. And Parliament, though packed with royalists, was not quite the compliant body which the monarch had expected; it enacted no "fixed liberty." But with the Pennsylvania-Maryland controversy pending, the Quaker leader dared not press the issue to the point where he might anger the King. Instead, he continued to speak optimistically: "My business here has been thrown off. . . first by the late king's death, then the coronation, next the Parliament, now this insurrection, almost over, for the Duke of Monmouth is defeated, and he and Grey taken, will be brought up to London next third day. I hope I may now be despatched."[9]

Parliament was prorogued after a brief meeting in November, 1685; no legislation concerning religious liberty had been enacted. Nor did James make any moves in this direction. Penn's business with Lord Baltimore was successfully concluded at this time, however, and now the Quaker spokesman saw that the cause of toleration could be dealt with. This was not to be done by publicly challenging the government's policy, an action which could result in arrest, trial, and notoriety. Rather, Penn issued a tract entitled *A Persuasive to Moderation to Church Dissenters, in Prudence and Conscience. Humbly submitted to the King and his Great Council.*

The opposition to toleration had come from those who believed that such freedom would present a dangerous challenge to the established church and that, furthermore, it would allow Dissenters to continue in their erroneous

---

instructed him to pay careful attention to the navigation laws. 17 March 1684/85, in ACM, XXVII, 191–196.

[9]WP to J. Harrison, 11 July 1685, in Janney, *Penn,* pp. 267–268.

ways. In his pamphlet Penn argued effectively against both beliefs, especially the first, in which case he cited historical examples from the ancient Jews to the contemporary Dutch in order to show that toleration not only worked, but worked well. He recalled that the Declaration of Indulgence issued by Charles II had had good results: "All dissenters seemed then united in their affection to the government."[10]

This pamphlet alone did not provoke James II's general pardon to all those in prison for conscience' sake. Instead, this act of March, 1685/86, should be seen as an early move in the King's policy of infiltrating the government with his own partisans.[11] But since James was offending the Anglicans, there can be no doubt that Penn's implication of Dissenter support influenced the King's decision to undertake a general pardon.

Penn was aware of the difficulties implicit in the King's action. The Houses of Commons and Lords both had been openly critical of the royal policy as it emerged in late 1685. To Sir William Trumbull, appointed to the Paris embassy in Rochester's interest but now passing into the Sunderland camp, Penn wrote that Parliament had been prorogued. But, he continued, if Trumbull would divert attention from the unpopular policy at home by creating an incident abroad, an incident which would range England on the side of the most esteemed Protestant ruler on the Continent, the effect would be most salutary.

[10]*Works of WP,* IV, 319–371.

[11]Compare Clarkson, *Penn,* I, 473–474, and Janney, *Penn,* p. 281, to the more recent interpretation in David Ogg, *England in the Reigns of James II and William III* (2nd ed.; Oxford, 1957), pp. 167–168. At this time James also ended, by royal warrant, all prosecutions against Quakers for recusancy. Lloyd, *Quaker Social History,* pp. 98–99.

"The name of Orange, so beloved of this people, will more easily dispose their representatives to close with the King in any honourable attempt."[12] This was not government policy; Penn was not acting as a mouthpiece for the Crown.[13] He had willingly entered the political arena in return for the support James gave to the cause of religious toleration.

So far, Penn had retained his confidence in the altruism of James and his advisers. In his letter to Trumbull he had remarked: "They talk of Quo warrantos against the Universities, which the King's Council have signed, and against four Bishops...but I give little credence to the Story." It was not until he was affected personally that his mind was changed. This was soon to happen. A few months earlier, in July, 1685, the Lords of Trade had asked that the Attorney General might "have directions to consider the several grants & Proprietyes of East and West New Jersey and of Delaware aforementioned & to enter like writs of Quo Warranto against the respective Proprietors if he shall find cause."[14] Nothing was done about this recommendation until the Lords of Trade revived it in April, 1686, at which time the King gave his approval to

[12]WP to Sir William Trumbull, 17 January 1685/86, in Historical Manuscripts Commission, *Report on the Manuscripts of the Marquess of Downshire* (4 vols.; London, 1924–1940), I, pt. 1, 99–100; Kenyon, *Sunderland,* p. 120.

[13]Kenyon writes that in February, 1685/86, "Trumbull, whose representation at Versailles on the question of the principality of Orange had far transcended the limits of normal diplomatic ettiquette, was at last reined in" (*ibid.,* p. 127).

[14]Lords of Trade to James II, 17 July 1685, in O'Callaghan and Fernow, *N. Y. Colonial Docs.,* III, 362–363. It was also recommended that proceedings begin against Rhode Island. This was, of course, the time when proceedings were actually begun against Maryland. That Penn was worried by these recommendations is evident in his

it. The following month the Attorney General was instructed by the Crown to begin proceedings against the Bahamas, the Carolinas, and Pennsylvania.[15] This was obviously part of a concerted royal effort to vacate the charters of all private colonies in America, irrespective of the individual merits of each case.

No longer could William Penn consider his province safe from attack. His confidence in the King and his advisers had now been shaken. Yet he was not too stunned to react quickly. Within a week after the Attorney General had received his first instructions, he got a message from Secretary of State Sunderland that the King "has thought fit to suspend the proceedings against the Proprietor of Pensilvania...his intention being nevertheless you should continue against the rest."[16] Rhode Island, Connecticut, and the Jerseys, along with New York, were to become part of the Dominion of New England—but, significantly, Delaware was not. As to Maryland, the Carolinas, and the Bahamas, they also escaped the King's clutches, but only because James' reign ended before they could be included under a royal government in America.

Penn had rescued his province from imperial control, but he had also learned his lesson. He must maintain a favorable relationship with the Crown if Pennsylvania was to remain autonomous. This could be done in two ways:

---

letter to Phineas Pemberton (see Chapter II, n. 65): "do not draw a storm on our River too. Wherefore be wise, few & safe in words, and In behaviour civil & obleidging to that officer or any else of the Kings."

[15]Grant and Munro, *Acts of Privy Council, Colonial,* II, secs. 193, 194, 209. Connecticut was included in the revived recommendation of April, 1686.

[16]Sunderland to Attorney General, 6 June 1686, in ACM, LXVIIᴬ, 93.

by remaining silent when he disagreed with royal policy and, more positively, by assisting in the implementation of the King's plans. He soon found himself in the latter position.

James' design was now becoming more evident: he had chosen judges who would assent to his interpretation of the dispensing power, and he had established an Ecclesiastical Commission to deal with recalcitrant churchmen. All this was done under the guise of religious toleration. But James was apparently aware of a growing restlessness and realized that, without parliamentry sanction, he would need firm backing from other quarters, preferably from his son-in-law, William of Orange. In Holland, William Penn was well known as a leading advocate of religious toleration; his philosophical brother, Algernon Sidney, had spent considerable time in The Hague. Henry Sidney was there now.

Consequently, Penn went as James II's emissary to the Court of William of Orange. The only record of this conference is that of Gilbert Burnet, a clergyman in exile from England who was understandably hostile to the Quaker's mission. But his acid account is worth repeating, if only as a forecast of the reaction against Penn in the next reign, when Burnet was again in England.

Complaints came daily over from England of all the high things that the priests were every where throwing out. Pen the quaker came over to Holland. He was a talking vain man, who had been long in the king's favour, he being the vice-admiral's son. . . . He undertook to persuade the prince [William] to come into the king's measures, and had two or three long audiences of him on the subject. . . . The prince readily consented to a toleration of popery, as well as of the dissenters, provided it were proposed and passed in parliament: and he promised his assistance, if there was need of it, to get it to pass. But for the tests, he would enter into no treaty about them. He said, it was a plain betraying the security of the protestant religion, to give them up. Nothing was left unsaid, that might move him to agree to this in the way of interest: the king would enter into an entire confidence with him, and would put his best friends in the chief trusts. Pen undertook for this so positively, that he seemed to believe it himself, or he was a great proficient in the art of dissimulation. Many suspected that he was a concealed papist. It is certain that he was much with father Petre, and was particularly trusted by the earl of Sunderland. So, though he did not pretend any commission for what he promised, yet we looked on him as a man employed. To all this the prince answered, that no man was more for toleration in principle than he was...but he looked on the tests as such as real security, and indeed the only one, when the king was of another religion, that he would join in no counsels with those that intended to repeal those laws that enacted them. Pen said, the king would have all or nothing: but that, if this was once done, the king would secure the toleration by a solemn and unalterable law. To this the late repeal of the edict of Nantes, that was declared perpetual and irrevocable, furnished an answer that admitted of no reply. So Pen's negociation with the prince had no effect.[17]

The fact that Penn carried overtures from the Catholic peers to William certainly did not improve his case.[18] The most obvious conclusion to be drawn from these overtures was that English Catholics were anxiously awaiting the repeal of the Test Act, that they were poised to swarm into offices for which they had been ineligible since 1673. The revocation of the Edict of Nantes in 1685 also damaged

[17]Gilbert Burnet, *History of the Reign of King James the Second* (Oxford, 1852), pp. 155–157.
[18]Kenyon, *Sunderland,* p. 150.

Penn's argument, especially since many of James' critics believed that he was modeling his reign after the absolutist regime of his French cousin, Louis XIV. There was, then, a just basis for Burnet's account, even though it was exaggerated. If the Anglican cleric had known the full background of Penn's visit, he would surely have been even more censorious. His greatest insight was to call Penn "a man employed"—an epithet which, though too strong, is a reminder that Penn was on the King's errand for reasons beyond the merits of religious toleration.

Penn left The Hague for Amsterdam, then traveled to Germany on a missionary journey before returning to England in September, 1686, to report on his unsuccessful discussion with William of Orange. He found that James had not waited for his report. The King had already begun to appoint Catholics to the Privy Council; by autumn there were five, one of whom took the privy seal from Clarendon in March, 1686/87. Two months before his brother was dispossessed, Rochester had been forced from office.[19] The demise of the Anglican interest was recognizable before the departure of the Hydes, however. On September 6, 1686, Henry Compton, Bishop of London, had been suspended from his post by the King's newly created Ecclesiastical Commission Court.[20]

This meant that the Dissenters would again have to be courted. In November, 1686, the King expressed his desire "not to have those people so troubled upon the account of their being Quakers only."[21] A more general and sig-

[19]The newly appointed councilors were the Earls of Tyrconnel and Porvis, and Lords Belasye, Dover, and Arundel of Wardour. The latter got the privy seal. Grant and Munro, *Acts of Privy Council, Colonial*, V, 648.

[20]Ogg, *James II and William III*, p. 179.

[21]Earl of Rochester to Sir Daniel Fleming, November 1686, in

nificant step was taken on April 4, 1687, when James issued his first Declaration of Indulgence.[22] All penal laws pertaining to ecclesiastical matters were to be suspended, while the Test Acts and the oaths of allegiance and supremacy were no longer to be applied to office holders. The Declaration concluded with the hope that when Parliament met in December it would approve this action by repealing the penal laws, Test Acts, and oaths.

It has been suggested that Penn's influence may be seen in this document.[23] He certainly believed in the course taken. To express his appreciation, he led a delegation of Friends to Whitehall to thank James personally for the measure. In view of the unpopularity of the Declaration, Penn was favoring James more than the Quakers in this action. To his steward in Pennsylvania he wrote: "I am engaged in the public business of the nation and Friends; and thos in authority would have me see the establishment of the liberty, that I was a small instrument to begin in the land: the Lord has given me great entrance and interest with the K[ing], *though not so much as is said*; and I confess I should like to see the penal laws repealed that are now suspended."[24]

Repeal of the penal laws was possible only by act of Parliament, and therefore Penn determined to get popular support for repeal. He went so far as to speak publicly in

---

Turner, *James II*, pp. 309–310. See also WP to Fleming, 6 and 9 November 1686, in HMC, *The Manuscripts of S. H. Le Fleming, Esq., of Rydal Hall* (London, 1890), p. 201.

[22]A copy of this is in Douglas, *English Historical Docs.*, VIII, 395–397.

[23]Ogg, *James II and William III*, pp. 180–181.

[24]Janney, *Penn*, pp. 294–297; WP to J. Harrison, 1687, in ACM, XXIX, 123 (italics mine). See also WP to R. Turner, May 1687, in *PMHB*, XXXIII (1909), 310–311.

favor of the King's policy, even after James tried to force a Catholic candidate for president of Magdalen College on the Oxford Fellows in June, 1687, a move which Penn disapproved of. A "News Letter" of September, 1687, reported:

Quaker Penn attends the King very close and preaches at the Bath in the Tennis Court but the report of his being made one of the King's Privy Council is false, though the King consults him in all matters of moment.[25]

Penn also gave positive support to the cause of repeal by writing. In 1687 he issued two tracts: *The Great and Popular Objection Against the Repeal of the Penal Laws & Tests Briefly Stated and Consider'd . . .* and *Good Advice to the Church of England, Roman Catholick and Protestant Dissenter. . . .*[26] The second of these treatises contains the more extensive exposition. In it Penn answered affirmatively the question "Whether it be fit to repeal the penal laws and tests in matters of religion, or not?" He argued: "That part of Popery which the Church of England with most success objects against, is her violence. This is that only she can pretend to fear: the doctrines she partly professes, or thinks she can easily refute." He accused the Church of England of guilt on that very score—violence—through laws which allowed persecution. He doubted their efficacy. "What, then is the use of the penal laws? Only

[25]HMC, *Downshire*, I, pt. 1, pp. 237, 243; Marquis of Lansdowne, ed., *The Petty–Southwell Correspondence, 1676–1687* (London, 1928), p. 280; Sir James Mackintosh, *History of the Revolution in England in 1688* (London, 1834), p. 171; Historical Manuscripts Commission, *The Manuscripts of His Grace the Duke of Portland . . .* (10 vols.; London, 1891–1931), III, 401, 403, and *The Manuscripts of the Earl of Westmoreland, Captain Stewart, Lord Muncaster and Others* (London, 1885), p. 376.

[26]The latter appears in *Works of WP*, IV, 373–435.

to show the sincerity of them that suffer, and the cruelty of those that make and execute them."

Yet Penn was aware of the objections which would arise to his proposition, and he dispelled them in order. The executive power in the hands of the King was but an "artificial strength." Furthermore, "we have his word to bind him. . . . Next, we have his age for security . . . , a greater age than most of his ancestors ever attained." Penn saw no reason to worry because the army was being staffed with Catholic officers, nor did he think there was cause to fear the intervention of Louis XIV. The essay closed with a special appeal to Dissenters: "Of all people, it would look the more disingenuous in you, and give you an air the least sensible, charitable and Christian, not to endeavour such an ease, that have so much so wanted it, and so often and so earnestly pressed it, even to clamour."

Although Penn declared, "Let us not therefore uphold penal laws against any of our religious persuasions, nor make tests out of each other's faiths, to exclude one another our civil rights," he had actually said virtually nothing in either tract about the implications of repealing the Test Acts. In an *unpublished* essay, also written in 1687, Penn stated: "I think it the true interest of all dissenters to repeale the penall Laws if they can, but to keep up the Test [,] of the Papists to take of both, & of the Church of England to preserve both. . . . Roman Catholicks have no needs of the repeale of the Test during this Reign. . . . I will rather lett the Penale Laws stand as they are then do any thing that may tend towards the repeale of the Test."[27] This disparity between Penn's private views and

[27]HSP, Dreer Collection, Penn Papers, p. 67. This important essay has been neglected both by those who would picture Penn as entirely blind to James' design and those who argue that Penn was, and rightly so, an apologist for the reign.

his public pronouncements is most striking. Yet it is not hard to explain. On the contrary, it demonstrates that he was not completely hoodwinked by James' tactics. The increasing infiltration of the government with Catholics made even the sanguine Quaker uncertain. But beyond this, Penn's repression of his doubts about James' intent is not only evidence that as a proponent of toleration he would go to great lengths to help the King obtain parliamentary support. It also shows that as a colonial proprietor he felt it necessary to stay on good terms with the Crown.

The prospect of an unfriendly House of Commons made it likely that James and his advisers would postpone a meeting of Parliament until at least March, 1687/88. Meanwhile, in October, 1687, the first attempt was made to obtain pliable MPs. This was to be accomplished by asking three questions of Deputy Lieutenants, Magistrates and leading gentry in the provinces: were they willing to live peaceably with their neighbors, of whatever religion; if elected to Parliament, would they support repeal of penal laws and Test Acts; and would they give their votes to candidates so pledged. Penn advised against the use of this scheme, possibly because he opposed such "packing" on principle and probably because he feared the repeal of the Test Acts.[28] But he still hoped that toleration could be accomplished. When the tactic of using the three questions backfired, Penn was willing to see the meeting of Parliament held off, but only temporarily. In January, 1687/88, he discussed with Sunderland, who was now virtually running James' affairs, the compromise measure by which Parliament was to repeal the Test Acts but Catholics were to be barred from the House of Commons. Penn agreed to

[28]Kenyon, *Sunderland*, pp. 165, 171–174. Penn's reasons are not given.

this when Sunderland promised a Parliament for spring. But he was less confident dealing with the crafty Secretary of State than with the straightforward King, with whom he could hardly discuss this measure. His uncertainty is evidenced in a conversation one James Johnstone reported having with him:

He [Penn] told me there would be a parliament at the end of May. I said I would wager twenty to one against. He began to laugh, and said I imagined Sunderland had more credit than he actually possessed—he hadn't the power to prevent it, and he would be ruined if he did not allow it. I replied that he had no need of power, he would use trickery instead. That is what I fear myself, he said.[29]

Meanwhile, the Crown's remodeling of parliamentary boroughs continued apace. And in April, 1688, the Declaration of Indulgence was renewed. "These two things, both superfluous, both unnecessary for the interests of English Roman Catholics, proved to be the undoing of James and the immediate causes of the Revolution."[30] Penn's role in both of these projects was ambiguous. He staged no strong opposition to tampering with the legislature, yet these steps ran contrary to his desires. He was offended to see Algernon Sidney defeated by such tactics in 1679 and, only months earlier, Penn had opposed the use of the three questions.[31] He approved of both Declarations of Indulgence, but he opposed commitment to the Tower of the

---

[29]*Ibid.,* pp. 186–187.

[30]Ogg, *James II and William III,* p. 186.

[31]Burnet, who was still in Holland, said that it was Penn and Father Petre who urged James to promise that Parliament would meet in November, 1688. The priest thought this would convince his monarch of the futility of parliamentary agreement; the Quaker "had still some hopes of carrying a parliament to agree with the king, if too much time was not lost" (*History of James II,* p. 252).

seven Bishops who had denounced the second Declaration and pressed for their release on the day the Prince of Wales was born.[32]

Furthermore, Penn did not have a realistic notion of the effect of these measures. He mistakenly believed that the Dissenters backed the King's position. As late as September, 1688, the Quaker leader was confident that James could summon a friendly Parliament.[33] So out of tune with public opinion was he that in the summer of 1688 he moved his residence to a site near Windsor, an act which could only further identify him with the King.[34] While Penn was apparently unaware of the unpopularity of the regime, and of the fact that his reputation was suffering because of this, other observers of the English political scene were more astute. One of these was William Popple, later a prominent figure in colonial administration, who urged Penn to make a public denunciation of the rumors concerning him. Popple pointed out that since Penn had such easy access to the King, and since it was generally accepted that James intended "to settle Popery in this nation," it was concluded that Penn was a Papist or, worse, a Jesuit. Penn had given abundant evidence, Popple agreed, of his opposition to the principles of the "Romish church." But, Popple added,

the general and long prevalency of any opinion gives it strength, especially among the vulgar, that is not easily shaken. And as it happens that you have also enemies of a higher rank,

[32]HSP, *Memoirs,* III, pt. 2, 230–231.

[33]Kenyon, *Sunderland,* pp. 208, 214. He even believed that he had undermined the Roman influence of Father Petre. S. W. Singer, ed., *The Correspondence of Henry Hyde...and Lawrence Hyde...with the Diary of Lord Clarendon...1687 to 1690* (2 vols., London, 1828), II, 178.

[34]HSP, *Memoirs,* III, pt. 2, 228.

who will be ready to improve such popular mistakes by all sorts of malicious artifices, it must be taken for granted that those errors will be thereby still more confirmed, and the inconveniences that may arise from thence no less increased. This, sir, I assure you, is a melancholy prospect to your friends; for we know you have such enemies.[35]

Penn's reply was immediate—not because he cared what the world thought of him but, he said, because of his friendship for Popple. It is likely, however, that the news of the Dutch invasion, which reached the Quaker at the same time as Popple's letter, prompted his haste.[36] Penn doubtlessly believed his reply would reach the Prince of Orange. In his letter, the Quaker leader ridiculed the notion of his being a Papist and pointed out that it was "not impossible for a true Protestant Dissenter to be dutiful, thankful, and serviceable to the king, though he be of the Roman Catholic communion," especially when that monarch advocated liberty of conscience. Whitehall, he pointed out, was a place "no more forbid to me than the rest of the world."

Penn knew this statement had a false ring to it, and so he asked rhetorically: "Why must I have preferable access to other Dissenters, if not a Papist?" He recalled that he had been visiting Whitehall for the past sixteen years in the interest of religious toleration. The deathbed promise made to his father by the Stuarts explained his easy access to the Crown. But his frequent presence in Court did not make him "the author of all that is done there that does

[35]William Popple to WP, 20 October 1688, in Janney, *Penn,* pp. 337–341.

[36]See WP to Earl of Dartmouth, 23 October 1688, in Historical Manuscripts Commission, *The Manuscripts of the Earl of Dartmouth* (3 vols.; London, 1887–1896), I, 170.

not please abroad." He held no official position; he had no obligation to oppose royal measures if his opinion was not solicited.[37]

These explanations were less than candid. While Admiral Penn was initially responsible for the good relationship between his son and James Stuart, the Quaker's recent access to the King came primarily as a result of the political power of the Dissenters and his own prominence within that group. Penn was too wise not to know this. Furthermore, he came close to denying that he had acquiesced in certain measures—even when his own principles were violated—though he was in a position to take a strong stand. Finally, he did not mention his reasons for spending so much time at Whitehall: his need to protect Pennsylvania and his desire to advance the cause of religious toleration. He was more than a little naive as to James' intent with regard to the latter, but he knew what was happening. The reason he so seldom publicly criticized measures he disapproved of can be traced to an anxiety to protect his province from the treatment the rest of the plantations were receiving from the government.

Penn's letter to Popple was, therefore, not entirely honest. But given the circumstances in late October, 1688, the Quaker leader can be forgiven a few half-truths. It is harder to forgive him his real error, his belief that he could influence James II without bearing the onus of the King's actions; in retrospect, the reverse seems to have been the case—without really changing the King's intentions, he had remained close enough to James to be discredited along with the reign.

[37]WP to William Popple, 24 October 1688, in Janney, *Penn,* 341–347.

There was irony, as well as error, in Penn's entanglement with the last male Stuart. Having returned to England to ensure his title to the Three Lower Counties, he remained to bolster the cause of religious toleration and to protect his enlarged province. The essence of his colonial experiment was democracy—the very thing which made it vulnerable to attack by a regime headed toward absolutism. In Pennsylvania, democracy threatened to degenerate into anarchy with the proprietor gone.

While Penn had been in the colony, his personality dominated the atmosphere and smoothed relations among contending factions. With his departure the rivalry between the powerful council, now exercising the executive functions of the colony, and the acquisitive assembly, determined to enlarge its role in provincial affairs, broke into the open. Since the proprietor was associated with the council, the assembly's hostility focused on him as well as on the council. Thus began the gradual erosion of respect for the proprietary privilege. It has been judged that when Penn left Pennsylvania, the failure of the "holy experiment" began.[38]

Illustrative of the general situation in the province was the case of Nicholas More, who apparently owed his position as chief justice to the fact that he had been speaker of the last assembly to meet before the proprietor sailed for England. Penn made a real mistake in appointing More, who turned out to be an arrogant and arbitrary man, especially in his dealings with the lower house. The assembly retaliated against More by impeaching him, although most of the council refused to cooperate.[39]

[38]Edwin B. Bronner, "The Failure of the 'Holy Experiment' in Pennsylvania, 1684–1699," *Pennsylvania History*, XXI (1954), 93–108.
[39]George, *et al., Charter to William Penn*, pp. 496–509. This oc-

This and other difficulties between the two legislative
bodies resulted in mutual recrimination and finally a
conference, at which "there arose a Long Debate about the
Privileges of the Assembly, wch not being granted by the
Councill, and that no president [precedent] should be Left
upon Record whereby to prejudice the Privileges of the
Assembly. The Genall Assembly did Unanimously agree
that all things Relating to the premises should remaine in
the same State and Condition as they are at this present
time, until the Governor shall arrive and the Contraversie
determined before him."[40] But Penn's coming, expected
daily, was over a decade away. In this sense his relations
with the Crown, or rather the necessity to be in England
to maintain these relations, adversely affected the operation
of the Pennsylvania government.

To complete the vicious circle, Penn saw that the tumult
in Pennsylvania could offset his efforts to protect the
province from the aggressive imperial policy of the home
government. He wrote to the Quakers in his colony: "Cannot more friendly and private courses be taken to set
matters to rights in an infant province whose steps are
numbered and watched; for the love of God, me and the
poor country, be not so governmentish; so noisy and open,
in your disaffections"; and later, "The noise of some differences that have been in the Province have reached these
parts with no advantage to the reputation of the country."[41]

It was his fear of royal action against the restive colony
which caused the proprietor to send Thomas Lloyd, presi-

---

curred in the first assembly after Penn's departure, which met on 10
May 1685. Other assemblies held during the reign of James II met
on 10 May 1686, 1687, and 1688, all in Philadelphia (*ibid.,* pp. 505–
518).
[40]18 May 1686 (*Colonial Recs.,* I, 184).
[41]Cited in Peare, *Penn,* p. 293, without exact dates.

dent of the Pennsylvania council, an extremely bold plan of action:

Our laws with the laws of other Provinces are like to be called before the Commit of Lords for Plantations, and because I know the franchises and constitution of them, Exceed wt is elsewhere: to the end we may use the advantages the Pening of my charter gave us...with what success we are able, Know that if once in five years, ours are presented to the said Commtt, or the King rather, it is as much as we are obliged to. my Councell therefore advises, that the very next Session after the receipt of this, a Bill be prepared to vacat all the Laws as they now stand, & prepare another with such abrogations, altera-tions & additions of laws as shall palliate the thing, that shall be read next year to the other, so that the distance will be but the time of reading one & the other, and by this, the laws will have been put probationary, and will take a new altera-tion, from Experience, & thus have a speedy resurrection.[42]

In other words, Penn's strategy was twofold. The present laws were to be repealed and passed in modified form, that is, with the more liberal features eliminated or moderated. The second step was to send both old and new laws to the Lords of Trade. But the new laws needed to be only temporary, since the charter allowed five years before laws had to be reviewed, and therefore they could be returned to the province and further amended to conform to the wishes of the Lords of Trade.

Penn's plan was to be "insinuated to the wiser only," and if its logic was not convincing then it should be "discreetly and closely intimated" that he would—as he could—simply annul all the laws. As he said, his plan was "for their sakes not mine, for the less free they are, the more free I am." Expediency was not the only issue

[42]WP to Thomas Lloyd, 21 and 22 September 1686, in ACM, XXVIII, 280–308. (Also cited in Chapter I, note 59.)

involved. The plan was totally in opposition to the spirit of the "holy experiment" and, for that matter, to the spirit of the royal charter. Penn naturally believed that he would meet opposition in trying to dictate policy to the colony. He did not suspect that the council would flatly and unanimously reject his plan.[43] The Quaker leader had been absent from the province only two years, but he was already out of touch with those whom he counted as his closest friends. And it is easy to see why. Penn was pre-occupied with the protection of his colony from the threat of royal centralization. The Pennsylvanians, lacking the proprietor's perspective, were primarily concerned with the defense of their local liberties.

Penn acted in such a way as to give substance to the colonists' concern. In February, 1686/87, he divested the council of its executive functions and appointed five commissioners of state to run the affairs of the province. "I judged it a way to quiet things till I came," the proprietor later wrote, but the council was angered and no one else was placated.[44] Nor was this Penn's final recourse. To replace an elected executive with an appointed one symbolized the Quaker leader's progressive disillusionment with the "holy experiment." When the commissioners of state did not work out as he had hoped, he decided that the executive would better rest in the hands of a single individual, one who stood above the contending factions.

As deputy governor of Pennsylvania the proprietor appointed John Blackwell.[45] He was not a Quaker but a former officer in Oliver Cromwell's army. He had the

[43]*Colonial Recs.*, I, 198–199.

[44]Bronner, *Holy Experiment*, pp. 101–104.

[45]A brief background to this appointment and a summary of Blackwell's brief term of office appear in Nicholas B. Wainwright, "Governor John Blackwell," *PMHB*, LXXIV (1950), 457–472.

character and experience to rule wisely and firmly. Yet Penn's announcement of his appointment undermined the deputy governor's authority from the start: "Let him see wh[at] he can doe a while. . . . If he do not please you, he shall be layd aside."[46] Blackwell was instructed that the sole purpose of the assembly was to approve or disapprove laws, a difficult rule for him to enforce under the most favorable conditions. In this and other ways Penn told the deputy governor to discipline the colonists, yet he placed the power of Blackwell's removal in the hands of those who would be most affected by his policies.[47] Small wonder that Blackwell received a rude reception from the leaders of the province, that within four months he sent Penn his resignation. He stayed in the colony only a little over a year.

The Blackwell fiasco was due in part to the Quakers, especially the small inner group headed by Thomas Lloyd—whom the deputy governor tried to impeach until Penn made him desist. Blackwell's parting remark was certainly apropos: "I have to do with a people whom neither God nor man can prevayle with [for they] despise all Dominion & dignity that is not in themselves."[48] But Penn must bear as much responsibility as the Pennsylvania Friends. It was he who sent Blackwell to the colony under circumstances which rendered the deputy governor powerless. The ambiguity of the proprietor's directions stemmed from his uncertainty about the "holy experiment." While he mistrusted the direction it took once it had begun, he did not want to undermine it completely. The result was

[46]WP to commissioners of state, 11 September 1688, in HSP, Penn Letters.

[47]Wainwright, "Blackwell," p. 459.

[48]Quoted in *ibid.,* p. 472; from Blackwell to WP, 11 January 1690, in HSP.

continued chaos in the colony, the very situation which he had hoped to eliminate.

In 1682 William Penn had sailed for America in order to set the "holy experiment" in motion. He left England with the royal blessing, most recently demonstrated in the grant of the Three Lower Counties. He was not long in Pennsylvania before he discovered two things: the experiment was developing in a direction he had not anticipated and did not like, in so far as it infringed on his proprietary privilege; and the region along the lower Delaware was not undeniably his, although he had already incorporated it into the Pennsylvania government.

In order to guard against the loss of the Three Lower Counties, Penn returned to England where he could exercise his influence over the men who would decide the issue. But his absence from the province resulted in the further development of its democratic tendencies, a phenomenon exactly opposite to the increasing absolutism of the Stuart regime. As this domination was extended to the plantations, Penn feared for the fate of the liberal government in Pennsylvania. He therefore remained in London to guard against imperial control of his colony.

In the authoritarian atmosphere of England, Penn could but view with alarm the increasing liberty in Pennsylvania. His unsuccessful attempt to have the province amend its laws to conform to the standards of the home government was followed by the removal of the executive office from the management of the colonists. The appointment of John Blackwell, because it demonstrated the proprietor's disillusionment with the democratic process, must be viewed as a blow to the "holy experiment."

Simultaneously, Penn had become more and more involved in the reign of James II. Having obtained the Three Lower Counties as a result of Stuart favoritism, he depended on royal beneficence not only to protect Pennsylvania but to advance the cause of religious toleration. In so doing, he occasionally sacrificed principle to expediency. But this was not the only way he hurt himself. His close association with James II led to his downfall when William and Mary took the throne. The irony of the situation was that throughout the late 1680's, Pennsylvania retained its autonomy in spite of the fact that it did not heed the pleas and warnings of the proprietor.

CHAPTER IV

Frustrated Fugitive

(1689–1694)

THE Revolution of 1688 was not glorious for William Penn. During the two previous reigns, he had been accepted, even welcomed by Charles and James Stuart. But his ideals had been rejected. Now the situation was reversed. The Toleration Act of 1689 embodied the religious principles he had been striving for: no longer were the penal statutes concerning Protestant Dissenters to be enforced against those who would fulfil certain inoffensive conditions; nonconformists would now meet openly and without fear of prosecution.[1] Penn's political tenets of limited monarchy and a government of laws, rather than men, were insured by the very circumstances under which William and Mary took the throne. The ideals of the Quaker leader were accepted by the new government, but he himself was rejected.

Penn's troubles began in December, 1688, when he was summoned to the Privy Council. Whereas he had formerly

[1]William & Mary, c. 18, in Douglas, *English Historical Docs.*, VIII, 400–403.

known the important statesmen on intimate terms, he was now appearing before an unfriendly group. He candidly admitted—how, indeed, could he have denied—his friendship for the deposed James Stuart. His declaration of faith in Protestantism and England was only temporarily satisfactory to the councilors. He was released but then called to court during both the Hilary and Easter terms of 1689, though in neither case could evidence be offered against him for the part he had played in the previous reign.[2] Before attending court the second time, he wrote to the Earl of Shrewsbury, assuring the new secretary of state that he had "no hand or share in any conspiracy against the king or government, nor do I know of any that have." Penn professed surprise that the King should take him for a plotter, since James II had always thought him too partial to William. In view of his peaceful intentions—and the press of "affairs of great consequence to me and my family now in hand that require to be dispatched for America"—he asked that he be allowed to carry on his business from the seclusion of his country house.[3] Having consorted with one king, Penn was now forced into the position of pleading for leniency from his successor.

His plea, if it ever had a chance of success, was doomed by developments on the foreign scene. In May, 1689, England declared war on France, and the Quaker's relationship with James Stuart, who was now openly in league with Louis XIV, took on a more sinister appearance. The former monarch was in Ireland with a squadron of ten ships, hoping to invade England.[4] On the other side of

[2]*Works of WP,* I, cxviii–cxix.
[3]WP to Shrewsbury, March 1689, in Janney, *Penn,* pp. 353–354.
[4]The account of James' sojourn into Ireland is in Turner, *James*

the Irish channel, Penn was begging the Marquis of Halifax for an "increase of his generosity in proportion to my unhappiness; for tho no man desired more to live with respect & submission to the Government, I am to be ever uneasy under it." He complained that he had forfeited two-thirds of his estate in Ireland, had suffered a long and expensive attendance at court to get clear of his bail. Now, having just returned to his family in Sussex, he was taken away again.[5] But this application to Halifax was no more effective than his plea to Shrewsbury three months before; the harrassment continued. A year earlier, Penn could have carried his complaints directly and personally to the most important men in the government. Now he could only communicate by letter with his few remaining friends in office.

Fearing for his reputation in the midst of all this, Penn published late in 1689 *An Epistle General to the People of God, Called Quakers, by Their Friend and Brother, William Penn.* "But of one thing be assured," he stated, *"I am innocent* both of the imputation of Jesuitism, Popery, and plots, and my God will in his good time confound their devices that trouble you and me with their false things."[6] Gone was the confidence Penn displayed in his letter to William Popple, when it seemed incredible that anyone could believe such things of him. He could not but realize that Popple had been right.

In early 1690 Penn was again called before the Privy

II, pp. 464–492. In May 1689, the French ambassador to James' Court, Avaux, sent Louis an optimistic report from a Jacobite spy in England, whom Avaux called M. Pen. While Turner is convinced that the spy was not William Penn, a rumor to the opposite effect could have circulated.

[5] WP to Halifax, 28 June 1689, in ACM, XXX, 179–185.
[6] c. 30 December 1689, in Janney, *Penn,* pp. 362–366.

Council, this time on charges of holding correspondence with James Stuart. It is extremely doubtful that he was guilty of this charge, for he was well aware of the dangers it would have entailed.[7] James had written to him, however, requesting his assistance. The government had intercepted the letter and questioned the Quaker about its meaning. Penn said he supposed the former monarch meant that he should aid in a restoration, but his loyalty to the present reign was unswerving. He had loved James II in his prosperity, and he could not hate him in his adversity. He was, in fact, obliged to him for many favors. But he never "had the wickedness even to think of endeavoring to restore him that crown, which had fallen from his head."[8] Nevertheless, Penn was held on bail, though cleared again in court during Trinity term, 1690. The story is told that William III, after talking with the Quaker for several hours, was inclined to acquit him immediately rather than hold him for bail, but some members of the Privy Council held out against the King.[9]

The truth of this tale may be doubted. Unlike the situation during the previous two reigns, Penn's relations with William III were neither warm nor close. The new

[7]He was, indeed, quite touchy on this issue. To a Friend who had been collecting his letters to the Duke of Buckingham, the Restoration statesman, Penn wrote: "In the rubbish of those times and the late extraordinary Revolution let them lie" (c. June 1690, in Clarkson, *Penn*, II, 56–58).

[8]*Ibid.*, pp. 59–60.

[9]*Works of WP*, I, cxix. It is not possible to tell from Penn's correspondence at this time who his friends and enemies were on the Council. It may be guessed, however, that Henry Compton, Bishop of London, was his most hostile critic in that body. Compton believed that Penn kept James II from appointing him Archbishop of Canterbury (Allison G. Olson, "William Penn, Parliament, and Proprietary Government," *William and Mary Quarterly*, XVIII [1961], 184 n.).

King held most men at a distance, and the Quaker leader was no exception. On the few instances when the two men met, the atmosphere must have been chilly. Penn's charm had from time to time affected the capricious Charles II, but William III always subordinated personal inclination to public policy. The Quaker's appeal to James II had stemmed largely from a similarity in temperaments; such could not be the case with the Dutch Prince. William's character has been described as "a grim edifice or institution, divided into separate, independent compartments, connected by a few corridors, and known to the world only from its cold, forbidding ante-chamber."[10] Penn had been unable to pass through this exterior when he visited The Hague in 1686, and there is no good evidence that he was more successful at a later date.

Nor did Penn exercise any influence with the King's wife. In the summer of 1690, William III took an army to Ireland to fight the French and Irish forces assembled there under the command of James Stuart. Queen Mary, left in charge of the government, was afraid that her father's allies in England might seize on this as an opportunity to rebel. Consequently, she issued a proclamation for the arrest of eighteen persons supposedly disaffected from the government. They were mostly nobles and military officers, but Penn was included among them.[11] Although in bad

[10]There is a brief character sketch of William and Mary in Ogg, *James II and William III,* pp. 319–323.

[11]The others were Edward Henry, Earl of Litchfield; Thomas, Earl of Aylesbury; William, Lord Montgomery; Roger, Earl of Castlemain; Richard, Viscount Preston; Henry, Lord Belasyse; Sir Edward Hales; Sir Robert Thorold; Sir Robert Hamilton; Sir Theophilus Oglethorpe; Colonel Edward Sackvile; Lieutenant Colonel William Richardson; Major Thomas Soaper; Captain David Lloyd (not Pennsylvania's David Lloyd); Edmund Elliott; Marmaduke Langdale; Edward Rutter (Clarkson, *Penn,* pp. 62–63).

health, he turned himself in and requested bail. Even this small favor was denied him by the daughter of his former benefactor. Instead, he was imprisoned for a month, the first time he had been jailed since his youthful passion for religious controversy had gotten him in trouble.[12] Again he appeared in court; the absence of evidence led to his discharge by order of King's Bench, Westminster, on the last day of Michaelmas term, November 25, 1690.[13]

Penn was now convinced that his tribulations were ended. Unfortunately, the worst was yet to come. In January, 1690/91, he was accused of treason by one William Fuller, a spiritual descendent of Titus Oates, and a warrant was issued for his arrest.[14] This came as a severe jolt. Realizing that clemency was unlikely, the Quaker leader resisted capture by going into hiding, probably at the home of William Popple.[15] While Charles II and James II had shown Penn favoritism, he could not even expect a fair hearing from the new rulers.

Meanwhile, his reputation continued to suffer. On January 1, 1690/91, three men had been caught leaving for France with a packet of treasonable letters addressed to James Stuart. They were Richard Graham (Viscount Preston) and Major Edmund Elliott, both of whom had been arrested with Penn the previous July, and John Ashton, who had been closely associated with James and

[12]Newsletter, 19 July 1690, 18 August 1690, in HMC, *Le Fleming*, 280, 285; WP to [Henry Sidney], 31 July 1690, in Historical Manuscripts Commission, *Report on the Manuscripts of Allan George Finch, Esq.* (3 vols.; London, 1913–1957), II, 391.

[13]*Works of WP*, I, cxix.

[14]*Ibid.*, pp. cxix–cxx.

[15]See Robert Henley to William Blathwayt, 3 July 1696, in Jacobsen, *Blathwayt*, pp. 299–300.

Penn for over a decade.[16] Ashton, on whose person the letters had been found, was hanged on January 28, 1690/ 91. Preston was sentenced to death, but found that he could obtain a reprieve by revealing the plot of which he was a part. He therefore confessed his guilt and named as his accomplices the Earl of Clarendon; the Baron Dartmouth; Francis Turner, Bishop of Ely; and William Penn.[17] Preston attached to this confession a long list of persons who, he said, Penn had assured him were friendly to James. Already a proclamation for the Quaker's arrest had been issued as a result of his association with the three captured conspirators. Now suspicion of his guilt was confirmed by the confession of an alleged confederate.[18]

From January to June, 1691, Preston and Matthew Crone, another former Jacobite, testified to the culpability of Penn and others.[19] The Quaker leader had no choice but to remain in seclusion. He could not take his case to the King, and he had no close friends in high government circles. However, he felt he was well enough acquainted with Algernon Sidney's brother Henry, whom William III

[16]On Preston, see *DNB,* VIII, 355–356; on Ashton, see Chapter I, note 25.

[17]Clarendon and Dartmouth were both arrested, the former obtaining bail that summer, the latter dying from apoplexy in the Tower on October 25, 1691. Turner, like Penn, went into hiding (*DNB,* XIX, 1263; X, 389–393; IX, 1263–1264). For correspondence between Penn and Turner during the reign of James II, see HSP, Penn–Forbes Collection, II, 44–45.

[18]The proclamation was issued on 5 February 1690/91: HMC, *Le Fleming,* p. 314. The Earl of Danby, Lord President of the Privy Council, believed in Penn's guilt; see his letter to the King, 3 February 1690/91, in Andrew Browning, *Thomas Osborne. Earl of Danby and Duke of Leeds. 1632–1712* (3 vols.; Glasgow, 1944–1951), II, 191–193.

[19]HMC, *Finch,* III, 43–44, 309, 311, 316–317, 321–322, 325–334, 337, 338, 343, 344.

had titled Lord Romney, to request intercession with the Crown.

Allow me to live quietly anywhere, [Penn wrote to Romney] either in this kingdom or in America. And that the king may be secured that I will make no ill use of his favour, I do not only humbly offer my solemn promise of an inoffensive behaviour, *but the security of a society of honest, sober people.*

My old and good friend, let me say with decency to the king, he owes thee as great a favour; and I will only add, that the king shall never have cause to repent of granting his request.... To conclude, if I am not worth looking after, let me be quiet; if I am of any importance, I am worth obliging.

Romney's answer was noncommittal, so Penn wrote again, pleading his innocence to the charges against him. But Romney would do no more than promise to approach the King.[20]

While Penn awaited the results of this audience, an indictment of high treason was found against him in Ireland in May, 1691.[21] Secretary of State Nottingham was anxious to proceed against him in England, but during the summer of 1691 his case, while discussed, was not decided.[22] Impatient, frustrated, angry—in this mood Penn inquired of John Tillotson, Archbishop of Canterbury, whether his offense was unpardonable or the King implacable.[23] His question was soon answered, but not by Tillotson. The long-awaited message from Henry Sidney provided the reply: "When I speake to the King about

[20]WP to Lord Romney, 22 April 1691 and after, in Janney, *Penn*, pp. 367–369.

[21]Robert Harley to Sir Edward Harley, 16 May 1691, in HMC, *Portland*, III, 466.

[22]HMC, *Finch*, III, 47, 128, 401, 404.

[23]ACM, XXXI, 284–291. For correspondence between Penn and Tillotson in 1685 and 1686, see Janney, *Penn*, pp. 273–276.

you, his answer to me is that you have done him all the harm you could, and he does not know why he should doe you any good till he see you have changed your mind, which cannot be done, but by your doing him some service, what am I to say to this, you must tell me"[24]

Penn had been of service to James II, but he was in no position to be of use to William III. There is no record that he even answered Sidney's letter. His secluded existence continued, broken only by an occasional plea for clemency,[25] an infrequent lament at the injustice of it all: "I have been above these three years hunted, up and down, and could never be allowed to live quietly in city or country, even then when there was hardly a pretence against me, so that I have not only been unprotected, but persecuted by the government."[26]

Few people were more affected by the Revolution of 1688 than William Penn. The man who had traveled freely in royal circles was reduced to hiding from the government and begging for mercy. The change in his relationship with the Crown could hardly have been more striking.

Penn's association with James II stemmed not only from personal friendship but from the Quaker's desire to end religious persecution and protect Pennsylvania. Yet, ironically, when he was accused of treason as a result of his connection with the former King, some of the Dissenters openly doubted his innocence. Even the Society of Friends was not free of such ungrateful skepticism. Penn wrote to the Yearly Meeting, assembled in London in 1691, that his

[24]H. Sidney to WP, 7 November 1691, in ACM, LXVIII, 219–131.

[25]See, for example, his letter to secretary of state Nottingham, 12 June 1692, in ACM, XXXII, 64–67.

[26]WP to ?, n.d., in Janney, *Penn*, pp. 378–379.

hiding was the consequence of false charges against him. He reminded the Quakers that his enemies were theirs also.[27] This message was not altogether appropriate for an assemblage of peaceful people, but Penn was understandably distressed by their attitude.

His real worry, however, was for Quakers on the other side of the Atlantic. The sudden change in his standing with the Crown meant that the Pennsylvanians should have been on their best behavior, since the proprietor could no longer serve as their apologist when they acted irresponsibly. His role as protector was ended, at least temporarily. Blackwell, had he remained deputy governor, would probably have recognized the new circumstances and acted accordingly. But Penn had returned the executive office of the province to the council, a body noted for its astigmatic view of colonial affairs. Nine months after the Glorious Revolution the Lords of Trade found it necessary to order Penn to have the accession of William and Mary published in his province. Still later in 1689 the Lords received a report that a justice of peace in New Castle had been removed from office for expressing his desire that the new King and Queen be proclaimed.[28]

The logical thing for Penn to do was leave England, where he could be of no aid to the colony, and go to Pennsylvania, where he could take affairs into his own hands. And, indeed, this is what he intended to do. In 1690 he published *Some Proposals for a Second Settlement in Pennsylvania,* a broadside depicting the many natural endowments of the province, its virtue as a commercial center and the proprietor's intention to return there him-

[27]WP to London Friends, 30 May 1691, in *ibid.,* p. 367.
[28]*BTJ,* VI (1686–1690), 265; HSP, *Memoirs,* IV, pt. 2, 246–247.

self as soon as possible.[29] When Penn had been cleared of charges of disaffection to the government in November, 1690, he was able to get from the secretary of state an order for a convoy. He was on the verge of leaving England when the accusations of William Fuller forced him into hiding.[30] There he remained for three years while relations between the Quaker colony and the home government went from bad to worse.

Pennsylvania has escaped the political control of the Crown during the reign of James II. The expression of this control, the Dominion of New England, collapsed when the tremors of revolution in Britain reached America, although the idea of such a colonial structure was not quickly forgotten. However, William III's concern with the colonies did not stem from anything so abstract as the concept of a political dominion. The war with France forced colonial affairs on his attention. In fact, hostilities in the upper reaches of New York against the French and their Indian allies had preceded the official pronouncement of war. And no sooner had battle begun that the Privy Council reported to the King that "the Proprietary Governments are worthy the consideration of the Parliament for the bringing them under a nearer dependence on the Crown."[31] William III took no immediate action on

[29]*PMHB*, XXVIII (1904), 60–61.
[30]*Works of WP*, I, cxix.
[31]HSP, *Memoirs*, IV, pt. 2, 246; *CSP, 1689–92*, secs. 102, 123–124. It is significant that the Corporations Restoration Bill of January 11, 1689/90, stated that "nothing in this Act contained shall extend to prejudice their Majesties or their successors in any of their rights or titles to the Bermudas, Maryland, Pennsylvania, Carolina, New York or Long Island" (HMC, *The Manuscripts of the House of Lords;* 13 vols. [1678–1714]; London, 1887–1953; o.s., II [1689–1690], 422–433).

this recommendation. He was not reluctant to draw the colonies closer to him, but he was unwilling to have Parliament act in a sphere heretofore considered his own.

Not only did the war with France make the home government especially aware of conditions in the plantations; it also provided the issue on which relations between the Crown and Pennsylvania finally foundered. One reason for this was evident in the first reports concerning the war to come from New York, for in these documents the ability, and even the willingness, of the Pennsylvanians to defend themselves was questioned.[32] It was more than the pacifism of the Quaker province which undermined its autonomy, however. A strategic motive had led the Crown to consent to its establishment in 1681: it would fill the sparsely settled gap between New York and the southern colonies. The central location of Pennsylvania made it tactically necessary that the colony prepare to fight; its weakness would seriously cripple the defense of the whole region. This situation was noticed first by Francis Nicholson, lieutenant governor of Virginia and former lieutenant governor of the Dominion of New England. He was not merely concerned with the unwillingness of the Quakers to fight, but with the antagonism and confusion which marked the policy of the Middle Atlantic colonies regarding the French threat as well. The central role of Pennsylvania in this situation was obvious.[33] The logical conclusion from Nicholson's observations was drawn by Henry Sloughter, who had recently been nominated governor of New York. In October, 1689, he told the Lords of Trade that it would be necessary to unite Connecticut, the Jerseys

[32]These reports were sent on 19 December 1689 and 7 January 1689/90. See *CSP, 1689–92*, secs. 646, 690.

[33]*CSP, 1689–92*, secs. 1023, 1164, 1302, 1324, 1583, 2344, 2346; *DAB,* XIII, 499–502.

and Pennsylvania to New York for defense purposes. This was, of course, a revival of the Dominion plan which Pennsylvania had been able to sidestep earlier as a result of the influence of its proprietor. Sloughter again brought up the idea in July, 1691, after he had reached New York.[34] A month later the Pennsylvania government rejected his request for troops to be used against a French invasion from Canada.[35]

Upon receiving this news, the Lords of Trade recommended that Pennsylvania be brought under the King's immediate government and annexed to an adjoining province. This recommendation coincided with Sloughter's advice. It also conformed with the imperial policy which had been taking shape since the accession of William and Mary. In 1689 many of the British colonies in America had experienced revolutions similar to that of the mother country. In contrast to England, the policy in the plantations was to restore the legitimate rulers to power.[36] To accomplish this the home government was forced to compromise with the provincials: the popular legislature could remain, but it would be countered by a royally appointed executive.[37] Now Pennsylvania was to be molded in this pattern.

In February, 1691/92, William III and his Council decided to include Pennsylvania, and East and West New Jersey as well, in the commission to Benjamin Fletcher, newly appointed governor of New York. On reconsidera-

[34]*CSP, 1689–92,* secs. 1638, 1671. Sloughter died in July 1691, but his plan appealed to prominent New Yorkers.

[35]*Ibid.,* sec. 1708.

[36]The exception was Maryland, where the Catholic proprietor, upset by a "Protestant Association," was not reinstated.

[37]Hall, *Randolph,* pp. 136–137.

tion, it was decided to submit the clauses in the commission concerning these proprietary governments to the Lords of Trade for further examination. Meanwhile, in March, Fletcher was issued instructions and a commission for New York only.[38] An analogous situation had occurred in the previous reign, when writs of *quo warranto* were issued against the proprietaries. Penn had intervened, and his colony was the only one to escape the proceedings. But in 1692, this course of action was impossible. The Quaker proprietor was in hiding and could not emerge to plead his case. Nor did he have friends in high office to intercede in his behalf. Indeed, William III was openly hostile to him.

In November, 1692, Fletcher was issued a commission for Pennsylvania, granting him the same governing power as he had in New York. In the two Jerseys, however, he was to control only the militia and not the government—an indication of the difference in influence between Penn and the Jersey proprietors.[39] It should be added that in

[38]Grant and Munroe, *Acts of Privy Council,* II, sec. 437; *CSP, 1689–92,* sec. 2701. Sir George Treby, the Attorney General, examined and revised the clauses concerning the proprietary colonies. O'Callaghan and Fernow, *N.Y. Colonial Docs.,* III, 818–825, 827–833, 835–836; *BTJ,* VII (1691–1695), 90, 96, 99; *CSP, 1689–92,* secs. 2134, 2179, 2194, 2214, 2227.

[39]In Shaw, *Cal. Treas. Books,* XVII (1702), 677, there is the following listing, dated 16 November 1692: "'Secret Service Payments' paid to Mr. John Kynvin in satisfaction of so much money...expended for fees and charges in passing with their Majesties' letters patent to appoint Geo. [sic] Fletcher as Governor of Pennsylvania and other islands and territories: clear [of fees]...£100." Compare the statements in the commission to Fletcher: "And whereas by reason of great neglects and miscarriages in the Government of our Province of Pensilvania in America, and the absense of the Proprietor, the same is fallen into disorder and confusion...." "Whereas we have been informed of the good affection of the Inhabitants of our colonies of

East and West New Jersey, the only region other than Pennsylvania where Quakers predominated, a militia was created in 1692. Penn did not instruct his colonists to recruit troops after their government was threatened, and there is abundant evidence to show that the Pennsylvania Friends would not have heeded such an admonition from the proprietor had it been given.[40]

The issue of defense caused Penn to lose control of his government. Had the pacifism of his colony been challenged directly by French invasion at the beginning of the war, Pennsylvania would undoubtedly have come under royal control much earlier. As it was, the Crown did not act until the Quaker province explicitly rejected a request for troops. There were two other reasons, as well, why Pennsylvania was slow to come under royal scrutiny. As mentioned, the major objective of colonial policy in 1689 and immediately thereafter was to control the local revolutions that had broken out in the colonies. This took about three years but did not concern Pennsylvania, since

---

East and West New Jersey in America, and that the Militia of those colonies consist of fourteen hundred men." For Fletcher's instructions and commission see O'Callaghan and Fernow, *N.Y. Colonial Docs.*, III, 856–861; *CSP, 1689–92*, secs. 2573, 2584. All three branches of the Pennsylvania government fell under the scope of his power. He could assemble and adjourn the legislature and deprive nonjuring members of their seats. He could erect both civil and admiralty courts and appoint the judicial officials. He was authorized to appoint a lieutenant governor. Dr. Daniel Coxe, the chief proprietor in West Jersey and powerful in East Jersey as well, was partly responsible for his colonies' good fortune (Pomfret, *East New Jersey*, pp. 276–277).

[40]O'Callaghan and Fernow, *N. Y. Colonial Docs.*, III, 838–840. One of the major sources of disagreement between the deputy governor and the provincial council had arisen over the issue of defense (*Colonial Recs.*, I, 299–319). The council won the battle with Blackwell's removal.

no rebellion had taken place there. The Quaker province benefited from this neglect, as it did from the fact that William III's interest was to the east rather than the west of the British Isles.[41] Not until the defeat of the French at La Hogue could he turn full attention to domestic and colonial affairs. It was at this critical juncture that a new government for Pennsylvania was being considered. Penn, friendless and in hiding, was unable to influence the outcome.

Fletcher, therefore, got his commission, but he was unable to resolve the defense issue. Not only did the Pennsylvanians retain their independent attitude in the face of royal control, but Penn encouraged them to do so. He advised them to communicate every instance of arbitrary government on Fletcher's part to the Lords of Trade or Westminster and promised that, as a last resort, "the House of Lords will do us right." (Penn, like William III, recognized Parliament's increasing role in colonial affairs.) To one of the members of the provincial council he expressed his hope that the Quakers would stand together "upon their patent against the commission of the governor of New York."[42] It was therefore not surprising that in March, 1693, Thomas Lloyd, still president of the provincial council, informed Fletcher that Pennsylvania commiserated with New York's plight but was unable at that time to send war supplies.[43] Angered by this insolence, Fletcher went to the Quaker colony in April and demanded assistance. When he finally obtained a grant from the assembly,

[41]See the brief chronicle of his activities from 1689 to 1692 in *DNB*, XXI, 313–315.

[42]WP to Friends in Philadelphia, [December] 1692, in *CSP, 1689–92*, sec. 2668; WP to Robert Turner, 29 November 1692, in Janney, *Penn*, pp. 375–377. Both quotations are from the latter.

[43]*CSP, 1693–6*, sec. 218.

it was with the proviso that the money would not be used for waging war.[44] Fletcher was under no illusions about his accomplishment. He wrote to William Blathwayt, secretary to the Lords of Trade, that the people of Pennsylvania would rather die than employ carnal weapons; that his trip had been unsuccessful; and that the minutes of the council and assembly, transmitted to the Lords of Trade, "will appear a farce."[45]

Fletcher received little cooperation of any sort from the officials of Pennsylvania. William Markham consented to be deputy governor, but a number of men who had previously served in the government refused the New Yorker's commissions. Fletcher warned Secretary of State Nottingham that these same men were sending delegates to Court with the hope of getting Penn restored or themselves empowered to act. Furthermore, the royal governor had found on the rolls of Pennsylvania some two hundred acts which had never been transmitted to England.[46] In February, 1693/94, the Lords of Trade decided to register a formal protest to the King against the Quaker Colony, based on the information received from Fletcher and from one of the

[44]*Colonial Recs.*, I, 398–433.

[45]*CSP, 1693–6*, secs. 395–396.

[46]On the appointment of officials, see Fletcher to Nottingham, 18 April 1693, *ibid.*, sec. 507. In April, 1694, a petition from these Pennsylvanians did reach the Privy Council, as Fletcher had predicted it would. The Council shuttled it off to the Lords of Trade and, thus, to oblivion (Grant and Munro, *Acts of Privy Council, Colonial*, II, sec. 555). Concerning Pennsylvania's laws, see E. B. Russell, *The Review of Colonial Legislation by the King in Council* (New York, 1915), pp. 37–38, and William H. Lloyd, *The Early Courts of Pennsylvania* (Boston, 1910), pp. 50–51. At the request of the assembly, Fletcher later accepted eighty-six of the untransmitted laws temporarily, many of which were subsequently re-enacted and considered by the Board of Trade after 1696.

letters Penn had written advising his people to protest against Fletcher's commission for the province.[47] The Lords of Trade took this action because the status of Pennsylvania was uncertain, as Penn himself realized. He informed Fletcher from his seclusion: "There is noe Quo Warranto brought nor Tryall or Judgment Judicially past in that Afair, and I therefore must impute it [the loss of the government] to some Missinformation given the Lords of the Committee of Plantations and an excess of Care in them over the English Territories."[48]

But even before the Lords of Trade registered their protest against Pennsylvania, Penn's situation took a sharp turn for the better. In December, 1693, William III granted him complete freedom. Penn attributed this action to the intercession of the Earls of Ranelagh, Rochester, and Romney. All three men were members of the Privy Council, and Romney has been called the only Englishman for whom the King felt any affection.[49] Nevertheless, Penn put too high an estimate on their aid. Ranelagh was not an important man, Rochester's stock was on the decline, and the King had no reason to be more receptive to Romney's request on Penn's behalf in 1693 than he had been earlier.

[47]*CSP, 1693–6,* sec. 860; *BTJ,* VII (1691–1695), 261.

[48]On 5 December 1692 (ACM, XXXII, 111–113; see also *CSP, 1689–92,* sec. 2667).

[49]WP to Thomas Lloyd, 11 December 1693, in Janney, *Penn,* pp. 386–387. Members of the Privy Council at this time are listed in Grant and Munro, *Acts of the Privy Council, Colonial,* V, Addendum. The statement concerning Sidney is in Kenyon, *Sunderland,* p. 243. Although he was freed, as late as October, 1695, Penn felt compelled to request from the secretary of state a letter protecting him "from the ignorance or prejudice of any busy person." Historical Manuscripts Commission, *The Manuscripts of his Grace the Duke of Buccleuch and Queensbury, K.G., K.T.* (3 vols.; London, 1899–1926), II, pt. 1., 232.

But the situation differed now in one very important respect, which Penn did not mention: the complexion of William III's government had changed. Whether this change should be interpreted as an alliance with the Whigs or as an effort to build a Court party in which former members of the Green Ribbon Club happened to figure prominently, the result was salutary for Penn.[50] The King's attitude toward him became neutral, if not warm, and among the new royal advisors were a number of his friends.

The Earl of Sunderland, who had been *persona non grata* in the government immediately after the Revolution as a result of his conversion to Rome and his deep involvement with the despotic measures of James II, had climbed back into power in his own agile way. Of more immediate importance to Penn, however, was Sir John Trenchard, who was a member of the Sunderland circle but actually joined the Privy Council as a Secretary of State in March, 1692/93, that is, before Sunderland's ascendency. Exiled from England by Charles II because of his political principles, Trenchard was readmitted in 1687 after Penn pleaded his case before James II.[51] Not only could the Quaker expect to collect on this debt, but there was another factor operating in his favor. Old-line Whigs such as Trenchard were less hostile to James II than to his older brother, who was held responsible for the executions of William Russell and Algernon Sidney in 1683.[52] Penn was in America at the time of these executions and therefore had taken no public position on them, but his friendship for Sidney was well known. It was Trenchard, having moved from the

[50]The former interpretation is in Ogg, *James II and William III,* pp. 390–392; the latter is in Kenyon, *Sunderland,* pp. 254–262.

[51]HSP, *Memoirs,* III, pt. 2, 220.

[52]Kenyon, *Sunderland,* p. 235.

northern to the more powerful southern department in November, 1693, who served as the King's instrument to grant Penn his freedom the following month.

The Quaker proprietor was again in a position to lobby for his colonial interests, and he lost little time in doing so. On July 5, 1694, he petitioned the Privy Council for the return of the Pennsylvania government. The request was forwarded to the Attorney and Solicitor Generals, who delivered their decision within a week.[53] Pennsylvania, including the Three Lower Counties, had been deeded to Penn, according to the two legal officers. But "the Government thereby granted to Mr. Pen was subject to Their Majesties Soveraignty in case of Extraordinary Exigencies happening or Arising through Default or Neglect of the Petieoner or of those Appointed by him to protect or defend the said Province or Inhabitants in time of War or Eminent Danger.... Their Majesties might Lawfully grant such Commission [as Fletcher's] but that when those reasons and grounds do fail or cease the Right of Government doth belong to the Petitioner."[54]

Three years earlier the Attorney General had used similar language, declaring that in a time of extraordinary emergency the King could commission a governor, even though the proprietor's charter remained intact. The

[53]*CSP, 1693–6,* sec. 1127; Grant and Munro, *Acts of Privy Council, Colonial,* II, sec. 561. The apparent speed may be deceptive. In February, 1693/94, the King-in-Council, on receiving the representation of the Lords of Trade concerning Pennsylvania (see n. 58, below), had instructed the Attorney General to peruse the patent granted to Penn (*ibid.,* sec. 539).

[54]*CSP, 1693–6,* sec. 1138; *BTJ,* VII (1691–1695), 299. The Attorney General also reported favorably on Penn's right to the New Castle area, which had been challenged by New York in 1691. *CSP, 1689–92,* sec. 1691; *CSP, 1693–6,* sec. 1164; *BTJ,* VII (1691–1695), 305.

colony specifically referred to was Maryland, which became a royal province in June, 1691. The emergency did not involve defense, as in Pennsylvania, but a Protestant revolution directed at the authoritarian policies of the Catholic proprietor. Lord Baltimore's religion had not aided his cause during the reign of James II. It definitely prejudiced the government of William III against him, the parallel between the revolutions in England and Maryland being so obvious. The colony remained royal until 1715, when it was restored to a Protestant Lord Baltimore.[55]

Charles Calvert was as unsuccessful in his dealings with the Crown in the 1690's as he had been in the 1680's. William Penn's fortunes were different. His setbacks in the early years of William III's reign were reversed when his friends came into office, while Baltimore had not developed such useful connections. A further clue to the advantage enjoyed by the Pennsylvania proprietor was his ability to convince royal officials that he knew what needed to be done and would do it. Summoned before the Lords of Trade, where the opinion of the Attorney and Solicitor Generals regarding the return of Pennsylvania was read, Penn promised that if his government were restored to him he would go to Pennsylvania, provide for the safety and security of the province, and transmit to the provincial council and assembly all royal orders—including that calling for "the supplying [of] such Quota's of Men or the defraying [of] their part of such charges as their Majesties Dominions in that part of America." The proprietor then produced two acts of the assembly, one for submitting to the royal will, the other providing support for the government. The Lords of Trade responded immediately with

[55]Andrews, *Colonial Period,* II, 368–376.

the recommendation that the government of Pennsylvania be returned to its original owner.[56]

Such an important decision was not likely to have been made at a brief meeting of the Lords of Trade, but earlier. It came because Penn's hand had been strengthened with the appointment of more of his friends to high places. John Sheffield, Earl of Mulgrave, was given the title Marquis of Normanby and a position on the Privy Council in the spring of 1694. The Earl of Shrewsbury was put back on the Council at that time as a secretary of state, thereby undermining the influence of Secretary to the Lords of Trade William Blathwayt, who was a staunch opponent of corporate and proprietary colonies.[57]

Pennsylvania was returned to its proprietor on August 20, 1694, but not until he had agreed to appoint William Markham, who had served under Fletcher, as deputy governor; to retain the laws passed during the Fletcher regime and confirmed by the Crown; and to submit to the Act of Fidelity to the King and Queen.[58] Soon thereafter, Penn wrote to the Friends in Pennsylvania:

By this you will understand that by the good providence of God, I am restored to my former administration of government, which I hope will be some relief and comfort to you

[56]This was on 13 July 1694. *BTJ*, VII (1691–1695), 299–302; *CSP, 1693–6*, secs. 1144, 1145.

[57]Kenyon, *Sunderland*, pp. 262–266; Jacobsen, *Blathwayt*, p. 141.

[58]*CSP, 1693–6*, secs. 1152, 1163, 1166, 1181, 1186–1188, 1238; *BTJ*, VII (1691–1695), 302, 307, 309; Grant and Munro, *Acts of Privy Council, Colonial*, II, sec. 561. Penn's final agreements pending restoration, made on August 3, coincided with the date the Attorney General gave his opinion on twenty-seven acts of the Pennsylvania assembly passed under Fletcher, thus accounting for that stipulation in the agreements.

Insofar as Markham was concerned, it would seem his appointment as lieutenant governor was dictated by the Lords of Trade, probably

that have been exercized by the late interruption upon us. That things are not just now put into that posture as you may reasonably desire, you must not take amiss, for neither will the straitness of the times, nor the circumstances we are under to the Lords of the Plantations, permit another method at this time. And as soon as I can make my way to that which is as much my inclination as yours, (and which I hope to do in a short time,) depend upon it, I shall do my utmost to make you entirely easy.

The proprietor did not pinpoint the source of discomfort, though it was doubtless his promise that Pennsylvania would cooperate in the defense effort, taking for granted that the colonists knew what he had in mind: "You know, I believe, as well as I, what has been a main obstacle and is still." Penn had temporarily denied the conflict between Quaker pacifism and imperial war by promising to supply troops or money for colonial defense. Again he had transgressed the high ideals of the "holy experiment" in order to save it as a physical reality, but his hope was to salvage the experiment *and* the ideals. He concluded the letter with a statement that revealed his desire to renege on his promise to the Lords of Trade eventually, and at the same time he forecast the bourgeois wisdom to be made famous by another prominent Pennsylvanian: "We must creep where we cannot go, and it is as necessary for us, in the things of this life, to be wise as to be innocent. A word to the wise is enough."[59]

---

because he had served under Fletcher. Yet four months later, Penn's financial agent, Philip Ford, wrote to Blathwayt, secretary to the trade committee, that Penn hoped the Lords of Trade would allow Markham to remain in his post of lieutenant governor. *CSP, 1693–6,* sec. 1601.

[59]WP to Pennsylvania Friends, 24 November 1694, in Janney, *Penn,* pp. 396–397.

Although Penn assured both the Lords of Trade and the Pennsylvanians that he was about to embark for America, he put off his trip for another five years. He remained at home in 1694 because he felt Pennsylvania's situation was still precarious, especially in view of the stronger role being played by the home government. His connections with those responsible for colonial policy had improved considerably over the past year. But while his presence might influence these men, he was uncertain of their allegiance in his absence.

Nevertheless, to stay in England had its drawbacks, too. If the Pennsylvanians were to be brought into line with the demands of the mother country, a strong hand was needed to make them change their ways. William Markham was not equal to the task. On August 21, 1694, the Crown ordered that the Quaker colony furnish eighty men or the equivalent in money to New York. When Markham presented this requisition to the provincial council and assembly in May, 1695, neither body bothered to respond.[60] A year later Benjamin Fletcher, who had remained in America as governor of New York, complained that he had yet to receive a man or a penny from Pennsylvania. And Markham warned him not to expect either.[61] Whether Penn could have gotten the necessary appropriations from the colonists by going to Pennsylvania is, of course, a moot question. But it was with a certain amount of justice that the governor's council of New York blamed him for the

[60]*CSP, 1693–6,* sec. 1252; *Colonial Recs.,* I, 491–495.
[61]*CSP, 1696–7,* secs. 14, 27 x, 27 xi. Markham was by this time exasperated with the legislature and wrote to Fletcher: "I never was for the Proprietor's form of government and doubted if he had the power to grant many things in it; but I know very well that it was forced from him by friends who unless they received all they demanded would not have settled the country."

negligence demonstrated by the Quaker council and assembly, claiming he had not instructed his government to comply with the military needs of its northern neighbor.[62] Indeed, Penn's promise to the Pennsylvania Quakers—"I shall do my utmost to make you entirely easy"—made them anything but compliant with imperial needs. Finally, in November, 1695, Penn wrote to prominent members of his government, taking them to task for refusing aid to New York.[63] His action was triggered not only by complaints from the latter colony, but also by the revival of the Dominion idea as an answer to the defense problem.[64]

The assembly and council of Pennsylvania still refused to cooperate in the war effort. Yet the proprietary remained firmly in Penn's hands. Several factors may account for this. The vitality of the Lords of Trade was visibly declining. More important, during the final years of King William's War the major colonial battles were fought on sea rather than land. Consequently, Pennsylvania's failure to contribute to the defense of New York was not of major importance. But most important of all was the proprietor's decision to remain in England where he could use his connections to best advantage.

Penn had traveled a hard trail since 1689. His fortunes declined precipitously after the accession of William and Mary, reaching bottom when he was forced into seclusion to avoid imprisonment. During this period Pennsylvania was subjected to royal rule as a result of its unwillingness

[62]On 11 July 1695 (*CSP, 1693–6,* sec. 1956).

[63]WP to Arthur Cook *et al.,* 5 November 1695, in HSP, Gratz Collection.

[64]See "Memorial of the Lords Justices of England," 16 July 1695, in *CSP, 1693–6,* sec. 1964.

to aid in the war against France. When, because of his improved connections with important government figures, he was able to come out of hiding, he managed to get his colony back from the Crown by promising that it would assume a defensive posture. Although the proprietor was willing to violate the Quaker conscience in order to hold onto his province, the Pennsylvanians were not. Council and assembly refused to designate funds for bellicose purposes. Nevertheless, the colony did not revert to the Crown again, primarily because the proprietor continued to pay close attention to his connections. This required more effort than it had in the reigns of Charles II and James II, since neither William nor Mary was friendly to him. Yet for all the energy Penn had exerted since the Glorious Revolution, it could be said that he had gotten nowhere. He was simply fighting to maintain the *status quo*.

CHAPTER V

Defensive Statesman

(1695–1698)

FROM 1689 to 1694 the Crown had been concerned with the plantations because of two separate happenings: local rebellions and the war with France. Many provincial governments had to be reorganized because of revolution; Pennsylvania was the only colony whose status had been radically, if temporarily, changed because of the issue of defense. From 1695 to 1699 the Crown's main interest was commerce. Not Pennsylvania's pacifism but the prosperous trade of the Quaker colony would be of central importance now.

This was not the only new development. The increased concern with commerce provided another entering wedge into colonial affairs for Parliament. Trade considerations also changed the nature of the Crown's approach to the plantations through the creation of an executive agency staffed by professional men concerned solely with the colonies. Up to this time Penn had depended on his friendships with important courtiers to protect the interests of his province. He would now have the added task of building or maintaining connections in other areas of the government.

In the early 1690's, commercial restrictions stemming from the war with France, as well as French naval depredations, were deleterious to British shipping. English merchants did not, however, assign the blame for trade difficulties to war. They saw it rather as the result of lax enforcement and wholesale breaking of the navigation acts in the colonies. An attempt to alter this situation was made in March, 1695, when a bill "for the better securing the plantation-trade" was brought into Parliament. But it reached only a second reading.[1] British legislators were not yet worried about the commercial situation. Three months later they, like the merchants, had cause for anxiety. In June, 1695, the Scottish Parliament passed an act authorizing the creation of a Company of Scotland, trading to Africa and the Indies, which was granted the power to colonize and build factories in areas not already possessed by other English peoples, given the consent of the local inhabitants.

The Scots were already active in the British colonies, and especially Pennsylvania. In 1684 Penn had been fined as a consequence of illicit trade between his province and Scotland. Ten years later the Quaker colony, along with Maryland and Virginia, was again accused of direct trade with England's northern neighbor.[2] Edward Randolph

[1]Leo F. Stock, ed., *Proceedings and Debates of the British Parliament Respecting North America* (5 vols.; Washington, 1925–1941), II, 112.

[2]*Ibid.*, pp. 195–196; see also Hall, *Randolph,* p. 156. The illegality of such commerce was currently under debate in England; but the Customs Commissioners, before whom the imputation was laid, had given as their opinion a decade earlier that such traffic was unlawful

warned that the Scots contemplated "purchasing a settlement in one of the three lower counties. . ., as being no part or parcel of the lands granted to Mr. Penn in his Province of Pennsylvania."[3] When Parliament convened in November, 1695, the House of Lords immediately moved to consider the state of trade of the nation; the first order of business was a reading of the Scotch act passed the previous June.[4]

The outcome of parliamentary concern was the passage in April, 1696, of "An Act for preventing Frauds, and regulating abuses in the Plantation Trade."[5] It was the last in a series of statutory regulations governing the trade and navigation of the empire, and it was intended primarily to strengthen the previous acts. The new law also contained several important innovations; conditions in Pennsylvania played no small part in necessitating these.

Sections II and VII of the law mentioned "the courts of admiralty in England, Ireland, or the said colonies or plantations" and "the court of admiralty held in his Majes-

(Shaw, *Cal. Treas. Books,* VIII [1685–1689], 212; *ibid.,* X [1693–1696], 571–572; Joseph Reddington, ed., *Calendar of Treasury Papers* [6 vols.; London, 1868–1889], I [1557–1696], 348, 354; Grant and Munro, *Acts of Privy Council, Colonial,* II, sec. 558).

[3]Randolph called for general colonial reorganization into units lying about each of the principle bay areas on the Atlantic Coast. Thus, the Three Lower Counties on the Delaware were to be annexed to Maryland; West Jersey was to be annexed to Pennsylvania "and an active governor there appointed" (Toppan and Goodrick, *Randolph Letters,* VII, 474–477. Also printed in HMC, *MSS, House of Lords,* n.s., II [1695–1697], 447–449).

[4]HMC, *MSS, House of Lords,* n.s., II (1695–1697), 3.

[5]7–8 William III, c. 22, in Douglas, *English Historical Docs.,* IX, 359–364. The most comprehensive treatment of this legislation is in Michael G. Hall, "The House of Lords, Edward Randolph, and the Navigation Act of 1696," *William and Mary Quarterly,* XIV (1957), 494–515.

ty's plantations" as the agency for trying breaches of the navigation acts. Edward Randolph, in a paper titled "An Account of severall things whereby the illegal Trade is encouraged in Virginia, Maryland and Pennsylvania, together with methods for prevention thereof," had proposed that "a Court of Exchequer be erected in all the Plantations on the coast of America to try all causes, criminal excepted, relating to the Crown; the Judges and Attorney-General to be appointed by his Majesty."[6] Francis Nicholson, now serving as royal governor of Maryland, had suggested that a court of Exchequer be set up in Pennsylvania since there was so much illegal trade and piracy there. "I do not understand," Nicholson wrote, "that Mr. Penn is Vice-admiral of Pennsylvania, Newcastle and territories, so if the King would appoint some other person, it would be better, because under the Acts of Trade and Navigation some vessels are to be tried in the Admiralty Court."[7] The House of Lords was responsible for substituting vice-admiralty for exchequer courts, and consequently for the unprecedented expansion of admiralty jurisdiction.[8]

The Navigation Act of 1696 required that royal governors take an oath to uphold the trade laws, as before, but now violation of the oath could mean not only removal from office, but also a £1000 fine (Section IV). Furthermore, it was specified that governors appointed in the

---

[6]Toppan and Goodrick, *Randolph Letters*, V, 117–124. Also printed in HMC, *MSS, House of Lords*, n.s., II (1695–1697), 449–451.

[7]Nicholson to Shrewsbury (secretary of state), 14 June 1695 (received 25 September 1695), in *CSP, 1693–6*, sec. 1897.

[8]Hall, "The House of Lords," pp. 503–504. Vice-admiralty courts had no juries, whereas section XI of the new law mentioned trial by jury in the case that the navigation acts were transgressed. A brief discussion of this internal contradiction appears in Andrews, *Colonial Period*, IV, 168–171.

proprietary colonies or elected in the corporate colonies must meet the King's approval (Section XVI). This was a sharp limitation on charter rights, but one forecast in 1694 when it was insisted that Penn accept William Markham as his deputy. These governors had also to take the oaths required of the royal governors, a demand not earlier made on Markham.

Section XI specified that juries trying breaches of the navigation acts were to be composed only of British, Irish, or plantation-born subjects, and Section XII extended this limitation to "all places of trust in the courts of law, or what relates to the treasury of the said islands." One of the distinguishing features of Pennsylvania was its attraction to settlers from outside the realm; before 1700 this meant dissenting sects from Germany and Scotland. Penn did not look on his "holy experiment" as exclusive to Englishmen, although it was not until after the founder's death that the character of his province became noticeably heterogeneous. Nevertheless, Edward Randolph was soon able to find many Scots in the Pennsylvania government.[9]

Yet for all these inhibitions on Pennsylvania and the other private colonies, none of the proprietors or colonial agents were asked their opinion of the threat posed by Scotch trading ambitions or the consequent Navigation Act.[10] There is no doubt, however, about the way Penn

[9]Hall, *Randolph*, p. 185. He pointed out that the naval officer, John Donaldson, and the secretary of the province, Patrick Robinson, were both Scots.

[10]One of the Customs Commissioners suggested to the Select Committee of the House of Lords considering the question of trade that the proprietors ought to be called in and admonished. Yet the Committee did not even do this (HMC, *MSS, House of Lords,* n.s., II, [1695–1697], 7). C. M. Andrews claims that the proprietors protested vigorously against the clause in the bill calling for royal

would have testified had he been allowed. He later told Edward Randolph that the Act "was made to ensnare honest men." To his friend Robert Harley, a prominent member of the House of Commons, Penn wrote: "Wee extreamly suffered by the last act of [16]96, in divers respects against the plantations, at large, and particularly injurious to our people, to say nothing of the blow that is given to jurys, in favour to the Court of Admiralty." It was the judicial provisions that were particularly irksome to the Quaker proprietor. He informed the Board of Trade: "The Law is so darkly, & If I may say so, inconsistently worded, that in Sect. 10 in the middle of it [actually, Section XI] jurys are taken for Graunted to be the way of Justice in all cases relating to forbidden Trade."[11] But Penn's later lamentations were of no value in ameliorating the provisions of an act already passed by Parliament.

The passage of the Navigation Act of 1696 was part of an effort to rationalize colonial policy and strengthen its administration. The creation of the Lords Commissioners of Trade and Plantations, commonly known as the Board of Trade, to replace the declining Lords of Trade had a similar purpose. This was "a body destined from the first to have very intimate relations with the colonies and to represent in its policies and recommendations the leading principles that were to guide England's rulers in their

---

approbation of their deputies (*Colonial Period,* IV, 171). However, there is no evidence that they were allowed to do so before Parliament or the Privy Council.

[11]Memorandum of Edward Randolph, 18 January 1696/97, in HSP, Photos of Originals in Other Liberties; WP to R. Harley, 30 January 1698–1699, in HMC, *Portland,* III, 601–602; WP to Board of Trade, 19 December 1698: *BTPr.,* II (1697–1698), B 38 (see also *CSP, 1697–8,* sec. 1060).

control of colonial affairs until after the Seven Years' War."[12] The Board possessed no executive, financial or penalizing powers. Rather, it supplied advice and information to the Crown, other administrative agencies, and Parliament, basing its recommendations on a constant stream of correspondence with the colonies. Its influence was great and frequently determinative; its collective opinion was consistently mercantilist.

While the new council of trade was to have sixteen members, only eight were paid, and they were the ones who attended regularly and carried on the business of the Board. The original appointees were John Egerton, third Earl of Bridgewater (president); William Blathwayt; John Locke; John Pollexfen; Abraham Hill; Ford Grey, Earl of Tankerville; John Methuen; and Sir Philip Meadows. There is no evidence that William Penn had a personal relationship with any of the Board members except Blathwayt and Locke. But these two men and Bridgewater were unquestionably the important members. Bridgewater was conscientious but overburdened; apparently he relied heavily on Blathwayt for advice.[13] Consequently the Quaker's association with Blathwayt and Locke was significant.

William Blathwayt, whose knowledge of colonial affairs was greater than that of any other member of the Board on which he served until 1706, was a staunch royalist. It was natural that he should be a close friend of Edward Randolph; the two men not only shared a similar distaste for independent colonies but even had the same patrons.[14]

[12]Andrews, *Colonial Period*, IV, 290. Chap. ix of Andrews' book describes the origin and work of the Board.
[13]Andrews, *Colonial Period*, IV, 292–293.
[14]Hall, *Randolph*, p. 171; Jacobsen, *Blathwayt*, p. 120.

They were joint authors of the clause in the Navigation Act of 1696 which declared that governors of proprietary colonies must have royal approbation. Randolph had written to Blathwayt in February 1695/96: "Since you are pleased to think it necessary that a clause should be provided for investing the Governments of the proprietyes [in the Crown] be pleased to oblige Mr. Pen and the Jersey Gentlemen with a draft of such a clause, that I may have it ready against the next tyme I attend their Lordships; it will save a great deale of tyme and putt a speedy issue to their uncertain expectations."[15]

When he drafted the royal charter to William Penn, Blathwayt did so grudgingly. At the time of the boundary controversy between Penn and Baltimore, his friendship with the Catholic proprietor was established. He surely resented the partiality shown to Penn then as well as later in James II's reign, when the Quaker's colony remained exempt from *quo warranto* proceedings. The secretary to the Lords of Trade was an activist, and his course was opposite to Penn's. But he was often absent from England, for his language proficiency and administrative abilities made him an invaluable aide to William III on the Continent.[16] Obviously his influence on plantation affairs would be a function of his presence in England.

[15]*Ibid.*, p. 335.

[16]*DNB*, II, 668. Miss Jacobsen says that Blathwayt was absent the greater part of each year from 1692 to 1698; in 1697 he was away from April to November. She points out that he was distracted by the European situation until 1702 and that he did not reside in England during any summer from 1696 to 1701. Nevertheless, she maintains that he missed less than one-quarter of the meetings during the first six years of the Board's existence and "never lost sight of the main thread in colonial administration" (*Blathwayt*, pp. 260, 331). This feat seems improbable.

John Locke, for whom Blathwayt had no respect as a Board member, was not a Tory in philosophy but a Whig.[17] His acquaintanceship with America came by way of his association with Sir Anthony Ashley Cooper, later first Earl of Shaftesbury. An initial interest in Carolina alone was broadened when Locke was appointed to the Council of Trade and Plantations in 1673. Locke may have met Penn when he was lecturing at Oxford and the admiral's son attending. In any case, he examined and commented on the proprietor's first Frame of Government for Pennsylvania. Like Penn, Locke was expelled from Christ Church, Oxford, though at a later time. Unlike Penn, he was forced into exile. The Quaker pleaded his friend's case to James II, who was willing to grant Locke a pardon. Locke declined on the grounds that he had committed no crime. He then took up residence in Rotterdam with Benjamin Furley, a Quaker and close friend of Penn's, until the Glorious Revolution.[18]

Locke is well known as the apologist for this Revolution. He has received considerably less renown as a member of the important Board of Trade. Yet he attended faithfully until 1700, and it has been judged that he "dominated the first meeting and continued to dominate the Board while his membership of it lasted. His most powerful rival was Blathwayt."[19] As mentioned earlier, Blathwayt's disadvantage was his frequent absence from England. This was aptly illustrated at the outset of the Board's existence.

[17]Blathwayt regarded all his colleagues on the Board "as poor Whigs, with a most pathetic lack of any practical knowledge of the colonies and trade" (*ibid.*, p. 317).
[18]*DNB*, XII, 27–36; Maurice Cranston, *John Locke, A Biography* (London, New York, 1957), pp. 153–156, 260–263, 280–281, 298.
[19]Cranston, *Locke,* p. 406.

In May, 1696, Blathwayt had to leave for Flanders with William III, yet he felt sure that his candidate for secretary of the Board, John Povey, would be named to that post. But Povey's availability was ignored by the Board. Chosen instead was the man who had written a preface to and translated from Latin Locke's *Letter on Toleration;* who was secretary of the Dry Club, which Locke had organized; and who had kept Locke posted on the progress of a bill to create a council of trade in the parliamentary session of 1695/96. That man was William Popple, the same William Popple who had secluded Penn a few years earlier.[20] Over the next several years the Quaker proprietor could expect fair consideration, if not some degree of partiality, from the Board of Trade.

It has been estimated that the Board's period of peak activity and effectiveness stretched from 1696 to 1712.[21] The friendship between John Locke and William Penn should not disguise the fact that during these sixteen years the proprietor and the Board were working at cross purposes. Inevitably, the reinvigorated colonial policy met opposition from the Americans. And because the privileges of the private colonies, more than those of the royal, were infringed upon, it was logical that greater opposition would come from the representatives of those provinces. It was

[20]On 3 July 1696, Blathwayt was informed that a majority of the Lords were for Povey, "yet that was obviated by my Lord Keeper [Somers] who very early disclosed...that one Mr. Popple was nominated thereto by his Majesty, and so there was no room to propose any other." Sir John Somers, who was a close friend of Locke's, had been appointed to the Privy Council on the same day as Penn's friend, Sir John Trenchard, and for the same reason (*ibid.,* pp. 260, 321, 361–362, 401–402; Jacobsen, *Blathwayt,* pp. 297–300; Kenyon, *Sunderland,* p. 255).

[21]Russell, *Review,* p. 48.

both significant and unique that the private colonies banded together for mutual protection against the common threat, although this came more in the form of spontaneous reaction than calculated policy. The spokesman for this group was William Penn. His antagonist was Edward Randolph, the staunch and tireless defender, and in some cases the creator, of the home government's policy.

The opening salvo in the battle between royal innovation and colonial conservatism was fired by Randolph. In July, 1696, he submitted to the Customs Commissioners a paper entitled, "Proposalls humbly offred, for the more effectuall putting in Execution the Act for Preventing Frauds and Regulating Abuses in the Plantation Trade."[22] As the title indicates, Randolph was anxious to set in motion the administrative machinery that would implement the Navigation Act of 1696. The first two "Proposalls" were of particular interest to Penn because of their direct application to his situation: the governors of proprietary colonies should be appointed by the Crown in accord with the new act and "fitt persons [should] be appointed to be the Govrs. of Carolina & Pensilvania." Of the three other proposals, which were intended for more general application, the most significant one called for the appointment of "a Judge, a Register, a Marshall of the Courts of Admiralty, and an Atturney Genll. in all the Colonyes." Within the next few weeks Randolph went so far as to suggest who should be appointed for each office in each colony.[23]

Some colonies already had attorneys general, a fact which

[22]Toppan and Goodrick, *Randolph Letters*, V, 135–136; see also HMC, *MSS, House of Lords*, n.s., II (1695–1697), 419.

[23]Toppan and Goodrick, *Randolph Letters*, V, 136–138; see also HMC, *MSS, House of Lords*, n.s., II (1695–1697), pp. 422–424.

would prove troublesome for Randolph's intended appointees. He therefore took it upon himself to show that these men would be unreliable when it came to prosecuting cases for the Crown in the projected admiralty courts. Again the situation in Pennsylvania was pertinent, as Randolph pointed out in a report to the Board of Trade in August, 1696: "David Koid [David Lloyd], a Quaker is the Attorny Genll. for the Province, he refused me, to put severall forfeited Plantacon Bonds in Suite, saying he was Attorny Genll. for the Province only."[24] Randolph's account of judicial conditions in the plantations was convincing; the Board approved the plan of appointing attorneys general. But before the Crown would act, the plan had to be submitted to England's Attorney General, Sir Thomas Trevor, for his opinion.[25]

Up to this point, neither Penn nor any other agents of the private colonies knew what Randolph was doing. It was Trevor who informed them of the Surveyor General's actions.[26] Whether Trevor was motivated by a respect for property, dictated by his Whiggery, or by a personal regard for William Penn cannot be known.[27] But it is clear that when the Penn group was warned of Randolph's machinations, it was not even able to see the papers he had submitted to the Board of Trade, although it petitioned the King in this regard and Penn tried to use a connection on the Privy Council to influence the Board.[28] Apparently there was a united desire within the administra-

[24]Toppan and Goodrick, *Randolph Letters,* V, 143.

[25]*Ibid.,* VII, 493, 493 n.

[26]Toppan and Goodrick, *Randolph Letters,* V, 146.

[27]Trevor, a "lukewarm Whig," had been educated with Penn's close friend, Robert Harley (*DNB,* XIX, 1155–1156).

[28]Toppan and Goodrick, *Randolph Letters,* V, 146–149; Earl of Monmouth to WP, n.d., in HSP, Penn-Forbes Collection, II, 71.

tion to put the new policy into action quickly, effectively, and without opposition.

At least Edward Randolph thought this was the case. Confident in the outcome of his cause, he pleaded that Trevor be hurried in rendering his decision so that the attorneys general might be sent immediately to the colonies.[29] But the eagerly awaited opinion was not the complete victory the Surveyor General was hoping for. Attorney General Trevor stated that nothing in the charters of the private colonies prevented the King from erecting vice-admiralty courts, and that the King could appoint "Advocates General and other such officers for the prosecution of suits in such Admiralty Courts as shall be thought convenient."[30] This meant that Crown cases not falling within the vice-admiralty jurisdiction would still be determined by a colonial attorney general, a development Randolph could not have cherished.[31]

Trevor's decision was no less disconcerting to William Penn and the agents of Carolina, the Jerseys and Connecticut. These men now, rather belatedly, asserted that their respective charters allowed them to set up their own admiralty jurisdictions. Such action, they said, had not been taken earlier because the navigation acts passed before 1696 allowed trial in common law courts, thus eliminating the expense of a parallel system of admiralty courts.[32]

[29]Toppan and Goodrick, *Randolph Letters,* V, 150–151.
[30]HMC, *MSS, House of Lords,* n.s., II (1695–1697), 428.
[31]Hall, *Randolph,* p. 170.
[32]Toppan and Goodrick, *Randolph Letters,* V, 149–150. This had been hinted, but not explicitly stated, in the petition sent earlier to the King; see n. 28, above. Soon after this, in mid-November, 1696, the Lords of the Admiralty reported that the governors of all colonies had commissions to be vice-admirals, or might have them if they made application for same. *BTPG,* IV (1681–1684), pt. 1, A25; HMC, *MSS, House of Lords,* n.s., II (1695–1697), 427.

Penn appeared with several other colonial representatives before the Board of Trade to testify that "tho they insisted on it [the power to erect vice-admiralty courts] as a right, they would accept it as a favour."[33] At this point the Board, previously so confident in its position that it had ignored the agents of the private colonies but now given pause by Trevor's decision and Penn's protest, submitted the case to the King. It claimed that a resolution of the matter exceeded the limits of its competence.[34]

This development gave Penn cause for new hope. To his long-time friend William Trumbull, who was now a secretary of state, he poured out the arguments against vice-admiralty courts in the colonies which he had already given to the Board. He concluded his letter: "The business comes up the 7th inst. [January, 1696/97] Mention it to Lord S [Sunderland] to speak, as he promised me he would, to the King and all the Lords of his acquaintance, to use us well."[35] Sunderland, whose relationship with Penn at this time was cordial, held the upper hand in a Privy Council split between Court Whigs and Junto Whigs; either group might be expected to take a fairly scrupulous approach to proprietary rights.[36]

The other aspect of Penn's strategy in his battle against the erection of vice-admiralty courts in the private colonies was diversionary, rather than straightforward. In December, 1696, he proposed to the Board of Trade a plan which would enable New York to obtain its troop quota assign-

[33]*BTJ*, IX (1696–1697), 279.

[34]On 17 December 1696, in HMC, *MSS, House of Lords*, n.s., II (1695–1697), 427–428.

[35]c. 4 January 1696/97, in HMC, *Downshire*, I, pt. 2, 727–728.

[36]Sunderland to WP, 30 August 1696, in HSP, Penn-Forbes Collection, p. 88; Kenyon, *Sunderland*, chap. viii.

ments from neighboring colonies with a minimum of resistance: deputies from each province would meet in a common assembly to discuss problems of defense.[37] This plan should not be interpreted as an attempt to solve the military issue which had irritated relations between Pennsylvania and the Crown. The war in the colonies had virtually ended, and the Pennsylvania assembly had voted £300, not directly for defense, but at least for "the Relief of the distressed Indians inhabiting above Albany, late sufferers of the French."[38] Nor should the Quaker proprietor's plan be viewed as a genuine and unique effort at general government for the British colonies in America. His project was not without precedent; a similar plan had been put forth in 1694 and several other such schemes were proposed two years later. Furthermore, Penn's sketch was so incomplete that the Board asked him to draw it up more carefully and present it again, although the problems it sought to remedy had existed for some time.[39] In fact, Penn's proposal had been recently and quickly conceived. It must be understood as an attempt to divert attention from the issue of vice-admiralty courts and to cast a favorable light upon himself as a man who took the general interests of the Crown to heart. His intent emerges from a letter written to Fitz-John Winthrop, agent for Connecti-

[37]*BTJ*, IX (1696–1697), 275.

[38]George *et al.*, *Charter to William Penn*, pp. 253–260. Root (*Relations*, p. 267) misinterprets this as an attempt to solve the defense imbroglio.

[39]*CSP, 1693–6*, sec. 999, 1964; L. P. Kellogg, "The American Colonial Charter," American Historical Association, *Annual Report for 1903* (2 vols.; Washington, 1904), I, 280–283. *BTJ*, IX (1696–1697), 275. See S. G. Fisher, *The True William Penn* (Philadelphia, 1900), p. 340, for an interpretation of Penn's proposal which does not recognize these qualifying factors.

cut: "The scheam begins to entertain me, I hope it will the Lords, to our genll. ease."[40]

But Penn's diversionary tactic failed. When in February, 1696/97, he submitted the finished draft of "A brief and plaine Scheame how the English colonies in the North parts of America may be made more useful to the Crown and one another's peace and safety with an universal concurrence," the Board of Trade rejected it as impractical, recommending to the Privy Council a military union instead.[41] Nor was the technique of banding together representatives of several colonies in opposition to the Crown successful. A petition from the proprietors, asking that their governors be appointed vice-admirals, was brushed aside in favor of Randolph's nominations, and on February 22, 1696/97, an Order in Council established vice-admiralty courts in all the colonies.[42] The third and most durable aspect of Penn's strategy, his political reserves, had also failed him. In the winter of 1696/97, Sunderland was completely absorbed in other business and Locke's ill health

[40]WP to Fitz-John Winthrop, 27 December 1696, in Massachusetts Historical Society, *Proceedings* (Boston, 1879), XII, 42. Winthrop's answer showed his belief in the plausibility of Penn's strategy as well as his acknowledgement of Penn's dominant position in the proprietary group (*ibid.*).

[41]*CSP, 1696–7*, sec. 694, 762; O'Callaghan and Fernow, *N.Y. Colonial Docs.*, IV, 259. The military union was put into action before the year was out, although Pennsylvania was not included in it (*ibid.*, pp. 261–262, 266–273, 284–292, 302).

[42]Although the petition went to the King, it was referred to the Board of Trade. By early March, 1696/97, the Board had laid before the King the list of officers for the Courts. Randolph's suggestion that colonial governments should be realigned about the great coastal bays was followed in laying out the vice-admiralty districts, which was probably why Penn's request that the same officers serve Pennsylvania and Delaware was granted with no difficulties (HSP, *Memoirs*, IV, pt. 2, 265–268; *BTJ*, X [1697–1698], 9, 11, 14; Hall, *Ran-*

kept him away from London. Blathwayt, on the other hand, had returned to England in October, 1696, and remained until the following April.[43] The consequent balance of power favored Randolph rather than Penn. Since he had come out of hiding the Pennsylvania proprietor had recovered enough strength to give battle, but victory was still out of reach.

Nor was he given time to marshall new forces. No sooner had Penn finished with the executive branch than he was under fire from the legislature. This was a new development, although both the King and the Quaker had recognized the increasing interest in the plantations shown by Parliament. Neither man welcomed this intrusion. It was a challenge to the King's prerogative. As for Penn, he had often depended on his connections with Court figures to facilitate colonial business. Now he was faced with a new task of maintaining parliamentary connections also. Had he been younger, he might have welcomed this development as a workable alternative to royal favor. Instead, it simply meant more work.

On February 10, 1696/97, the House of Lords appointed a committee to consider the trade of the Kingdom. Its chairman was the Earl of Rochester, who had come to Penn's aid in 1685 and 1693. Its membership included some old allies of the Quaker proprietor—the Earl of Sunderland, the Earl of Romney, and the Marquis of Halifax;

---

dolph, p. 168; *CSP, 1696–7,* secs. 812, 853). The officers of the Pennsylvania–West Jersey region, as well as an interpretation of their jurisdiction, can be found in Root, *Relations,* pp. 94–97. *BTJ,* X (1697–1698), 6. In November, 1697, the Attorney and Solicitor Generals ruled that offenses against the Navigation Act of 1696 could be prosecuted in colonial vice-admiralty courts.

[43]Kenyon, *Sunderland,* pp. 281–290; Cranston, *Locke,* pp. 411–412; Jacobsen, *Blathwayt,* p. 485.

and some new friends—the Earls of Devonshire, Somerset, and Dorset, the Marquis of Normanby, and Lord Poulett.[44] Two of the members were colonial proprietors, the Earls of Bath and Berkeley, but this did not work to Penn's advantage. Rather, it meant that the affairs of the Carolinas and the Bahama Islands, the bailiwicks of Bath and Berkeley, were dismissed from the Committee's scrutiny, shifting a disproportionate amount of attention to Pennsylvania. Other factors also worked to the disadvantage of the Quaker province. Rochester was more Edward Randolph's patron than Penn's.[45] William Blathwayt, Randolph's friend and colleague, made his presence felt and probably exercised his influence over the Earl of Bridgewater, who was also a Committee member. Finally, the port of Philadelphia would have to receive considerable attention since it dominated the trade of western New Jersey, Delaware, and northern Maryland, as well as Pennsylvania.

The first several meetings of the Committee were devoted to a resumé of the past year's activities of the Board of Trade and the Commissioners of Customs, both of whom had been in close working relationship with the Surveyor General during that period. Edward Randolph resurrected his report of July, 1696, which made general reference to abuses of trade in Pennsylvania. Having heard this report, the Committee ordered that a copy of Penn's deed to Delaware be brought in, since the trade laws were

[44]Later letters reveal these earlier friendships. See Marquis of Normanby to WP, 17 July 1698, in HSP, Penn-Forbes Collection, II, 72; Lord Powlett to WP, 22 April 1699, in HSP, Penn-Forbes Collection, II, 79; WP to C. Lawton, 27 August 1701, in HSP, Penn Letter Book (1699–1701), pp. 114–117. The membership of the special committee of the House of Lords is in *Journals of House of Lords* (vols. 11–19 [1660–1714]; London [c. 1767–1772]), XVI, 94.

[45]Hall, *Randolph,* p. 171.

badly abused there.[46] This was a strange demand in view of the fact that Randolph's paper nowhere mentioned specific violations in Delaware, although they surely existed. The fact was that a sustained attack on William Penn had begun, to the virtual disregard of the proprietors and agents of other private colonies. This development can be attributed to the commercial importance of the Quaker province, as well as its record of trade violations. Randolph's rather than Penn's testimony was accepted because of the nature of the Committee.

Since Randolph was unable to locate the leases by which Penn held Delaware, the proprietor was ordered to attend the Committee. Meanwhile Randolph, working in conjunction with William Blathwayt, introduced a new issue by bringing in a list of proprietors independent of the King and, coincidentally, a copy of Benjamin Fletcher's commission for the government of Pennsylvania. Simultaneously, the Board of Trade was ordered to submit to the Committee the papers concerning the problem of vice-admiralty courts in the colonies, the affair in which Penn had played the leading role.[47] There could no longer be any doubt that Penn would be the center of the Committee's attention.

Randolph's list of the independent proprietors was supplemented with a damning description of every colony that was in any way independent of the Crown. About Delaware he noted: "Mr. Penn is the Proprietor of the soil only...great quantities of tobacco are some years brought over land [from Maryland] to Delaware and shipped directly for Scotland.... Pirates are harbored there." As to

[46]HMC, *MSS, House of Lords,* n.s., II (1695–1697), 411.

[47]*Ibid.,* p. 411. This was six days prior to the Order in Council which established vice-admiralty courts.

Pennsylvania: "The Acts of Trade are not observed in this Province.... It will soon become a staple of Scotch and Holland goods." Randolph climaxed his dogmatic report with the recommendation that the governments of all the proprietaries be invested in the Crown.[48] By his own account, he made a good impression. He wrote immediately to Blathwayt: "The Lords are of the opinion that the 3 lower Countyes are holden by lease from the Duke of Yorke & Mr. Penn has not the Gomt. of them.... I did offer the proposall in writing about having the Gomts. in the proprietyes to be invested in the Crown. Some of the Lords presently agreed to have a clause to that purpose But others agree that their Titles (such as they bee) should be well looked into. not by the present Atturney Genll. because he with Mr Serjeant Ward reported upon it but by one more of the Judges."[49] Apparently the Committee thought Sir Thomas Trevor was too friendly to the interests of the Pennsylvania proprietor.

This was the atmosphere of the Committee when, three days later, Penn came before it to testify. He brought the deeds for Delaware which had been granted him by the Duke of York in August, 1682. These, he claimed, allowed him, as they had allowed the Duke, the right to appoint the governor there.[50] When Randolph's most recent charges

[48]*Ibid.,* pp. 440–444.
[49]20 February 1696/97, in Toppan and Goodrick, *Randolph Letters,* VII, 504.
[50]The Duke of York did not get actual title to the Lower Counties from the King until 22 March 1683. In the opinion of one historian: "The deeds of enfeoffment [given to Penn] therefore were worthless, except possibly to show an intention of the duke, which at a later time he might more fully carry out. In 1685, however, when the duke became James II, the title to the Lower Counties was vested legally in the crown, and so remained until the Revolution. Hence the right which Penn claimed to both the soil and the government of

were made known to him, he asked and was granted time to prepare a reply. At the same time, Penn told the Committee he was preparing a paper to show how the trade of the kingdom could be advanced. Again the proprietor was employing his dual tactic of showing deep interest in England's well-being while diverting attention from the real issue. And again he failed. The Committee was definitely set on getting his reply to Randolph's charges.[51]

Less than a week later, on March 1, 1696/97, Penn gave his answer. The burden of his defense was that Maryland ("where he [Randolph] chiefly resides," Penn pointed out), a royal colony, violated the acts of trade with greater frequency than Delaware. Penn, as usual, had slight compunction about accusing his southern neighbor.[52] Little was said about the abuse of the navigation acts in Pennsylvania. In rebuttal, Randolph deluged the Committee with facts and figures to demonstrate his contention that the trade of Pennsylvania and, especially, Delaware was preponderantly non-English, and that the officials in the region either did nothing to prevent or directly instigated the foreign intrusion.[53] Penn attempted to answer some of these charges, but apparently not to the satisfaction of the Committee. It wondered what objections he could make to the investiture of Pennsylvania's government (includ-

---

that region rested merely on the acquiescence of the crown" (Shepherd, *Proprietary Government,* p. 322). The issue did not, of course, seem so clear-cut at the time.

[51]HMC, *MSS, House of Lords,* n.s., II (1695–1697), 412.

[52]However, Penn did have to fend for the chief officers of the province: Deputy Governor Markham, who was accused of harboring pirates; Secretary Patrick Robinson, whose allegiance was supposedly to Scotland; and Attorney General David Lloyd, whose earlier-mentioned offenses to Randolph were minor compared to those he would later give to Penn (*ibid.,* pp. 412–413, 456–457).

[53]*Ibid.,* pp. 413, 458–459.

ing Delaware) in the hands of the King. He answered that the province and territories were worth nothing to him if he should lose the government, which was his right and the support of his family.[54] Finally, pressed to the wall, Penn proposed that his deputy governor should be approved by the King and give security for his term of office.[55] The first point was already required by the Navigation Act of 1696, although it had not been put into practice as yet. But the question whether a deputy governor should put up security as a means of ensuring his good behavior in office had been considered moot until this time, due to the ambiguity of the Act. Penn's concession, a minor victory for Randolph and the royalists, demonstrated the feebleness of his counterattack in the face of charges which he really could not answer.

The same day on which this interrogation took place, Penn submitted a "Proposal for the advancement of trade in America" to the Committee. The most significant aspect of the paper lay in the fact that it hardly dealt with the point at issue—violation of the Navigation Acts. Again

[54]Actually, Penn never could support his family from the proceeds of Pennsylvania, nor would that province pay the costs of his present battle against the Crown. He wrote on 2 May 1698: "Loving Friends: I am surprised to hear my bills for three hundred and odd pounds should be refused. Is not my right by public obligation to six hundred pounds, in consideration of the law I relinquished of customs; my expenses in coming over and prosecuting the dispute with Lord Baltimore, which held near a year; all my expenses in two years' withstanding of Edward Randall [Randolph], &c., at my great charge; and, last of all, my quitrents, of which I have not seen for twelve years one sixpence: I say, are not all these credit enough to give a governor and proprietor, too, his bills acceptance, or honour at least, for three hunderd and odd pounds?" (Janney, *Penn*, p. 413.) There is no record that this plea was answered.

[55]HMC, *MSS, House of Lords*, n.s., II (1695–1697), p. 413.

the weakness of the proprietor's position was illustrated. His paper did, however, include a brief plan "for the prevention of frauds from the tobacco Colonies to the King." This was enlarged into a paper entitled "An Expedient against Fraud in the Plantation Trade," about which the Customs Commissioners observed that it contained no proposal that was not already provided for by legislative enactment or executive decree.[56]

The Commissioners were correct, insofar as the letter of the law was concerned. But there was a real innovation in Penn's plan which was not immediately apparent. He would have shifted the burden of obedience to the Navigation Acts almost entirely from the provincial officials to the masters and commanders of ships involved in the colonial trade. Had his plan (which was probably unworkable) been accepted, the cause for attacks on the private colonies would have been considerably weakened.[57] In a larger sense, Penn was changing the strategy of his dealings with the English government, at least temporarily. Since he could not rely on friends in prominent positions for his relief, he was attempting to succeed by beguiling his opponents.

Meanwhile, Randolph had launched still another attack on the Quaker proprietor and his province. The Surveyor General's most important point (which had wider application than to Pennsylvania alone) was that in the Navigation Act of 1696 the clause which concerned proprietary

---

[56]*Ibid.,* pp. 470–472, 490–494.

[57]The Customs Commissioners were told by the Lords' Committee to make no report to their superiors in the Treasury until Penn had drafted a more finished plan for the Committee to consider. But when Penn submitted this draft in April, 1697, the Committee was no longer in existence (*ibid.,* pp. 414, 500–504; *CSP, 1696–7,* sec. 987).

nomination of a governor for royal approval gave no power to the King "to remove such Governor for misdemeanor or to appoint another in his stead, in case the Proprietor neglect to nominate one." Nor was there a penalty provided for disobedience to the existing clause.[58] This immediately caught the Committee's attention, for the problem of instructions to colonial governors was presently under discussion with the Customs Commissioners, who complained that the governors in proprietaries would take no notice of any instructions sent them. Accordingly, Chairman Rochester told Penn the Committee believed that the governors appointed by the proprietors should receive the same instructions regarding trade from the King as royal governors; that the proprietors should be under obligation that those instructions be observed and should also be liable for the misbehavior of deputies; and that "if there be any further complaint against the proprietors after this, the Parliament may possibly take another course in the matter, which will be less pleasing to them."[59]

When the Committee prepared an address to the King, however, it apparently did not feel bound by its statement to Penn. In addition to the terms mentioned to the Quaker proprietor, the Committee recommended that in every private colony the proprietor should give security for the governor, and that the governor should be made to forfeit his position if he failed to carry out the laws and instructions sent him.[60] William III answered that he would "take Care to comply with their Lordships Advice therein, so as to make the same effectual."[61] Soon a circular letter was

[58]HMC, *MSS, House of Lords*, n.s., II (1695–1697), 488–490.
[59]*Ibid.*, pp. 413–414, 472–488.
[60]*Journal of H. of L.*, XVI, 126–128 (includes text).
[61]*Ibid.*, p. 131. Four days later the Committee's address was before the Board of Trade. *BTJ*, X (1697–1698), 47.

sent out to all private colonies under the King's name, warning the governors of their new responsibilities. Pennsylvania was the only proprietary colony threatened with the loss of its patent for further willful failure to enforce the acts of trade.[62]

The Attorney General drafted the bond which the proprietors and corporations would have to take for their governors, while the Customs Commissioners set the sum of the security. By early May, 1697, the Board of Trade was prepared to have the proprietors and colonial agents fulfill their obligation. Yet despite the recommendations of Randolph and the Committee of the House of Lords, no provision was made for the removal of a governor for disobedience.[63] While it is unlikely that such an important point was dropped inadvertently, there exists no evidence that Penn or anyone else was responsible for its removal. In either case, the result was only a minor victory for the private colonies.

By the spring of 1697, William Penn could attest to the new vitality of England's colonial policy. The Navigation Act of the previous year had mentioned vice-admiralty courts, and these courts were set up in spite of the vigorous protests of the proprietors and agents of the private colonies. This Act also tightened restrictions on governors in both royal and private plantations. While Edward Randolph's attempt to have proprietary governors named and removed by the Crown failed, as had his plan for royally appointed attorneys general in the private colonies, the

[62]The corporate colonies of Connecticut and Rhode Island were similarly warned. *CSP, 1696–7,* secs. 958–961.

[63]*BTJ,* X (1697–1698), 64–66, 69, 94; *BTPr.,* Entry Book A, pp. 62, 64, 68, 74–75, 79; Entry Book D, p. 165. The amount of security varied from £2000 to £5000, depending on importance of the trade of the colony.

final policy established was more stringent than the Navigation Act of 1696 indicated it would be. Penn had led the group which fought this development, but collective action met with only minimal success: the most radical of Randolph's proposals were not heeded. Nor had Penn's connections saved the day. This can be partially attributed to the fact that in 1697 policy-making decisions were coming from both the executive and legislative branches, a new development which made the Quaker proprietor's task of protecting his interests more difficult. He would have to enlarge his circle of political friends, and this would necessitate remaining in England awhile longer.

In the meantime, Penn did not accede to the new policy gracefully. When he learned he would have to give bond for his deputy governor, he answered that he thought "it hard that the Proprietarys should give security for the Deputys of the King's approbation; Since it is the same thing for therefore we should be excused because the King approves or disapproves our Nomination." In June, 1697, the Board of Trade noted that he had yet to give security for his deputy, and that he had not even acknowledged the Board's letter of May 8, which specified the type of bond he must put up. Penn promised to act on this matter in due haste, but he did nothing for eight more months.[64] The same perversity marked his attitude toward other issues as well. In February, 1696/97, he protested against the quota of men which Pennsylvania was to provide for the defense of New York.[65] He complained in September, 1698, of a man-of-war cruising in Delaware Bay, although he had recently endorsed such naval tactics before the

[64]*BTPr.*, II (1697–1698), B 8; Entry Book A, pp. 189–194; *BTJ*, X (1697–1698), 117, 119, 385.
[65]*CSP, 1696–7*, secs. 695, 697.

Committee of the House of Lords.[66] In other words, Penn was doing his best to impede increasing royal control in the plantations.

The proprietor was not chastised for his contrariness, because the complexion of the Board of Trade had changed in his favor. From 1697 to 1699, William Blathwayt was more often out of than in the country, while Edward Randolph had sailed to America.[67] Even while he was in England, Blathwayt's attention was not, technically speaking, to be focused on Penn's province. In January, 1696/97, the Board of Trade had distributed its work load to facilitate affairs, and Blathwayt received Barbados, Jamaica, and the Leeward Islands. This was far too important an area to allow his attention to wander to other regions, especially when he had other duties besides the Board of Trade.[68] The Board member in charge of proprietary and charter colonies was John Pollexfen, whose chief interest in the colonies was commercial, and not governmental.[69] For these several reasons, and perhaps because, with the termination of King William's War, the home government had temporarily spent its energy insofar as colonial affairs were concerned (indeed, the end of the war marked the return of colonial prosperity), no serious attacks were launched against Pennsylvania from England in the last three years of the seventeenth century.

[66]*Ibid.,* sec. 1305: HMC, *MSS, House of Lords,* n.s. II (1695–1697), 490–491.

[67]Hall, *Randolph,* p. 177; Jacobsen, *Blathwayt,* p. 485.

[68]Board of Trade meeting mentioned in Cranston, *Locke,* p. 419. In addition to his trips abroad with William III, Blathwayt was Surveyor and Auditor General of Plantation Revenues. See Jacobsen, *Blathwayt,* chaps. vi, xi.

[69]Andrews, *Colonial Period,* IV, 292; *DNB,* XVI, 62–63.

The same was not true of America, from which place came letter after letter complaining of a variety of ills in the Quaker province. Leading the assault on Pennsylvania was Francis Nicholson, whose hostility to the Quaker colony was by now well established. Governor of Maryland since 1694, his record showed him to be a good administrator but a man of uncontrollable temper.[70] Perhaps the latter quality played too great a role in stimulating an animus toward Pennsylvania, but there were more concrete reasons for his enmity. Not only was the Quaker colony filling a trade role which Maryland felt was its own, but Nicholson and William Markham were having a dispute concerning commerce between Maryland and the Three Lower Counties.[71] A large part of Penn's trouble in these last years of the 1690's stemmed from the economic success of his colony and, consequently, the jealousy it aroused in others.

Simultaneously, governors Markham and Nicholson were quarreling over the boundary between their respective colonies, and Nicholson was accusing the Pennsylvania government of countenancing illegal trade and piracy. While the Quakers had often been charged with illicit commerce since their settlement along the Delaware, the allegation of piracy was novel.[72] Piracy was, however, an

[70]*DAB,* XIII, 499–502.

[71]*CSP, 1696–7,* secs. 478, 716; *CSP, 1697–8,* secs. 35, 49; *BTJ,* IX (1696–1697), 273, 275; HSP, *Memoirs,* IV, pt. 2, 266–268.

[72]Markham to WP, 22 February 1696/97, in *ibid.,* p. 266; Nicholson to Board of Trade, 27 March 1697, in *CSP, 1696–7,* sec. 862. The Board appointed Nicholson to run a boundary between the two colonies, allowing the decision of 1685 to stand. The boundary was not run, probably because Nicholson was appointed governor of Virginia in 1698 (*ibid.,* secs. 1253, 1262, 1265, 1285, 1292, 1296; ACM, XXXVᴬ, 95, 99–100; HSP, Penn Papers, Official, I, 15). As to piracy, there seems to have been only one complaint about this in

almost inevitable outcome of war. Privateers, commissioned to prey on enemy commerce, could easily cross the fine line which divided them from pirates. Other colonies besides Pennsylvania were warned against harboring these outlaws after the war ended.[73] Yet—because of the feeble Quaker government, the central location of the colony, and the sparsely populated regions along the west bank of the lower Delaware—it was practically foreordained that Penn's province would become a haven for pirates.

Nicholson was quick to point this out to the home government, as was Robert Snead, a justice of the peace in the Three Lower Counties. Both blamed William Markham, even alleging that the lieutenant governor received gifts from the pirates. Nicholson went even further, accusing the proprietor himself, and in such a way as to arouse attention at home: "The government of Pennsylvania, as he [Penn] now manages it, is every way prejudicial to the King's interests."[74] Sensing the danger in this situation, Penn wrote to Markham and the provincial council: "The Accusations of one sort, & the reports of another that are come for England against your Govermt. not only tend to our ruine but our Disgrace." He emphasized the charges of piracy and illicit trade, warning that such activities had to be suppressed.[75] But while Penn was admonishing the members of his government, he would not admit their

---

Pennsylvania before the end of King William's War (*CSP, 1693–6,* sec. 1916).

[73]On 9 February 1696/97. See *CSP, 1696–7,* secs. 696–701.

[74]*BTJ,* X (1697–1698), 275, 286–287, 308; *CSP, 1696–7,* secs. 1144, 1178, 1331, 1348, 1373; Nicholson to James Vernon (secretary to Duke of Shrewsbury, a secretary of state), 30 June 1697, in *ibid.,* sec. 1127.

[75]*BTJ,* X (1697–1698), 271–274. Quary thought the solution lay in having a vessel cruise around the mouth of the Delaware. Penn was

culpability to Nicholson, whom he accused of pretending friendship when he left England for Maryland, so that "I feared no nightStabs, or secret Designs against me and my Interest." The Maryland governor also feigned friendship with Markham and "at the same time [endeavored] to encourage Edward Randolph to impeach him [Markham] and the province here, two years successively." Much of the trouble in Pennsylvania, Penn claimed, resulted from the dissension that Nicholson consciously fomented.[76]

But the proprietor's letters to America could not mend the damage already done to the reputation of his province in England. In October, 1697, he was summoned to attend the Board of Trade. From his home in Worminghurst, Penn replied that over the past three months he had come several times to London and checked at the Board's offices, but that he would not make a special trip now unless the Board persisted. In defense of Markham, Penn pointed out that the deputy governor was being judged *ex parte*. In defense of himself, he recalled that the Crown had wanted Markham retained. He revealed his plan to leave soon for Pennsylvania, where he would "be able to recommend [himself] and the province to the Council of Trade in a very convincing manner." In the meantime, he proposed an impartial investigation of the colony by the royal governor of New York.[77]

Penn honestly felt that complaints against the province

---

complaining of the presence of a man-of-war in that very region. This was the earliest indication of future relations between the judge and the proprietor.

[76]WP to Nicholson, 22 November 1697, in Browne *et al., Md. Archives,* XXV, 573–576.

[77]*CSP, 1696–7,* secs. 1362, 1371; WP to Board of Trade, 15 October 1697, in *ibid.,* sec. 1383. There is no evidence that he prepared to go to Pennsylvania the following spring.

arose from the spite of his enemies. To the leader of this group, Edward Randolph, Penn wrote that he would oblige Markham to pursue the interest of the Crown, but expected in return that "those which have been the Instruments of raising this smoake agst my Province will quench that fire which feeds it, or I must fling away my scabbard and openly detect and impeach too."[78] The charm which had characterized Penn's letters in the 1680's was gone; his frustration and exasperation were now too great to be concealed.

Nevertheless, the Quaker proprietor saw the necessity of defending against the attacks on Pennsylvania in a more positive way than by threat, and so he presented to the Board a collection of papers regarding the colony. These included a series of letters from Markham, written in explanation and defense of his action. Of even greater importance was a letter from Francis Jones, whom Nicholson had named as an informant against the lieutenant governor of Pennsylvania. Jones wrote: "Notwithstanding the heats that has hapened between Coll. Markham & myselfe...in my judgemt. there can be no fitter person for the King's interest and the Interest of the Province than himselfe." Markham, Jones continued, was working diligently to eliminate piracy. Tobacco was not carried from Maryland into Pennsylvania, as Nicholson asserted, but in the opposite direction. Finally, Maryland was trying to subvert the government of Pennsylvania and was discriminating against the trade of that province.[79]

[78] WP to E. Randolph, 16 October 1697, in Browne *et al., Md. Archives,* XXV, 572–573.

[79] W. Markham to WP, 13 and 22 February, 1 March, 1696/97; 24 April, 1 May 1697, in *CSP, 1697–8,* sec. 76; F. Jones to WP, 13 November 1697, in *BTPr.,* II (1697–1698) B3; see also *CSP, 1697–8,* sec. 45.

Penn was hopeful that Jones' letter, supplemented by similar information from Robert Quary, who had been appointed judge of the vice-admiralty court for the Pennsylvania–New Jersey region, would bring the Board over to his side. He even expected better treatment from Edward Randolph.[80] At the same time, Penn maintained a close contact with those people in the government from whom he could expect aid. Francis Nicholson could not have been happy to hear from a friend in December, 1697, that "Mr. Pen was in great Esteem at Court, and by what I have seen & heard he has been very instrumental to displant Col. Fletcher from the Government [of New York]."[81] After all, Nicholson's situation was very similar to Fletcher's.

The Court and the Board of Trade, however, were different entities. The latter was not converted to Penn's point of view on illicit commerce in the plantations,[82] but

[80]See WP to the provincial council, 1 December 1697, ACM, XXXVᴬ, 156–160. For Quary's letter, as well as one from Jeremiah Basse which also showed Pennsylvania in a favorable light, see CSP, 1696–7, secs. 1203, 1338; BTJ, X (1697–1699), 271–274. Basse was later appointed governor of West New Jersey.

[81]Nicholas Bayard to F. Nicholson, 30 December 1697, in HSP, Photos. It might have been added that John Locke played a role in Fletcher's removal, also (Cranston, Locke, p. 420).

[82]Note its message to a secretary of state on 26 February, 1697/98, in CSP, 1697–8, sec. 265: "Again, the chief support of these pirates lies in your Colonies, and particularly in those under Proprieties and Chartered Governments. The Proprietors have not yet presented their Governors and Deputy Governors to you for approbation, according to the late Act of Parliament, nor given security for them according to your order made in pursuance of the address from the House of Lords. If the said Proprieties and Chartered Governments do not speedily comply with what is required of them, as abovesaid, we see no means to prevent the continuance of this mischief without calling in the further assistance of Parliament." Penn was protesting the injustice of having to give security for his deputy governor at this time (ibid., secs. 132, 173, 222; BTJ, X (1697–1698), 385; BTPr.,

it had to be satisfied with the feeble measure of requesting the proprietary and chartered colonies to pass acts for the suppression of piracy.[83] The last word was with the Crown, which refused to act forcefully. In the wake of war and colonial activity had come a slack period, and Penn took advantage of this relaxation to use his influence in dissuading royal action.

Yet the removal of Francis Nicholson was beyond the Quaker proprietor's power, and this proved unfortunate. In December, 1697, Edward Randolph had landed in Maryland. Due to the weather, he was forced to remain there for two months, and he occasionally sat as a member of the Maryland council. It takes little imagination to reconstruct the unsavory tales he must have heard about Pennsylvania from Nicholson, stories which Randolph doubtless was willing to believe. He had no love for that colony anyway: it was proprietary, it was Quaker, it was pacifist and non-juring.[84] These considerations were all on his mind when he left Maryland to visit Pennsylvania.

Before Randolph reached the Quaker colony, its inhabitants received the reproachful letter from Penn which, having delineated the charges against Pennsylvania received by the Board of Trade, concluded: "For my sake, for your own sake, and above all for God's sake, Let not the poor province Longer suffer under such grievous and offensive Imputations."[85] Soon Randolph arrived for a brief stay. After his departure, Markham was warned that

---

II (1697–1698), B 8. Two years later the Board was still vainly requesting action concerning the posting of security (*CSP, 1697–8,* sec. 943).

[83]*Ibid.,* secs. 307–311; *BTPr.,* II (1697–1698), B 8.

[84]Hall, *Randolph,* pp. 178–180.

[85]See n. 75, above.

the Surveyor General was spreading scurrilous stories about him and gathering unfavorable reports to be sent to England. Impelled by these warnings and the reproof from Penn, the provincial council and assembly took uncharacteristically hasty and decisive action to clear the colony. A lengthy vindication from the charges of the past was sent to the King, subjecting Randolph to special censure: he "puts himself & the rest of the King's Officers here upon Methods that will render most of the Inhabitants of the countrey Uncapable to trade. . . . He also carries himself abusive to the Governor and endeavours to render him and his acts contemptible here and elsewhere."[86]

But Randolph was also busily writing letters, fully acquainting the Board of Trade with his point of view.[87] The Surveyor General was censorious of the Pennsylvania government in general, which pretended to be totally independent of the Crown, and of its Quaker character in particular, which dictated that at trials no judges, juries, or witnesses should be sworn. But Randolph's major criticisms concerned commerce, and particularly "An Act for preventing frauds and regulating abuses in trade, within the Province of Pennsylvania & Counties annexed," confirmed by Markham on May 10, 1698. If the title recalled the English navigation act of two years before, the content did not. The new law sought to substitute common courts for vice-admiralty courts; it doubled the penalties for trade violations, although there was no intention of

[86]*CSP, 1697–8,* 759 i, xi; *BTPr.,* II (1697–1698), B18, B29; *Colonial Recs.,* I, 562. Relations between Randolph and the Pennsylvania government are described in Hall, *Randolph,* pp. 180–187.

[87]These letters were written between April 25 and September 12, 1698, and read by the Board during October of that year. *CSP, 1697–8,* sec. 451; Toppan and Goodrick, *Randolph Letters,* V, 169–178, 189–192; VII, 527–528, 535–543, 546–549.

enforcing these penalties; it attempted to restrain customs officials and to frighten officers from searching ships. Finally, the act allowed a merchant to attest, rather than take the oath necessary for registering a ship.[88] Randolph claimed that Penn devised this latter provision in England and that David Lloyd, Pennsylvania's attorney general, said that the proprietor never intended it to be observed in the province. If this law was not bad enough, the Surveyor General pointed out that foreign traders were still tolerated in Pennsylvania, that aliens remained in positions of high trust in the Quaker government, and that the local merchants continued to trade directly with Scotland. Yet there was no one in the colony to prosecute cases for the Crown, certainly not the Quaker David Lloyd. Such were the consequences, Randolph implied, of dismissing his proposal to place royal attorneys general in the plantations.

The Surveyor General laid much of the responsibility for this state of affairs at the feet of the deputy governor, who remained the "steddy friend" of pirates. Markham's daughter, so it was said, was married to a pirate. Markham had no respect for the oath administered to him by Randolph, nor for any act of Parliament. He resorted to such tricks as adjourning the courts for six months, in order that those accused of trade violations would have ample time to cover up their offenses. Yet the really insidious

[88]Randolph's description of the law was reasonably accurate, at least concerning oaths and vice-admiralty courts. The provision made for cases concerning violation of the acts of trade stated: "The mean or manner of trial shall be according to the course of Comon Law, known practice of the courts of records within this government by twelve Lawful men of the neighborhood, where the offense is committed" (George *et al.*, *Charter to William Penn,* pp. 268–274. Randolph's annotated copy of the law reached the Board later. *CSP, 1697–8,* sec. 949).

influence in Pennsylvania was the power behind Markham: William Penn. The people in Pennsylvania had no fear for the consequences of their illegal actions because they knew their proprietor's interest would prevail in England. Randolph insinuated that Penn was involved in the passage of the Scotch Act of 1695, which was intended to be so detrimental to British trade. He boldly concluded that "Mr. Penn's Governt. has as little regard to the Acts of Trade as Mr Penn himselfe has to his Promises which he makes to the Ministers of State & others in England in relacon to Mr Markham his Governts putting in Execution the Acts of Trade in his Province of Pensilvania." Randolph suggested several minor remedies to the situation, such as discharging Markham and sending more vessels to patrol the area. But the only real solution, cited again and again, was that Penn's government be taken over by the Crown.

Randolph's accusations were soon substantiated by letters received from Robert Quary and Francis Nicholson.[89] Quary, who had previously testified in behalf of the Pennsylvania government, was now serving as judge of the vice-admiralty court in that region and seeing provincial affairs from a different vantage point. Quary confirmed Randolph's charge that the newly passed Pennsylvania act for preventing frauds excused the inhabitants from swearing to uphold the acts of trade and rendered the vice-admiralty courts extraneous and, therefore, worthless.[90] He also gave credence to Randolph's accusations of illegal trade. Nichol-

[89]*CSP, 1697–8,* secs. 633, 760, 786, 796, 813, 827.

[90]On the other hand, Quary was not at all pleased with Randolph's appointees to the vice-admiralty courts: the register lived one hundred miles from Philadelphia; the marshall was out of the province; the advocate lived in England, where he expected to remain.

son, too, corroborated the unfavorable reports on Pennsylvania.

The Board notified Penn of its objection to the act for preventing frauds and its decision to take the affairs of Pennsylvania into special consideration.[91] The Quaker proprietor's response was immediate. He first sought to show that Deputy Governor Markham recommended the law in question to the assembly as the best means of adapting the Navigation Act of 1696 to local conditions. Three days later, Penn reported that he had vetoed the law because of one disagreeable clause, which he did not specify.[92] This satisfied the Board, which now made no move to act on letters received from Robert Quary, who continued to bemoan the state of affairs in the Quaker province. The vice-admiralty judge adopted a plaintive tone: "This is the 4th time I have troubled yr Lordships"; "This is the 6th time I have troubled yr honrs without the favour of receiving any orders or Instructions." Finally, he made a charge which he thought would surely arouse the Board:

By some late accoumpt from Mr. Penn to those in Governt here, he acquaints them of severall complaints Sent home against yrs wch he hath (as they say) blown of[f]. wch is generally believed, and give cause of great Joy amongst them here [.] itt is the General discourse of this Place that Mr. Penn hath greater Interest at Court now than ever hee had in King James Raigne.... It is the Support for all irregular & illegal activity in this place.[93]

Meanwhile, pressure was being put on the Board from another quarter. The Customs Commissioners, who had

[91]*Ibid.*, secs. 901, 1005; *BTJ*, XI (1698–1699), 290.

[92]*Ibid.*, p. 305; *CSP, 1697–8,* secs. 1059, 1060, 1061; BTPr., II (1697–1698), B38.

[93]*Ibid.*, III (1699), C16, C28; *CSP, 1697–8,* secs. 811, 907; *CSP, 1699,* secs. 138, 426.

played an important part in drafting and passing the Navigation Act of 1696, also received letters from Randolph, Quary, and Nicholson recommending that Markham be removed and the Pennsylvania act for preventing frauds be disallowed. Extracts had been submitted to the Treasury Lords, who, unfortunately for William Penn, were also members of the Privy Council. Hitherto unaware of the uproar concerning Pennsylvania, the Council immediately ordered the Board of Trade to consider the Customs Commissioners' report, although the Board had previously reviewed all this material and considered the matter ended.[94] Similarly, a month later the Council ordered the Board to study a paper from the Lords Commissioners of the Admiralty, although the paper's primary concern was a letter from Quary which had been read before the Board six weeks earlier.[95] A discussion of affairs in Pennsylvania was resumed in July, 1699, after a lapse of seven months. It took the Board only a week to prepare for the Lords Justices a report calling for the dismissal of Deputy Governor Markham and the disallowance of the Pennsylvania act for preventing frauds.[96] Penn was not even consulted until the report was prepared. Then his protests against it were to no avail.[97]

In the past, Penn had never been averse to disregarding

[94]*Ibid.,* sec. 450; HMC, *MSS, House of Lords,* n.s., II (1695–1697), 7, 21–24, 446, 451–454; Reddington, *Cal. Treas. Papers,* II (1697–1701/02), 300–301; Grant and Munro, *Acts of Privy Council, Colonial,* II, sec. 743.

[95]*BTPr.,* III (1699), C27.

[96]*BTJ,* XII (1699–1700), 131, 135; *CSP, 1699,* secs. 679, 694. The Board advised the Lord Justices that Penn's disallowance of the law was insufficient, and that the Justices should make it official. In this manner the theory of royal disallowance put the proprietor in a weak position.

[97]*CSP,* 1699, sec. 692.

the regular channels of colonial administration if he could attain his ends by appealing to higher authority. Now the tables were turned; higher authority had dictated policy to a Board of Trade which, frustrated in its attempt to regulate Pennsylvania earlier, had been willing to let the issue die. Faced with the hostile attitude of certain high-ranking officials, Penn decided to follow through on a course of action he had been contemplating for several years. He would go to America, for he realized he could handle the affairs of his province better from abroad than at home. After all, the Board had acted in response to the demands of the Treasury Lords and the Lords Commissioners of the Admiralty, and these two groups were influenced by the views of their respective colonial agents, Edward Randolph and Robert Quary. By dealing with these men directly, as well as directing the affairs of Pennsylvania, Penn might end his difficulties at their source. At the same time, he was well aware of the dangers involved in leaving England. He had written earlier to his powerful friend, Robert Harley:

I have two things more to recommend to thy favour; one relates to America in case any thing should be started that should concern the plantations and especially those in propriety. Pray be a friend to the absent, and without vanity, the meritorious.... The next thing is, that if any persecuting temper should show itself in your house [of Commons], which I have some cause to believe will, at least, be attempted, thou would please to remember the house that liberty of conscience is one of the articles of the original contract of this revolution and most agreeable with that of the English Government at large.... I know thy double influence in the House, to moderate one sort and to excite t'other to help us.[98]

[98]WP to R. Harley, 30 January 1698/99, in HMC, *Portland,* I, 601–602.

It may be significant that, in continuing his pursuit of these two goals, Penn put the protection of Pennsylvania before the toleration of dissent.

The Board of Trade recommended that the proprietor be given certain instructions before he left England: remove David Lloyd and other officials of the colony who disregarded the King's interest; call for obedience to the vice-admiralty courts and encourage the customs men; observe the acts of trade; prevent piracy by law and punish pirates;[99] report to the King on the state of the province and carry on public affairs in the service of the Crown. It was also proposed that Penn establish a militia in his province.[100] The Lords Justices approved the Board's recommendations, and orders to this effect were sent to Penn. Both Quary and Nicholson were notified of the action and advised not to give the Quaker proprietor offense when he arrived in America.[101]

Actually, the instructions Penn took with him to Pennsylvania were not harsh, especially in view of the fact that many of them were based on the assumption that the Quaker colony was violating the commercial rules of the empire. Only two years previously, Penn had been threatened with the loss of his patent should these laws be broken. While the removal of Markham was the first royal action of its kind in a private colony, Penn himself had already agreed to such a course of action before the Committee of the House of Lords and the Board of Trade. The estab-

[99]On 10 August 1699 the Board sent a lengthier report about pirates in Pennsylvania and the Jerseys to the Crown. *CSP, 1699,* sec. 699; *BTJ,* XII (1699–1700), 142. However, a law against piracy had already been passed in Pennsylvania in May, 1699 (George *et al., Charter to William Penn,* pp. 284–285, 291, 578).

[100]*CSP, 1699,* sec. 706.

[101]*Ibid.,* secs. 750, 751, 778, 779; *CSP, 1700,* sec. 8.

lishment of a militia followed logically from Penn's promise in 1694 to have his colony cooperate in the defense effort. The real innovation in his instructions was the requirement that provincial officials hostile to the King's interest be dismissed from office. Here was a clear illustration of the dilemma Penn frequently faced: how to satisfy the demands of the home government and the desires of the Pennsylvanians. He was leaving for America in search of a solution.

In the 1680's William Penn had launched a bold and creative project in the New World. In the face of increasing imperial control, Pennsylvania had remained autonomous because of Penn's close friendship with Charles and James Stuart and their advisors. This situation changed drastically in the 1690's. Penn was thrown on the defensive as his relationship with the Crown disintegrated overnight; weary and discouraged, he remained on the defensive throughout most of the decade. His efforts were no longer devoted to experiment and change, but rather to maintaining the *status quo*. In this he met with a fair degree of success. Although he lost his colony, he regained it under the favorable terms which had earlier applied to his proprietorship. He did not win the battle waged over augmented royal control of the private colonies, but he retained his province and most of his rights there.

As in the 1680's, Penn's fortunes in the 1690's were closely related to his connections. His troubles in the early part of the decade were largely attributable to William III's enmity, as his later success was in part due to the King's neutrality. After 1694 Penn was likely to have the ear of the monarch's advisers, but so were the enemies of proprietary government. The professional nature of the Board of Trade probably diminished the role of politics in determining colonial policy, but the rivalry between John Locke and William Blathwayt precluded a policy of complete neutrality toward the Quaker province. In other words, Penn faced greater difficulties than he had previously encountered. In combating these difficulties, he showed that his innovating abilities were not completely lost. For the first time, the proprietors and agents of the private colonies banded together for mutual protection with Penn as their leader. His past experience and present connections with important statesmen, as well as the primary importance of Pennsylvania, qualified him for this position. Unfortunately, Penn was not influential enough, nor were his tactics so novel as to divert the home government from its intent of expanded authority in America.

CHAPTER VI

Beleaguered Proprietor

(1699–1701)

IN 1699 William Penn was returning to a colony quite different from the one he had left in 1684. The autonomy of the province, evident from the very beginning, continued in the face of increasing imperial control. While Penn worried his way through the 1690's, apprehensive lest Pennsylvania become a permanent possession of the Crown, the colonists behaved with abandon. Not only did they disregard the obligations of a plantation within an empire, but they gave little thought to the interests and requests of the proprietor himself. Related to this attitude was a second aspect of Pennsylvania's political life—the growing power of the provincial assembly. This body was already chafing at its restricted role in the legislative process when Penn left the colony in 1684. His absence eased the lower house's chosen task of augmenting its power.

Both features, the sustained autonomy of the provincial government and the increasing power of the assembly, were sometimes overshadowed by a third development. Although Penn had returned to England to secure the

Three Lower Counties to his province, there was no real community of interest between the Delaware territory and the three counties which originally comprised Pennsylvania. The proprietor had brought the two regions together, though the legality of this action was questionable at best; and with his departure they had begun to drift apart. The Three Lower Counties were sparsely settled by people of Dutch and Swedish descent, generally Calvinists, Lutherans, or Episcopalians. The three upper counties were inhabited largely by English Quakers. Between New Castle and Philadelphia there was for many years a commercial rivalry. Finally, the Three Lower Counties feared political domination by the Pennsylvanians, while the latter resented the fact that Delaware, with a far smaller population, had equal representation in the legislature.[1]

Following Lieutenant Governor Blackwell's departure in 1689, relations between the two areas had become especially strained. A major source of difficulty was the form of government to be adopted. Penn agreed to accept either a deputy governor or the investment of executive power in five commissioners of state, although he made clear his preference for the latter. The representatives from the Three Lower Counties sided with the proprietor, but the Pennsylvanians, as usual, won out. This was too much for their southern adversaries, who now departed from the council, joined by William Markham. Penn was not consulted about this withdrawal, but on hearing of it he naturally worried that the separation would endanger his precarious hold on the Three Lower Counties. Nevertheless, he finally agreed to let William Markham be deputy

[1]Shepherd, *Proprietary Government*, Pt. II, chap. vi, "The Three Lower Counties"; Richard S. Rodney, "Early Relations of Delaware and Pennsylvania," *PMHB*, LIV (1930), 209–240.

governor of that region; at the same time Thomas Lloyd held the same post in Pennsylvania.

Soon thereafter, Benjamin Fletcher arrived on the scene and ostensibly healed the breach by appointing William Markham deputy governor of the upper and lower counties, Thomas Lloyd having turned down the position.[2] But if Fletcher relaxed the sectional tensions which disturbed the province, he revived another and more permanent problem. In the late 1680's, the antagonism between the assembly and the council, which was then serving as the executive, was in the open. This conflict died down as a common opposition to Blackwell and the Delaware representatives brought the two bodies closer together. With the advent of royal rule, the assembly was strengthened at the expense of the council. Most of the former provincial officials refused to serve under Fletcher, a situation best typified by the actions of council member David Lloyd, who resigned in order to become an assemblyman and thus made that body the center of resistance to royal rule.[3] Fletcher abetted this development. His object was to raise funds for the defense of New York, and he was interested in little else. By ordering the assembly to initiate such legislation, he was going beyond the lower house's limited privilege of approving or disapproving the bills which came before it. David Lloyd, attempting to press this new power to its limit, asserted: "To be plain with the Governor, here is the Monie bill, and the house will not pass it untill they know what is become of the other bills that are sent up." This was too much for Fletcher, who

[2]The most succinct treatment of the Fletcher period is in Bronner, *Holy Experiment,* chap. ix, "Royal Interlude, 1693 to 1695."

[3]For this phase of Lloyd's career, see Roy N. Lokken, *David Lloyd, Colonial Lawmaker* (Seattle, 1959), chap. iii.

angrily threatened to annex Pennsylvania to New York or Maryland. The assembly backed down and passed a rather inadequate money bill. But in the long run the victory belonged to the lower house.[4]

The political ferment of the royal period did not end when Pennsylvania was returned to its proprietor. Markham remained as deputy governor, and he recognized that it was his duty to get money for defense. The assembly was not happy to resume its role as assigned by the second Frame of Government of 1683 after Fletcher had officially recognized its increased strength. It therefore refused to appropriate funds without the promise of a new constitution.[5] In an attempt to win support, Markham brought David Lloyd and others who shared his sentiment into the council. This tactic proving unsuccessful, the deputy governor consented to a third Frame of Government in November, 1696, in exchange for a supply bill.[6] This new charter recognized the assembly's right to initiate legislation. From this point on, the council's function was primarily advisory. There exists no record of Penn's immediate reaction to this new Frame of Government, but he was undoubtedly sensitive to it as a further infringement on the proprietary prerogative in Pennsylvania.

There was always a group of men in the colony who were friendly to the proprietor, and who were willing to support his interest. They assisted Blackwell as deputy governor,

[4]The exchange between Lloyd and Fletcher is quoted in Bronner, *Holy Experiment,* pp. 161–162. Bronner pictures this incident as another step in the gradual failure of the "holy experiment," in which the assembly bargained its principles (by contributing to the war effort) in exchange for enhanced liberties and privileges (Bronner, "Failure of the 'Holy Experiment,'" p. 105).

[5]William Markham to WP, 26 May 1696, in *CSP, 1696–7,* sec. 27 xi.

[6]Bronner, *Holy Experiment,* pp. 176–180; Shepherd, *Proprietary Government,* pp. 278–284.

they tried to heal the breach with the Three Lower Counties, and they attempted to restrain the lower house, being basically distrustful of democracy. The assemblymen, on the other hand, tended to be antiproprietary. David Lloyd was their leader, yet he served as attorney general for the province after Fletcher's departure. Both of these factions were Quaker, but there was a third force growing in Pennsylvania which was not. In 1695 Christ Church was established in Philadelphia and patronized largely by royal officials.[7] Here was the seat of hostility toward Quaker ways, specifically the attitudes toward oaths and war. While the Anglicans composed only a small minority of Pennsylvania's population, they were important out of proportion to their numbers as a result not only of the patronage of royal officials, but also of the backing of the Bishop of London and the Society for the Propagation of the Gospel in Foreign Parts.

William Penn was more disturbed about the potentially adverse effect of the Anglican group than he was about the emerging assembly party. This concern is evident from the account of the young Irishman who accompanied him to Pennsylvania as his secretary. James Logan described the proprietor's arrival in December, 1699:

The faction that had long contended to overthrow the settled constitution of the government received an universal damp, yet endeavoured what mischief they could by speaking whispers, that the proprietary could not act as governor, without the king's approbation, and taking an oath as obliged by act of Parliament; but that in great measure soon blew over. Colonel Quary, judge, and John Moore, advocate, of the

[7]Its chaplain was supported by a levy on Pennsylvania's commerce. Shaw, *Cal. Treas. Books,* XV (August 1699–September 1700), 106, 356, 402–403, 417–418; Reddington, *Cal. Treas. Papers,* II (1697–1701/02), 417.

Admiralty, the two ring leaders, went down to the water side among the crown to receive the governor at his landing. . . . [They] expected nothing but almost an open hostility from the proprietary as they were at before with Col. Markham, especially having heard that copies of Col. Quary's letters to the Admiralty at home against the governor were also brought over.

But, Logan continued, rather than give Quary offense Penn invited him to discuss provincial affairs; and in the course of this talk the proprietor promised the vice-admiralty judge that all parties not injurious to him would be treated with "equal civility." Penn even confessed that he believed occasion had been given for the complaints made to the home government, and he resolved to take up these matters with the council. He then listened to Quary's complaints against David Lloyd and William Markham, who were leaders of the two factions within the Quaker community.[8] Penn saw, if he did not admit, the truth in these accusations, and he wanted to pacify Quary. At the first meeting of the provincial council, it was decided to invite the vice-admiralty judge to attend that body and comment on the subjects of piracy and illegal trade. Meanwhile, Deputy Governor Markham was removed from office.[9]

[8]Logan also noted Penn's attitude toward the two men accused by Quary. "His [Lloyd's] obstinacy the governor could by no means brook; he could not but think there was more deference and consideration due to his character and station; the other [Markham] knew not what it was to bend, he was engaged in the cause [of defending the colony's every action], and would stand or fall by it, offering to plead it at Westminster Hall, but the governor, who was more sensible of the pulse of the court and affairs in general at home, knew this course would never take" (J. Logan to William Penn, Jr., 25 September 1700, in Janney, *Penn*, pp. 422–423).

[9]*Colonial Recs.*, I, 565–566. Quary spoke to the council on these subjects on 24 January 1699/1700 (*ibid.*, pp. 575–576). Not only was Penn trying to placate the royal officials in his own province. He also

Although Penn did not particularly like David Lloyd and was even under royal order to dismiss him from the office of attorney general—an expulsion Quary contemplated with relish—the proprietor had to move very carefully in dealing with the popular leader. As James Logan pointed out, Lloyd was "a man very stiff in all his undertakings, of a sound judgment, and a good lawyer, but extremely pertinacious and somewhat revengeful."[10] The proprietor could not afford to make an enemy of this powerful member of the council and assembly, at least not at present, for he was anxious to carry out his pledge to the Crown concerning maritime affairs and defense. In this he was successful. The assembly was convened on January 25, 1699/1700, and passed two bills—one against illegal trade and the other against pirates.[11] Meanwhile, David Lloyd remained the attorney general. Penn recognized the importance, if not the full significance, of the emerging popular faction.

The Quaker proprietor immediately broadcast the assembly's action, writing to the Board of Trade, the Customs Commissioners and the secretary of state for the northern division.[12] Quary verified the news of the proprietor's success in glowing terms:

---

wrote a friendly letter to Francis Nicholson, informing the Virginia governor of his plans to remedy piracy and illegal trade (12 December 1699, in ACM, XXXVII, 24–25).

[10] J. Logan to William Penn, Jr., cited in n. 8, above.

[11] Hazard *et al., Pa. Archives,* ser. 8, I, 221–231. For the text of the laws see George *et al., Charter to William Penn,* pp. 268–274, 284–285.

[12] WP to Customs Commissioners, 28 February 1699/1700, in HSP, WP Letter Book (1699–1701), p. 15; WP to Board of Trade, 27 February 1699/1700, in *ibid.,* pp. 11–12 (also in *CSP, 1700,* sec. 158); WP to Secretary of State James Vernon, 26 February 1699/1700, in *CSP, 1700,* sec. 156. To Vernon, Penn expressed the conviction that

Governor Penn is now arrived here: his coming hath made a very great change. He is so far from countenancing what hath been done that he hath publicly shewn his resentment and abhorrence of it all. He hath given ample assurance to all the King's Officers of his favour and encouragement to them in all matters relating to the King's service. . . . A demonstration of all his real intentions herein appears by these several weighty steps which he hath already taken. . . . I must do Governor Penn the justice to say he is very zealous in promoting all things that doth anyways concern the King's interest.[13]

Penn's old adversary, Francis Nicholson, took a more skeptical view of events in the Quaker province, but the Board of Trade ignored this sour note and expressed its satisfaction with the new turn of affairs to Penn, Quary, and Nicholson, as well.[14] The Board was also pleased with the leading role the Quaker proprietor played at a meeting of governors from the middle colonies held in New York during September and October, 1700.[15]

---

he ought to have a share in the seizures made by the vice-admiralty "as Lord of the soil, erected into a Seigneury, must needs have a royalty. . . ." To the Board he complained that the Navigation Act of 1696 did not allow Quakers to register their ships without taking oaths, whereas they were excused from this in England.

[13]6 March 1699/1700, in *CSP, 1700,* sec. 189. On 10 April 1700 Quary wrote the Board that Penn had vowed to root the pirates out of their habitat on the lower Delaware (*ibid.,* sec. 300).

[14]Nicholson to Board of Trade, 10 June 1700, in *ibid.,* sec. 523. Penn had also written to the royal governors in New York (and the lieutenant governor), Maryland, Barbados, Jamaica, and the Leeward Islands. These letters were sent in January, February, and March, 1699/1700. See HSP, WP Letter Book (1699–1701), pp. 4–7, 13–14, 16–21. His obvious intent was to establish good relations with those men in the plantations who were closest to the Crown. Board of Trade to Quary, 19 August 1700, in *CSP, 1700,* sec. 721; Board of Trade to Nicholson, 21 August 1700, in *ibid.,* sec. 728; Board of Trade to WP, 23 August 1700, in *Ibid.,* sec. 734.

[15]Board of Trade to Blakiston, 20 September 1699, in *CSP, 1699,*

But in satisfying the home government, Penn irritated a large number of his colonists. In May, 1700, he finally dismissed Lloyd from his post as attorney general, an action apparently triggered by pressure from Robert Quary. The new attorney general was John Moore, advocate of the vice-admiralty court.[16] Informing the Board of Trade that Lloyd had been dismissed, Penn lamented: "You cannot easily imagine the difficulties I lie under, what with the King's affairs, those of the Government, and my Proprietary ones. No King's Governor, without vanity, has had more care and vexation, tho' I receive nothing from the Crown to support me under it. . . . As for the people here, they are soured to see their accusers believed, and think themselves both innocent and meritorious. However, 'tis I that pay the reckoning."[17] Under these conditions, the proprietor felt it necessary to give the assembly leeway. When the legislature met during October and November, 1700, Penn was willing to approve a number of acts which transformed Quaker custom into Pennsylvania law. But this

sec. 798; Board of Trade to Nicholson, 4 January 1699/1700, in *CSP, 1700,* sec. 8; Nicholson to Board of Trade, 10 June 1700, in *ibid., sec.* 523; Earl of Bellmont to Board of Trade, 17 October 1700, in *ibid.,* sec. 845 (pp. 580–581, 598–599); WP to Board of Trade, 8 December 1700, in *ibid.,* sec. 984; WP to Board of Trade, 31 December 1700, in *ibid.,* sec. 1065; O'Callaghan and Fernow, *N.Y. Colonial Docs.,* IV, 724, 757; WP to Blakiston, 10 October 1700, in HSP, WP Letter Book (1699–1701), p. 41.

[16]Moore had met Quary in South Carolina in 1680; he migrated to Pennsylvania around 1695. Undoubtedly Quary influenced Penn to appoint Moore. He was a man who could serve King, colony, or both, since his first allegiance was to his own interests. In *DAB,* XIII, 130–131, there is a brief sketch of him with untrustworthy dates.

[17]*Colonial Recs.,* I, 602–604; WP to Board of Trade, 28 April 1700, in *CSP, 1700,* sec. 366. This letter would lead one to believe that Quary was dismissed in April, 1700, a month earlier than the date given in *Colonial Recs.*

legislation—laws banning rough games, cock fights, stage plays; laws numbering the days and months, regulating marriages and granting religious liberty in the latitudinarian tradition of Friends; and a law which allowed attestations or affirmations in place of oaths for provincial officials, judges, and juries[18]—was offensive to the Anglicans.

Now the proprietor was attacked by the very group he had been assiduously courting. The vestrymen of Christ Church wrote to the Board of Trade that they had submitted to earlier hardships, such as exposure to Indians and pirates, which were the consequences of Quaker pacifism. But they had at least exercised freedom of religion until Penn's arrival. "We should not have presumed to have laid our grievances now before you, had we not found that Governor Penn resolves not only to continue that uneasy and intolerable yoak and burthen, which we have so long groaned under, but is adding more weight to our former misery by making laws contrary to our religious rights and consciences." Already the vestrymen had written about this matter to the Archbishop of Canterbury and the Bishop of London, both of whom were privy councillors.[19] Two of the most prominent churchmen in Philadelphia signed this complaint—Robert Quary and John Moore.

Penn, of course, was not immediately conscious of this

[18]These acts may be found in J. T. Mitchell and Henry Flanders, eds., *Statutes at Large of Pennsylvania from 1682 to 1801* (17 vols.; Harrisburg, 1896–1908), II, 3–5, 14–15, 19–20, 21–23, 39–42. The law banning clandestine marriages was recommended to Penn by Governor Nicholson. Initially, both Quary and Moore approved it. See WP to Bellmont, 10 October 1700, and WP to Nicholson, 31 December 1700, in HSP, WP Letter Book (1699–1701), pp. 42, 81–86.

[19]Vestrymen of Christ Church to Board of Trade, 28 January 1700/01: *CSP, 1701,* sec. 101.

attack on his administration by the Anglican faction. His relations with the vice-admiralty judge remained smooth on the surface, although he was not above aiming an occasional barb at Quary.[20] And aside from his concurrence with the vestrymen of Christ Church, Quary was far more antagonistic toward the activities of the Quaker merchants than toward Penn, who, he said, "would have prevented [the Quakers] in greate measure, if it had beene in his power." Even toward the merchants Quary felt some sympathy, for he realized that the illegal exportation of tobacco was the only way the province could make returns to England, with whom it maintained an unfavorable balance of trade at the ratio of six to one.[21] Pennsylvania did not adopt paper money until a later period, although both barter and the procedure of inviting specie into the colony by accepting it at a higher rate than that of other colonies or the home government had been utilized by the assembly to combat the unfavorable balance.[22] Quary at least recognized the reason for the province's action.

It was not commerce per se, but the particular matter of the vice-admiralty court, which caused Penn and Quary to become openly hostile. The Quaker proprietor could not reconcile himself to the completed mercantilist system, symbolized by Quary's presence in Pennsylvania. The vice-admiralty judge had other colonial interests which too often kept him from carrying out his job properly, a defect

[20]See Penn's defense of Markham and other members of his government in a letter to the Customs Commissions, 7 May 1700, in HSP, WP Letter Book (1699–1701), pp. 31–36.

[21]Quary to Board of Trade, 6 March 1699/1700 and 14 November 1700, in *CSP, 1700,* secs. 190, 932.

[22]Shepherd, *Proprietary Government,* pp. 401–402; Root, *Relations,* pp. 180–183.

which was supplemented by his ignorance of the law.[23] But the conflict between the two men was also the result of a circumstance beyond their control: the fact that the rights and jurisdiction of the vice-admiralty courts were not clearly defined. Penn was caught in the dilemma caused by the obscurity of the law on the one hand, and the necessity for immediate action on the other. Could he appoint an official to carry out vice-admiralty functions where his authority to do so was doubtful, or should he bear the possible onus of illegal activity?[24] Quary's dilemma was of a different kind. He did not know whether a case tried in the colonial vice-admiralty court could be appealed in England. The judge of the High Court of the Admiralty in England said appeal was possible, but other English jurists of renown took the opposite position.[25]

The quandary Quary faced was well illustrated by an incident involving the ship *Providence,* owned by one John Lumby, who was brought into the vice-admiralty

[23]Penn's complaints about the vice-admiralty courts can be seen in his letter to the Board of Trade, 28 April 1700, in *CSP, 1700,* sec. 366. Quary himself did not "pretend to the law." (See his letter to the Admiralty, cited in n. 25, below). His career as a merchant is occasionally evident in the official records. See *CSP, 1702–3,* secs. 643–645; Shaw, *Cal. Treas. Books,* XVIII (1703), 84, 91–92, 459–460.

[24]Penn faced a similar dilemma with regard to customs, as illustrated when Samuel Lowman, collector of plantation duties at Lewes on the lower Delaware, inquired of Penn whether his (Lowman's) district extended through all of Sussex county or only the port of Lewes. This was important since vessels sailed up streams into the interior and violated the laws concerning enumerated commodities and bonding (Shaw, *Cal. Treas. Books,* XIV [September 1698–July 1699], 169; S. Lowman to WP, 10 October 1700, in HSP, Penn-Physick Collection, I, 14).

[25]Sir Charles Hedges was judge of the High Court in England. See Quary to Lords of the Admiralty, 14 November 1700, in HMC, *MSS, House of Lords,* n. s., IV (1699–1702), 341–342.

court because the registry of the ship was questionable.[26]
The court's advocate, John Moore, had to argue not only
against Lumby's counsel but also, according to Quary,
against all the Quaker magistrates in Pennsylvania. They
had attended the proceedings "not out of kindness to the
man [Lumby] but prejudice to the jurisdiction of the
Admiralty." When Quary judged the case in Moore's favor,
these Quakers convinced Lumby that he could reclaim the
Providence at no cost if he would obtain an inhibition
against the trial from the High Court of the Admiralty.
This Lumby was able to do, causing great dismay to the
vice-admiralty judge, who believed that such action involved more than the specific issue of appeal to England.
It went further than this, insofar as it encouraged the
Quakers to deny the very authority of the vice-admiralty
court. Quary noted that Pennsylvanians were already cir-
culating the rumor that he and Moore "were sent for to
England and there to be fined to our ruin; that whatever
we have or shall do will be made void at home."

Penn gave a different version of the incident, expressing
his belief in Lumby's innocence, and he used the occasion
to strike at Quary where he was most vulnerable.[27] The
inhibition against the trial was "a great change and a severe
disappointment to the Admiralty Officers here," Penn admitted, "especially if their judgmt. should be reverst."
The proprietor pointed out that it would be in the King's
interest to appoint someone who understood the practice

---

[26]Quary's account of this incident appeared in his letter to the
Lords of the Admiralty cited in the previous footnote, and in a
letter of the same date to an unidentified correspondent (*CSP, 1700*,
sec. 932 ix [see also sec. 932 vii]). Quotations from Quary in these
pages are from these sources, unless otherwise specified.

[27]WP to Board of Trade, 8 and 13 December, in *ibid.*, sec. 984.

of admiralty law and who could "preserve a faire understanding between the Civil and Maritime Courts." Furthermore, Penn presented "another unhappiness," which was "Col. Quarry's having no sallery to support him; for he is obliged to be frequently absent upon trading voyages to Maryland, Virginia and Carolina, for the Company he serves, and is certainly a dilligent factor, but as that has cost him neer eight months of the twelve that I have been here, so I do believe you cannot think it is for the King's service." Yet Penn continued to act in a friendly manner toward Quary, assuring the admiralty judge that he would proceed against "anyone of those that are called my friends that have made that report vizt that thou wert sent for to Engld and that the Admiralty proceedings from first to last are declared voyd."[28]

While Quary's dilemma was shown clearly in the *Providence* affair, Penn's own predicament was also being illustrated. Quary was complaining that the proprietor had violated "that solemn promise which he was pleased to give me and so often confirm, vizt., that he would not in the least invade the rights and jurisdiction of the Admiralty. . . ." According to Quary, Penn had commissioned sheriffs in all counties as water bailiffs and, when challenged about this, asserted that the vice-admiralty court had no jurisdiction over the interior waterways of the province. "For my part," Quary said, "I have charity enough to believe that he would never have taken those measures were he not under a necessity of complying with his Quaker friends, especially at this juncture when they are sitting in Assembly and he expects considerable supply

[28]WP to R. Quary, 11 November 1700, in Hazard *et al., Pa. Archives,* ser. 1, I, 137–138. The letter from Quary to Penn which provoked this response is not extant.

from them. . . . Governor Penn is reduced to this great streight, if he complys with his friends here, then he must violate all his promises, which he hath made at home for supporting the King's Authority in his Government, and if he doth not comply with them, he must not expect any mony from them."

Though the proprietor had admitted a few months earlier to the Board of Trade that he was caught between conflicting imperial and provincial issues, he now refused to accept Quary's explanation. To the Lords of the Admiralty Penn wrote that Quary had been absent five months from Pennsylvania, during which time a ship in the Philadelphia harbor fired a cannonball through a house. To guard against such incidents in the future, he had issued the water bailiff's commission.[29] Penn gave reasons why such action might be within the powers granted him by charter, although he was willing to concede them to the vice-admiralty court when it was inclined to act. "But," the proprietor concluded, "the peace must be preserved, and therefore I was obliged to do more than otherwise I should, not through any doubt of my power, but to prevent clashings and misunderstandings."[30]

As a result of their facing these ambiguous but real problems regarding the vice-admiralty court, an atmosphere of mistrust began to pervade relations between Penn and Quary. The latter told the Lords of the Admiralty that the proprietor's protestations of cooperation were "but pretense to serve an end, which he concludes is now fully answered, having made things easy and smooth at

[29]This was the only commission Quary sent to the Board of Trade, although he claimed there were others. *CSP, 1700*, sec. 932 i.

[30]WP to Lords of Admiralty, 10 December 1700, in *CSP, 1701*, sec. 1162.

home,...he is pleased to run counter to all." However, when he accused Penn of using his influence in England to obtain the inhibition in the Lumby case, Penn flatly denied the charge. Yet Quary's suspicion was well founded, and the proprietor's denial was less than honest. Within a month after stating, "I never concerned myself with any p'son at home that could give the least help to this issue...," Penn sent letters to Chief Justice John Holt, the Earl of Romney, and Lord John Somers. And to his agent in London, Charlewood Lawton, he sent equally compromising instructions and advice:

Salute me to Ld Haversham [one of the Admiralty Lords], & tell him the Admty is no Inheritance to him, but the common Law is, & Hope he will not Countenance their Ignorance.... Hinder Randal [Randolph], our enemy, a knave, & c., from returning...Sr. R. Southwell was his protector, & when I left London his great enemy for baseness: R. Harley has great power with him.

Penn had always been willing to use his connections to protect his interests. But malice was uncharacteristic of him.

He was obviously upset, and he even went so far as to suggest that bribery was acceptable under the circumstances. He concluded his letter to Lawton:

Coll. Bass and Coll. Barkstead are Alsatians, wooden Colonels, litle witt, &c., ingrate to the last, my great Enemies; Bass, & a Liar the Same, lett him not come hither...See R. West on this.... Give R. West a guinea now & then, I fear him in the surrender of the Jerseys, he has always profest friendship, putt him in mind of it; he advised me to stay & settle matters, but Coll. Quary, & c., with their artful Letters, helped by the Bp. of London and Gr Nicholson, who would not suffer it— Church is their Cry, and to disturb us their Merit, whose labours have made the place; they misrepresent all we doe, & would make us dissenters in our own Countrey.[31]

This final note of dejection typified the pessimistic attitude which gradually overcame Penn in the early years of the century; and perhaps this attitude can be accounted largely responsible for the proprietor's declining sense of ethics.

The despondent tone of Penn's conclusion, however, should not obscure its content. The proprietor had reaffirmed his allegiance to the colonists of his own persuasion, making clear that he considered Quary and the Anglicans to be outsiders. The members of Christ Church could be courted, but never loved. Toward the provincial Quakers, on the other hand, Penn had strong paternal feelings, and he simply assumed that the Pennsylvania Quakers reciprocated with filial devotion. It was for this reason that, on his arrival in the province, he had turned his attention to the alien church party and imperial problems—first, illegal commerce and piracy, then the vice-admiralty court. But Penn had to solve a third problem regarding the empire, one which would bring him face to face with the provincial Quakers. He was about to witness the strength of filial devotion after two decades of growth.

The problem was a military one. When his government was restored to him in 1694, and again when he took leave of England in 1699, Penn had promised to provide troops,

[31]WP to C. Lawton, 10 December 1700, in Hazard *et al., Pa. Archives,* ser. 1, I, 139–142. The letters to Holt, Romney, and Somers are mentioned in the Lawton letter. I have been able to find only a letter to Somers, dated 22 October 1700, in HSP, WP Letter Book (1669–1701), pp. 68–71. Somers had lost his seat on the Privy Council in April, 1700 (*DNB,* XVIII, 629–637).

or the monetary equivalent, for the defense of the plantations in America. As soon as he reached Pennsylvania, he informed the colony's neighbors of his intention to cooperate on this matter.[32] He was willing to sacrifice the principle of pacifism to the necessities of imperial existence, and he anticipated no serious trouble from the assembly. Informed by the King that Pennsylvania must provide £350 toward the construction of forts on the New York frontier, Penn confidently turned the matter over to the lower house on August 2, 1701. Within four days the royal demand was rejected on the grounds that such a defensive effort would require too much financial sacrifice for a struggling colony, that other plantations had done nothing in this regard, and that there was no real emergency anyway.[33] Like many a fond father, William Penn suddenly realized that he had not been sufficiently aware of the growing independence of his child.

At the meeting of the provincial council which followed the assembly's decision, the proprietor stressed the urgency of pleasing the home government. To emphasize his point, he described the attempt made in England during the past spring to secure an act of Parliament which would annul the proprietary charters. While such action had always been far more worrisome to Penn than to his colonists— indeed, the assembly faction welcomed any weakening of the proprietary prerogative—the members of the council were generally friendly to his interests. When he predicted that a fresh attack would be mounted against the charter

[32]WP to "Honored Friends" in New York, 17 May 1701, in HSP, WP Letter Book (1699–1701), p. 103; WP to N. Blakiston, governor of Maryland, 26 May 1701, in *ibid.*, p. 105.

[33]Board of Trade to King, and King to WP, 10 January 1700/01, in *CSP, 1701,* secs. 16, 20; *Colonial Recs.,* II, 28–31; Hazard *et al., Pa. Archives,* ser. 8, I, 280.

at the next session of Parliament, the council agreed to issue writs calling for a new assembly. When this body convened on September 15, 1701, Penn informed its members that they had been hastily reassembled because he would soon have to return to England to defend the colony against its enemies there. He charged the assembly to reconsider the issue of defense. In return, he offered the members compensation: "Review again your Laws, propose new ones that may better your Circumstances, and what you do, do it quickly, remembering that the Parliament sitts the end of the next month, and that the sooner I am there the safer."[34]

By springing the news of his impending departure on the assembly and suggesting that he was open to compromise, Penn did not gain the assembly's sympathy. Instead, he opened a veritable Pandora's box. His request that the defense issue be reconsidered was flatly rejected, but the assembly revived other matters which the proprietor would rather have left dormant. On September 20, 1701, he was presented with an address which, according to the speaker, was "encouraged by his [Penn's] favourable promises in his Speech, and incited by a Petition from a Considerable Number of the Inhabitants of Philadia." This address called for changes in the form of government, including the judiciary, as well as in the policies concerning real and personal property.[35]

Ever since his return to Pennsylvania in 1699, the proprietor had encountered agitation favoring a modification of the form of government. Penn himself was not averse to change. But in contrast to the popular faction, he envisioned a reactionary alteration of the present situation:

[34]*Colonial Recs.*, II, 32, 34–36.
[35]*Ibid.*, II, 37–39, 41.

"The ablest men have always been chosen to be of the Council to prepare Laws, & the Assembly to consent to them; wee are two bodies yet but One power, the one prepares, the other consents." In other words, he was rejecting the modifications accepted by Deputy Governor Markham in 1696. However, when he asked the assembly whether it wanted to return to the Frame of 1683, he received a resoundingly negative reply. Recognizing the strength of this sentiment, the proprietor gave up without a fight. He agreed that a new constitution could be drawn up. Work began on this project in the spring of 1700.[36]

The distribution of power between the upper and lower houses of the legislature was the issue providing most obstacles to agreement on a new constitution. There was, however, another stumbling block in the form of a debate over representation for the Three Lower Counties. Although delegates from this region had been attending meetings of the assembly since the Fletcher period (the legislature had even met in New Castle in 1700), the breach between the upper and lower counties was by no means healed. The validity of the Act of Union therefore remained a moot point, and at the New Castle assembly the members from Delaware proposed

that the Union shall be confirmed on Condition, that at no Time hereafter the Number of Representatives of the People in Legislation in the Province, shall exceed them of the annexed Counties; but if hereafter more Counties be made in the Province, and thereby more Representatives be added, that then the Union shall cease.

[36]*Ibid.,* I, 596, contains Penn's speech. Accounts of the movement toward a new Frame of Government appear in Shepherd, *Proprietary Government,* pp. 284–296, and Eshleman, "Popular Power in Pennsylvania," pp. 153–158.

The representatives from Bucks, Philadelphia, and Chester counties rejected this proposal, and a compromise suggested by Penn was not acted upon. The matter was left to the next assembly, which, as it turned out, was to be the last one where delegates from upper and lower counties would meet together.[37]

Penn was very troubled by the turn affairs had taken with regard to Delaware. He had just been reminded by the Lords of the Treasury that his deed for this region (except New Castle) specified that half the quitrents and other profits were to be paid to the Duke of York. The Lords assumed that this moiety reverted to the Crown when James became king; therefore, the Quaker proprietor was now in debt to William III.[38] Penn indignantly replied that neither the Lords nor William Blathwayt, Surveyor and Auditor General of the royal revenue in the plantations, understood the situation. But his answer clearly demonstrated that he was uncertain of his position.[39] Furthermore, at the same time that the Lords of the Treasury were demanding that Penn fulfill the terms of his grant, the Board of Trade was again raising the question as to whether he was legally empowered to govern the

[37]Hazard et al., Pa. Archives, ser. 8, I, 258–260. A succinct account of the differences between the upper and lower counties (sometimes distinguished as the Province and the Territories) at this time is in Rodney, "Early Relations of Delaware and Pennsylvania," pp. 230–240.

[38]Shaw, Cal. Treas. Books, XVI (October 1700–December 1701), 235.

[39]On the one hand, Penn claimed he had gotten another deed from James II (this was never confirmed); on the other, he argued that he was not in full possession of the area until a line be run between Delaware and Maryland (WP to Colonel Depeister, 20 September 1701, in HSP, WP Letter Book [1699–1701], p. 147–148). Depeister had recently been appointed deputy to Blathwayt (Shaw, Cal. Treas.

Three Lower Counties.[40] From Penn's point of view, his case would be strengthened if this area was firmly tied to the upper counties by the Act of Union—but this would depend on the assembly.

Among the delegates who convened in September, 1701, there was, ostensibly at least, a general agreement that the province needed a new constitution. Representatives from both Delaware and Pennsylvania were commissioned by the assembly to "wait on the Governor, to desire him to send to the House what he had drawn up relating to Privileges." Penn's response—he immediately sent the assembly two papers, containing "Heads of a Frame of Government"—was in part due to his desire to find a political vehicle acceptable to both upper and lower counties. But when the assembly appointed a four-man committee "to consider of some Privileges to be put in a Charter, and draw up some Articles to present to the Proprietary," only one member was chosen from Delaware. Soon thereafter, the cement binding the two regions crumbled completely. A bill was introduced which would have confirmed the acts passed at the New Castle session of 1700, the implication being that laws made in the Three Lower Counties were of doubtful validity. The members from this area angrily left Philadelphia, claiming that only by separation could they obtain equal privileges. Penn pleaded

---

Books, XVI [October 1700–December 1701], 256). Penn had warned Lawton of the sinister influence of Blathwayt, who may have been responsible for bringing up this issue with the Treasury Lords, but there is no record that such action was taken. Discussion on the subject ended when Penn offered to sell his government in 1703 (*ibid.,* XVII [1702], 189; XVIII [1703], 254, 354).

[40]Board of Trade to Attorney and Solicitor Generals, 28 October 1701, in *CSP, 1701,* secs. 973, 975–976. See also *CSP, 1702,* secs. 5, 316, 319. There is no record that the Board's question was ever answered by either of these men.

in vain against this rupture. In the end, he had to concede the split which the inhabitants of both the upper and the lower counties desired, even though it put his title to Delaware in greater jeopardy.[41]

In the summer of 1701 David Lloyd, leader of the antiproprietary Quakers but not a member of the current assembly, had attempted to convince Penn that a constitutional settlement involving the political separation of the Three Lower Counties and a greater measure of autonomy for the lower house would be to the proprietor's advantage. Penn had thought otherwise at the time, but in October he found himself virtually forced into this position. He later wrote to James Logan: "The Charter was never altered by me, but by the suggestions of. . . David Lloyd, to my regrets, as my letters before and my conduct after plainly shewed."[42] The proprietor's unhappiness is easily understood. The fourth Frame of Government, usually referred to as the Charter of Liberties, was an explicit rejection of Penn's ideas concerning the nature of political institutions. The devices that had characterized the Frames of 1682 and 1683—a bicameral legislature with a powerful upper house, the ballot, indirect election and rotation— were no longer the essence of Pennsylvania's government. Instead, the assembly became the sole law-making body, and the privileges it had claimed in the past were now

[41]Hazard *et al., Pa. Archives,* ser. 8, I, 306, 311; *Colonial Recs.,* II, 49–52. He did receive compensation for this concession, or so it would appear. He was informed on the same day that a bill granting him £2000 was in preparation.

[42]WP to J. Logan, 10 May 1705, in HSP, *Memoirs,* X, 17–18. In addition to his role with regard to legislative reform, Lloyd was the architect of the Judiciary Act of 1701 as well as the Charter of Property, a document concerning land reform, which Penn hastily but reluctantly signed as he was leaving America (see Lokken, *Lloyd,* pp. 89–117).

granted officially.[43] In a political sense, therefore, the "holy experiment" had been repudiated; but the Charter of Liberties explicitly stated that the principle of liberty of conscience was to remain "inviolably for ever."

Penn received no compensation from the assembly for granting this new instrument of government. Rather, he had seen no recourse but to accede to the colonists' wishes in this matter; he had neither the desire nor the energy to put up a battle. Nor did the assembly appear grateful. Several days after he had agreed to the Charter of Liberties, the proprietor recommended reconsideration of an act concerning marriage because it gave offense to some of the Anglicans. Instead, the legislature passed the law unaltered.[44] This action was an early indication of the fact that more than Penn's political principles had suffered as a result of the Charter of Liberties. The ascendancy of the assembly meant that the province would frequently be controlled by the faction which was not only antiproprietary but also indifferent, if not hostile, to imperial demands. Both of these characteristics would make Penn's task in England more difficult than it had previously been, particularly if the home government continued to pursue a tough policy. His return to England was prompted by this very expectation.

[43]The Charter of Liberties appears in *Colonial Recs.*, II, 56–60, and is reprinted in Douglas, *English Historical Docs.*, IX, 192–195. In his letter to Logan, cited in the previous footnote, Penn stated: "It [alteration of the Charter] was carried by so great a majority that I see no blame, and being nearer to English methods, which they called for so often, I acquiesced, having first shown my dislike, as at their disliking the model of an elected Council to prepare an Assembly to resolve, and at throwing away the use of the Ballot, which their children, as I told them, will have, perhaps, sufficient cause to repent of their folly therin."

[44]*Colonial Recs.*, II, 48, 56.

Penn had barely left London in late 1699 when the Board of Trade took a further step toward the regulation of the private colonies. In a report to the House of Commons the Board emphasized that violations of the mercantile system were always worst in these areas. And, it concluded,

being further sensible of the great irregularities in the proprieties, and charter-governments, not only in reference to illegal trade and piracy, but otherwise, we have, upon several occasions, represented the same to his Majesty...we do not see any thing, without some further provision by Parliament, capable to reduce them to a more regular conduct, and compliance with their duty.[45]

Parliament adjourned in April, 1700, without taking any action on this report. Nevertheless, the Board continued to look to the legislature for the implementation of colonial policy. In the case of private colonies, to have their charters vacated by the act of Parliament would be faster than prosecution in the courts, simpler than the piecemeal process of individual royalization, and more permanent than any other method, as the judicial decision which returned Pennsylvania to its proprietor in 1694 had demonstrated.[46]

Parliament was to meet again in February, 1700/01. In the interim Edward Randolph reappeared in England primed, as usual, with tales of disobedience in the plantations. Although he had not been in Pennsylvania or the

---

[45]Stock, *Proceedings*, II, 364–369.

[46]Not only was the Board looking more in the direction of Parliament. The Attorney General, queried about the way which proprietors in the plantations could be more effectively obliged to present the names of their governors to the King for approbation, said that the best remedy lay in an Act of Parliament. Sir Thomas Trevor to B. of T., 2 January 1700/01, in *BTPr.*, V (1699–1701), 537.

Delaware territory since 1697, he was not deterred from making the charge that illegal trade in tobacco in the Three Lower Counties had increased since Penn's arrival.[47] Also in London at this time was Jeremiah Basse, who had been appointed governor of New Jersey in 1697 to replace Andrew Hamilton, a Scot. This gesture of propitiation to the home government by the Jersey proprietors had worked to their disadvantage as Basse aligned himself with the antiproprietary factions. Penn, who apparently had played a large part in getting Basse appointed in order to insure the integrity of the Jersey government, had to warn Lawton that "Randal and Bass the two Poles formerly are joyned agst Proprietary Goernmts.... I lost him [Randolph] in a blanket & before the Attny General and 5 times afterwds before the house of Lords." But the Quaker proprietor was not confident of his ability to continue to stave off attacks on the private colonies as he had in the past. "Savage of the Custom house has that business under his power, can do as he will with him [Randolph].... Savage loves a token & I should not begrutch him 20 pcs of 8 or if it were 5 guineas."

Penn realized, however, that the security of the private colonies was dependent on more than the Surveyor General's impotence. His final advice to Lawton was more general in scope, and more characteristic of the methods he had used before. Pennsylvania's colonial agent was to contact all the proprietor's friends in the House of Commons, warn them of the impending attack on the private colonies, and prepare them to fight against it.[48]

[47]Toppan and Goodrick, *Randolph Letters*, V, 210–242. Interesting in view of what Penn had said about Quary's private activities was Randolph's proposal that no customs official be the owner of any vessel, nor an agent or factor for any merchant or company.

[48]WP to C. Lawton, 21 December 1700, in HSP, WP Letter Book

Lawton was not able to carry out Penn's first instruction, however. He could not prevent Randolph from submitting papers to the Board of Trade castigating the proprietary governments.[49] Furthermore, letters of a similar nature were reaching the Board from Robert Quary. Therefore, when the House of Commons called for an account of the action taken by the Board over the past year to improve trade, the response was in line with the sentiment expressed by the Surveyor General and the vice-admiralty judge: "We humbly conceive it may be expedient that the Charters of the several Proprietors and others, intitling them to absolute Government, be reassumed to the Crown, and these colonies put into the same state and dependency as those of your Majestie's other Plantations, without prejudice to any man's particular property and freehold, which being no otherwise so well to be effected as by the Legislative power of this Kingdom."[50] The House of Commons responded to the Board's recommendation with a request for an elaboration on the complaints submitted, which the Board furnished. Still the representatives of the private colonies saw

(1699–1701), pp. 74–81. The MP's to be contacted were Sir Edward Seymour, Sir Christopher Musgrove, Sir John Lowther, Colonel Norton, Sir Heneage Finch (first Earl of Aylesford), Charles Lord Spencer, Anthony Henley, Sir Simon Harcourt (first Viscount Harcourt), and Robert Harley. Harley was elected Speaker of the House in the session that convened on 6 February 1700/01. For Penn's explanation of his predicament to Harley at this time see HMC, *Portland*, IV, 30–32.

[49]*CSP, 1701,* secs. 180, 184, 203. Insofar as Randolph treated Pennsylvania, he discussed Penn's defective title to the Three Lower Counties, the illegal tobacco trade of Delaware, the proprietor's interference in the affairs of the customs establishment, and the poor state of defense.

[50]The House of Commons' request was on 12 March 1700/01, the Board's reply on 29 March 1701. See Stock, *Proceedings,* II, 378,

no cause for alarm. The response of the House of Commons was no more than standard procedure and, besides, Penn had alerted his allies in that chamber. But, to the great surprise of the colonial agents and proprietors, a bill to reunite the private colonies to the Crown was introduced suddenly in the House of Lords. This was undoubtedly the work of Randolph and the Board, who recognized Penn's strength in the lower house.[51]

The decision to introduce the bill in the House of Lords was an unfortunate one for Pennsylvania, which again bore the brunt of the attack against private colonies. The petition of William Penn, Jr., that counsel be allowed to plead against the bill, was granted. But testimony was heard only four times before the bill was given its second reading.[52] Of the six witnesses called to speak in the bill's favor, five were ill-disposed toward Pennsylvania, including Randolph, Basse, and George Keith, a Quaker schismatic who had caused considerable trouble in the colony before departing for England to become an Anglican minister. Not surprisingly, the House of Lords asked that all papers concerning William Penn be laid before it.

382–389. The Board made an almost identical presentation to the King on 26 March 1701, from which the quoted passage is taken (*CSP, 1701,* sec. 286). The Customs Commissions also declared in favor of investing the proprietary governments in the Crown (Reddington, *Cal. Treas. Papers,* II [1697–1701/02], 480–482).

[51]Stock, *Proceedings,* II, 389–390, 392–401; *Journals of H. of L.,* XVI, 659; HMC, *MSS, House of Lords,* n.s., IV (1699–1702), 314–315, 317. The colonies included Massachusetts, New Hampshire, Rhode Island, Connecticut, New Jersey, Pennsylvania and the Three Lower Counties, Maryland, the Carolinas, and the Bahamas.

[52]*Journals of H. of L.,* XVI, 660. The minutes of the four meetings, held on May 3, 8, 13, and 17, 1701, are in HMC, *MSS, House of Lords,* n.s., IV (1699–1702), 315–316. The papers submitted are in *ibid.,* pp. 317–355.

These, the only papers considered in regard to the bill, were the communications from Robert Quary to the Board of Trade, the Customs Commissioners, and the Admiralty. The House of Lords saw only one letter from Penn to these agencies, although he had written at least six others.[53]

It is not difficult to see why the Quaker province received such harsh treatment. It was the most important of the private colonies. The prosperous trading community in Philadelphia, supplemented by the tobacco growing area to the south, made the colony subject to complaints of illicit commerce. Resistance to the newly established vice-admiralty courts was strongest in Pennsylvania. Its form of government gave too much voice to a restless people, thus disturbing its royal neighbors. Quaker pacifism ran contrary to the defense requirements of the home government. Furthermore, the Board of Trade, which instigated the action against the private colonies in general and Pennsylvania in particular, was functioning without the services of John Locke. The antiproprietary influence of William Blathwayt was now supreme. Finally, Penn's absence from England meant that the attack on his colony could be mounted with far less opposition than his presence would

---

[53]The Penn letters (in chronological order) not forwarded to the House of Lords were WP to Board of Trade, 27 February 1699/1700 and 28 April 1700, in *CSP, 1700,* secs. 158, 366; WP to Customs Commissioners, 7 May 1700, in HSP, WP Letter Book (1699–1701), pp. 31–36; WP to Customs Commissioners, 9 December 1700, in Hazard, *et al., Pa. Archives,* ser. 1, I, 138–139; WP to Board of Trade, 8–13 December 1700, in *CSP, 1700,* sec. 984; same to same, 6 March 1700/ 01, in *CSP, 1701,* sec. 219; WP to Customs Commissioners, 6 March 1700/01, in HSP, WP Letter Book (1699–1701), pp. 90–91. The last letter written to the Board was received in London on 5 May 1701, four days before the House of Lords asked to see Penn's papers (*CSP, 1701,* sec. 422).

have permitted—a lesson which was not lost on the proprietor.

Nevertheless, the effort failed. Two weeks after the bill was read a second time, Parliament was prorogued. The Board of Trade attributed its lack of success to "the shortness of time and the multiplicity of other business." The agent for Connecticut, Sir Henry Ashurst, took credit for delaying the bill until Parliament adjourned. No doubt both of these explanations are valid. On one point the Board and Ashurst agreed: it was very probable that the same matter would again be under consideration the next session of Parliament, and at this time the private colonies would have more trouble defending themselves.[54] Perhaps this is why the House of Lords did not pursue the business more energetically. In any case, the Board immediately began its preparations for the next session by sending out requests to several of the royal governors to "get the best information you can relating to the conduct of Proprietary Governors and Governments upon the several heads of observations...here inclosed, and upon such other heads as you judge proper." Neither Randolph nor Basse needed such advice, since they instinctively followed that policy.[55]

[54]*Journals of H. of L.*, XVI, 700, 717, 726, 736; Board of Trade to Francis Nicholson, 22 July 1701, in *CSP, 1701,* sec. 661; Sir Henry Ashurst to Fitz-John Winthrop, 10 July and 1 November 1701, in Massachusetts Historical Society, *Collections* (7 ser., 79 vols.; Cambridge), ser. 6, III, 75, 85.

[55]Board of Trade to Nicholson, cited in previous footnote; Board of Trade to Nathaniel Blakiston, governor of Maryland, 22 July 1701, in *CSP, 1701,* sec. 662. Blakiston was instructed to pay special attention to Pennsylvania. See also *BTJ*, XIV (1701–1702), 107; *BTPr.*, VI (1701–1702), pt. 1, G 22. On Randolph, see *BTJ*, XIV (1701–1702), 55; on Basse, see *CSP, 1701,* secs. 564, 644.

William Penn was also preparing for the forthcoming session of Parliament. He called for an all-out fight against parliamentary action, conceding that a few concessions might have to be made in order to triumph.[56] Allies were to be marshalled not only in the House of Commons, but also among the peers. Penn did not want to be unprepared in the House of Lords again. Among the "Lords who I am Inform'd have been very Kind in my affair," Penn included the Dukes of Devonshire and Somerset, the Marquis of Normanby, the Earls of Romney and Dorset, and Lords John Poulett and George Jeffreys; all were men of influence.[57] In a moment of candor and confidence, Penn wrote to the Board of Trade: "By nothing but a downright Parliamentary omnipotency can my pretentions be over-

---

[56]The concessions Penn mentioned were these: "If nothing else will Serve Lett proprietaries be bound for themselves or Deputies for their Administration. The King has his own Vice Admrlty his Collector and Lett him name if he will his own Naval Officers: nay Lett him Appoint the Military Officers if he pleases Rather than tak the Civill Administration from those that had that Priviledge granted for the first Incouragemt" (see WP to C. Lawton, 2 July 1701, in HSP, WP Letter Book [1699–1701], pp. 106–107). The appointment of the naval officer, whether by the Crown or the governor, was at this time a moot point. For a discussion of this point and a description of the naval officer's function, see Andrews, *Colonial Period*, IV 184–191.

A second letter to Lawton was written on 26 August 1701 (HSP WP Letter Book [1699–1701], pp. 109–117). Other instructions from Penn, cited in the text, are from this letter.

[57]Devonshire, formerly a Lord Justice, was to support Penn's case before the Admiralty (*DNB*, III, 1279–1284; and see also WP to Devonshire, 25 August 1701, in HSP, WP Letter Book (1699–1701), p. 118). Romney was again to represent Penn's case to the King (see WP to Romney, 6 September 1701, in ACM, XLI, 4). Somerset was a member of the Privy Council and a Regent of England from July to November 1701. Normanby and Dorset were previously members of the Council and Dorset was three times a Regent. Letters from

ruled, but I hope by the lights they may receive before the next Sessions are over, those that are the Conservators of our Liberties and the last resort of Englishmen for right will not lightly suffer other men's mistakes or ill designs to prevail with them to ruin me and my family."[58]

However, the situation caused Penn too much apprehension for him to be satisfied with the efforts he had made thus far. England's champion of religious toleration suggested that his agent might use to good advantage the idea that the private colonies were being challenged because most of them were founded by nonconformists. "And if this were well Insinuated among the Chief of the presbyterians Independents & Baptist methinks they would See the common cause of Dessent at stake and Consequently make a bold Appearance & stand bothe within doors & without, agst the progress of such a Bill." Finally, Penn warned Lawton to "insist upon Time my case differing from all others & to the End I may come safely home to Negotiate my affairs of so great Importance to mee and my poor family." But it was surely wishful thinking to suppose that he could receive the special privileges granted him by James II.

Penn assured James Logan, whom he was leaving in Pennsylvania to handle his affairs, that "no man living

---

Penn to these three men and Poulett and Jeffreys are in HSP, WP Letter Book (1699–1701), pp. 118–124, 127–128. See also *DNB*, XVI, 230–231; XVII, 575–577, 1235–1237; XVIII, 13–15. With regard to the House of Commons, Penn told Lawton to contact Christopher Musgrave and Edward Seymour, while the proprietor himself wrote to Robert Harley (27 August 1701, in HMC, *Portland*, IV, 19–21), John Lowther (16 August 1701, in HMC, *The Manuscripts of the Earl of Lonsdale* [London, 1893], p. 246) and Henneage Finch (27 August 1701, in HSP, WP Letter Book [1699–1701], pp. 132–135).

[58]WP to Board of Trade, 26 August 1701, in *CSP, 1701*, sec. 791.

can defend us or bargain for us better than myself."[59] While there was more truth than conceit in this statement, the proprietor's position was not so strong as he thought. If his letters to Lawton suggest that he was returning to fight as vigorously for the preservation of his charter as he had in the 1680's, his position nevertheless remained defensive, as it had been in the 1690's. Furthermore, his health was beginning to fail, and at least three times in the first few months after his arrival in England he explained his absence from important meetings of the Board of Trade as resulting from his physical condition.[60] Finally, Penn faced a problem of a different nature, as he informed James Logan:

I must renew my pressing upon thee about returns, for I perceive by the votes of the day, the House of Commons have ordered the state of the plantations laid before them. And just now a lawyer sends me word he is offered to be feed against me by Col. Quarry, who is now come over to do us all the mischief he can. Hasten over rents, & c., all thou canst, for many call on me for old scores, thinking I have brought over all the world with me.[61]

Therefore, when attacks were launched on proprietary governments in both houses of William III's sixth Parliament, Penn's cause was weakened by his own ill health and lack of money.[62]

[59]WP to J. Logan, 8 September 1701, in HSP, *Memoirs*, IX, 56.

[60]WP to W. Popple, [14 January] 1701/02, in *CSP, 1702*, sec. 31; WP to Board of Trade, 7 April 1702, in HSP, WP Letter Book (1699–1701), p. 152; *BTJ*, 21 and 27 May 1702, in *BTJ*, XV (1702–1703), 40–42, 44–47; *CSP, 1702*, secs. 511, 531.

[61]WP to J. Logan, 3 March 1701/02, in Janney, *Penn*, p. 458.

[62]Stock, *Proceedings*, II, 425–443. The Board's position was put before the House of Commons on 5 February 1701/02 and before the House of Lords on 16 February 1701/02.

Penn's immediate tactic was to submit a plan which would serve as an alternate to the expected bill concerning private colonies. It followed closely the specifications stated in his letter to Lawton: all military, admiralty, and customs affairs would be solely the province of the Crown, while the civil government would remain firmly in the hands of proprietor or corporation; justice, however, would be administered in the name of the King, who would have a right of veto on every provincial law, and appeals to England would be guaranteed. When this plan was shown to the Board of Trade, it objected that Penn's scheme in no way contributed to the goals sought.[63] In truth, the Quaker proprietor was merely proposing to accept what was already the official, if not the actual, situation in Pennsylvania. The real problem which faced the royal agencies was that of enforcement, and the Board of Trade had concluded that this was possible only by uniting all private colonies to the Crown.

Although Penn's plan was rejected, a bill embodying the Board's desire did not reach Parliament. It has been surmised that the untimely death of William III on March 8, 1701/02, was responsible for this lack of action.[64] But there exists no evidence of a relationship between these two events; on the contrary, Parliament remained in session for over two months after the King's passing. The explanation for the failure to submit a reunification bill lies in the fortuitous juncture of several other factors. In the first place, Penn had his forces well organized, a situa-

[63]Secretary of state Manchester to WP, 16 February 1701/02, in HSP, Penn Forbes Collection, II, 68; Manchester to Board of Trade, 17 February 1701/02, in *CSP, 1702,* sec. 121; Board of Trade to Manchester, 18 February 1701/02, in *ibid.,* secs. 128, 135.

[64]Root, *Relations,* p. 350.

tion which could not escape the Board's notice. No doubt the Board would still have staged an assault had it not received a letter from Robert Quary pleading that no business concerning Pennsylvania be concluded until he reached England. Therefore, the Board was willing to wait for Quary's new evidence rather than risk loss of face in Parliament. It could, in fact, take consolation in the fact that the royalization of East and West New Jersey, which Penn had so feared, was completed in April, 1702.[65]

Queen Anne's first Parliament convened on October 31, 1702. The Board of Trade immediately renewed its attack on the private colonies. The issue again went into committee in the House of Lords and, as usual, most of the papers presented concerned Pennsylvania. Included were the denunciations of the province which Quary had brought back to England. Yet there was one notable difference between this situation and that of 1701, when most of the letters from William Penn to the Crown agencies did not reach Parliament. In the current session, Penn's answers to Quary's accusations against the Quaker province were included in the papers presented by the Board.[66] The proprietor's presence in London explains the difference. He had been back long enough to rebuild his connections. At one point, he was able to prevail on a Com-

[65]Quary to Board of Trade, [October] 1701, in *CSP, 1701,* sec. 985 (received in January 1701/02). Quary claimed that he had a "matter of moment to offer to your Lordships on that subject," and he added ominously: "I could inlarge, but I am afraid 'twill be intercepted." The surrender of the Jerseys is treated in Pomfret, *West New Jersey,* chap. xi, and in Pomfret, *East New Jersey,* chap. xv.

[66]Stock, *Proceedings,* III, 1–6; HMC, *MSS, House of Lords,* n.s., V (1702–1704), 81–92. The debate between Quary and Penn can also be followed in *CSP, 1702,* secs. 260, 269–282, 299, 304–306, 342, 356, 357, 375, 385, 391, 395, 462, 463, 498, 563, 568, 580, 612, 638, 648, 649.

mittee of the Privy Council to summon the Board before it to answer his charge that the Board had shown undue favor to Quary.[67] Soon thereafter, he wrote confidently to Logan: "I believe this Parl. will not meddle with our Grannts."[68] In this Penn had judged correctly. The Committee of the House of Lords did not even discuss the papers submitted by the Board, and no bill reached the floor of Parliament.

It was not Penn's connections alone which were responsible for this development. Quary had contributed no new or startling information to the case against proprietary governments. Yet Penn felt compelled to answer the charges. The consequent war of words between him and the vice-admiralty judge was long, complex, and oftentimes tedious—not the sort of exchange that would arouse legislators who understood the plantations only in the most general terms. The one issue which might have had an

[67]The Committee took no action against the Board. *CSP, 1702,* sec. 665. Penn's charges against the Board appear well-founded, to judge by a letter from the Board to the Customs Commissioners, 18 June 1702, in *ibid.,* sec. 610. Quary himself had protested to the Privy Council that "Mr. Pen by Vixatious proceedings here has Caused him to be arrested in severall Great Actions...purely to oppress him and oppose his Prosecuting Her Majesty's Interest...." No action was taken by the Council (Grant and Munro, *Acts of Privy Council, Colonial,* II, sec. 869).

[68]WP to J. Logan, 28 July 1702, in *PMHB,* XXXVI (1912), 303–308. Among those helpful to his cause Penn listed the Dukes of Somerset, Queensberry, and Normanby, as well as the powerful Earl of Godolphin. The recently favored Earl of Peterborough also promised him support. (WP to J. Logan, 23 September 1702, in HSP, *Memoirs,* IX, 136–137; Peterborough to WP, 3 and 6 October 1702, in HSP, Penn-Forbes Collection, II, 76–77. On Godolphin and Peterborough, see *DNB,* VIII, 42–46; XIII, 840–850.) The aid during the reign of Anne was comparable to assistance from Sunderland during the time of William III, although Penn was never as close to Godolphin as he had been to Sunderland.

impact because of its novelty and its particular pertinence to Quary—the issue of vice-admiralty courts—had actually been settled several months earlier by the Solicitor and Attorney Generals.[69] Penn had benefited by this decision in two ways. The official English legal opinion corresponded more closely to his than to Quary's view of the subject. It was judged, for example, that internal waterways fell within the jurisdiction of common law courts; the proprietor was therefore within his rights when he issued the bailiff's commission which Quary had so hotly protested. Secondly, the elimination of quarrels over the domain of the vice-admiralty courts—which was the effect of the legal decision—gave the home government one less excuse for proceeding against the proprietary governments. In other words, it was not Penn's friends in government alone, and certainly not the schemes proposed to Lawton, which saved his province from royalization. He was also aided by several developments which he had neither planned nor foreseen.

Penn's position seemed relatively secure in 1701. The Board of Trade did not give up easily, however. In 1703, 1704, and 1705 a reunification bill was put before committees of the Privy Council or the House of Lords, but without success. In 1706 William Blathwayt introduced a

[69]In these decisions, the Attorney General, Sir Edward Northy, was more favorably disposed toward Penn's view than the Solicitor General, Sir John Cooke, who tended to see things Quary's way. Cooke had been connected with the Admiralty since 1694. But Northy was the more powerful, and his view prevailed (*CSP, 1702,* secs. 585, 596, 708, 751, 778, 889; *DNB,* IV, 1015–1016; George Chalmers, *Opinions of Eminent Lawyers, on Various Points of English Jurisprudence, Chiefly Concerning the Colonies, Fisheries, and Commerce of Great Britain* [2 vols.; London, 1814], pp. 499–502, 504–507; D. S. Towle, ed., *Records of the Vice-Admiralty Court of Rhode Island* [Washington, D. C., 1936], p. 6).

similar bill into the House of Commons, and the Board made a concerted effort to have it passed. But the bill was defeated by a close vote on the second reading.[70] The failure of the bill has been variously attributed to the Whiggery of Parliament, the influence of the Connecticut agent, Sir Henry Ashurst, and the connections of William Penn. This third explanation differs from the first two; it rejects the notion that Whigs consistently supported the private colonies. Parliamentarians of this political persuasion were caught between commitment to chartered rights and religious dissent on the one hand, and recognition of the virtues of mercantilist regulation on the other. It has been pointed out that Penn was as likely to look to Tories as to Whigs for support, and that from 1701 to 1706 "Tory support for the proprietaries remained steady."[71] It is certainly debatable, however, whether there was a two-party system in England in the early eighteenth century.[72] If the traditional view is rejected in favor of the contention that Parliament was dominated by personal interest groups rather than Whig and Tory parties, then Penn's alliances

[70]The genesis and fate of the 1706 bill can be followed in *CSP, 1704–1705,* sec. 1525; *CSP, 1706–1708,* secs. 18, 88, 120; Stock, *Proceedings,* III, 113–114, 118.

[71]Root, *Relations,* pp. 360–361, subscribes to the Whig theory. Kellogg, "Colonial Charter," AHA, *Annual Report for 1903,* pt. I, pp. 298–305, gives credit to Ashurst and "his Whig influence," possibly because her discussion of the 1706 bill is focused on New England. The most recent interpretation, emphasizing the role of Penn and his Tory alliances, is put forward in Olson, "William Penn," pp. 176–195.

[72]"The more one studies the party structure under William and Anne, the less it resembles the two-party system described by Trevelyan in his Romanes Lecture and the more it seems to have in common with the structure of politics in the Age of Newcastle as explained to us by Namier" (Robert Walcott, *English Politics in the Early Eighteenth Century* [Cambridge, 1956], p. 160).

become more comprehensible. A careful examination of the House of Commons in 1701, a year for which figures exist, shows that Penn had connections with enough of these interest groups to expect about three-fifths of their votes.[73] Since the composition of these factions was not greatly altered in five years, the failure of the reunification bill in 1706 can be attributed primarily to the Quaker proprietor's influence. Not until 1715 did another bill of this nature reach Parliament. By this time, William Penn was no longer involved in politics.

In 1699, unable to restrain the home government from trying to increase its authority in America, Penn had traveled to Pennsylvania. His object was to remove the excuse the home government gave for its course of action— disobedience in the plantations, where the Quaker province was judged one of the worst offenders. On reaching

[73]The membership of the eight parliamentary groups, which included an estimated 250 out of 513 M.P.'s in 1701, appears in *ibid.*, pp. 198–215. Penn could hope for 164 of these votes, assuming that he could carry the Harley-Foley connexion (through Sir Robert Harley), the Hyde-Granville-Gower-Seymour connexion (through Sir Edward Seymour and Sir Christopher Musgrave), the Nottingham-Finch connexion (through Heneage Finch) and the Junto connexion (through John Somers, first Earl Somers; Charles Spencer, third Earl of Sunderland; Charles Powlett, second Duke of Bolton—the leaders of three of five subgroups in this connexion; and through Harry Mordaunt and John, Lord Mordaunt, whose father was Lord Peterborough—both of whom were in the fourth subgroup). It is unlikely that Penn had enough influence to carry the Court Peers (although Sir Harry Ashurst was the Earl of Pembroke's nominee), the Marlborough-Godolphin connexion (it is difficult to tell how well Penn knew Godolphin, but he certainly had access to the Lord Treasurer), the Newcastle-Pelham-Townshend-Walpole connexion, or the Government interest (although he was close to two members, James Vernon and Anthony Henley).

Pennsylvania, however, Penn got a rude shock. Not only was the colony torn by party strife, but it was no longer susceptible to the magic of his presence. The group of people who supported the proprietary influence was greatly diminished since his previous visit, while the assembly or popular party was rapidly gaining strength. Also growing in power was the Anglican party, which could depend on support from the home government. Finally, there was a sectional faction which represented the interests of the Three Lower Counties.

Initially Penn tried to placate the Anglicans, but he thereby affronted the popular party. In an effort to undo this offense and to tie the assembly Quakers and the members from the Three Lower Counties more closely together, Penn agreed to political concessions, the nature of which he did not approve. Even this tactic failed. The Delaware delegates left the assembly, never to return. The new Frame of Government, while it temporarily appeased the popular party, in essence meant that the Pennsylvanians could more easily violate royal and proprietary orders.

Penn's trip to America was a failure. On the other side of the Atlantic, however, his success continued. He had no sooner left England than an attack on the charters of the private colonies was begun. The assault was rebuffed, indicating that Penn could still depend on his connections in the home government for support. Nevertheless, the Quaker proprietor judged that his presence in London would be necessary to repulse future attacks. Since he could not alter the situation in Pennsylvania, the logic of circumstances impelled him to England. By staving off the successive reunification bills that arose from 1702 to 1706, Penn was still acting in the defensive manner which characterized his stance in the 1690's. But he was at least maintaining the *status quo* in Pennsylvania's relations with the home government, which was more than he had been able to accomplish with regard to the internal situation in the province.

The irony in this turn of affairs should not be lost. Penn was failing where he most wanted to succeed—in the creation of a "holy experiment." But he continued to succeed in the environment which he had ideologically repudiated in his conception of the experiment.

CHAPTER VII

Perplexed Courtier

(1702–1718)

SINCE the founding of Pennsylvania in 1681, William
Penn had spent considerable time and energy defending
it from the attacks of government officials who opposed
the private colonies. The initiation of the "holy experiment" was a task of creative statesmanship; thereafter, the
maintenance of the *status quo* required a defensive politician. This was the role Penn assumed, and his job became more arduous with the passage of time. At first he
had to deal only with the executive branch of the home
government. It was his good fortune to have useful connections with the Crown, although these were ruptured
temporarily by the Glorious Revolution. An equally important consequence of the Revolution for Penn was the
enlarged power of Parliament, bringing the legislature
into direct contact with colonial affairs. Although the
Quaker proprietor also had connections with important
members of this body, his defensive task was nevertheless
enlarged.

While changing conditions demanded more and more

of Penn, personal circumstances made him less and less able to keep up the pace. Age was taking its toll; more than once he collapsed as a result of physical strain. Furthermore, the defense of his colony was a costly affair, and he was sorely lacking in money. As the eldest son of Sir William Penn he had inherited estates, but as early as 1676 he was having monetary difficulties. The cost of settling Pennsylvania taxed his financial resources severely, and its maintenance proved expensive. The amount of quitrents and other revenue collected from the province was tiny. By 1688 he had poured over £13,000 into the "holy experiment," virtually without return. At the same time the revenue from his estates in Ireland declined precipitously.

While the proprietor's fortunes languished, Pennsylvania prospered, yet the assembly continually refused to help him. Finally, in an uncharacteristically petulant tone, Penn warned his steward: "I do desire thee to let no more mention be made of supply. I will sell the shirt off my back before I will trouble them any more."[1]

Just before Penn left Pennsylvania in 1701, however, the assembly granted him £2,000, apparently in gratitude for the Charter of Liberties. But this was not nearly sufficient for his needs in England, where he had not only to support his family but to foot the bills for his colonial business as well.[2] No more money was forthcoming from the colony, and the Irish estates yielded nothing.[3]

[1]Shepherd, *Proprietary Government,* p. 183; Peare, *Penn,* pp. 176, 294, 301.

[2]WP to J. Logan, 21 June 1702, in Janney, *Penn,* pp. 457–458.

[3]Logan wrote to Penn: "I dun for money to my utmost, showing to honest Friends and others to whom't is fit, the convenient parts of thy letters; but even of the quitrents, which the county would more willingly pay than any other debt; and in Chester County—always

The children of his first marriage made the financial situation even more difficult. His eldest son, William Penn, Jr., like many offspring of busy and important men, was extravagant and a waster, a source of personal and financial embarrassment to his father.[4] His daughter Letitia married in 1702 one William Aubrey, who objected to any delay in payment of the dowry. Penn characterized his new son-in-law as "a tyger against thee for returns."[5]

But the Quaker proprietor remained secretive about his greatest source of financial trouble—the dishonesty of his English steward. In 1669 he had appointed Philip Ford, an unsuccessful Quaker merchant, to manage his Irish estates. As a matter of course Ford came to handle the accounts for Pennsylvania, while Penn, who trusted his steward completely, was busy with other affairs. The proprietor's confidence was never more badly placed. By trickery, then by threat, Ford systematically defrauded the Quaker proprietor of money and land. In 1687 Penn signed an account for £5,282, 9s. 8d., and mortgaged his province for 5,000 years, unless he could pay £6,000 by

reputed the richest—a very good hand that I employed would in five weeks' time, spent almost wholly upon it, collect but about £30: though he went over the greatest part of it all. Of the supply from Bucks I have received but one ton and a half of flour.... Land, however, sells as well as ever, but they generally dissappoint wholly in their pay" (1 December 1702, in HSP, *Memoirs*, IX, 147). On 24 March 1702/03 Penn wrote to Logan: "I was never so low and so reduced.... This year the customs upon goods from Pennsylvania amount to £8000. The year I arrived there, 1699, but to £1500, at the most" (Janney, *Penn*, p. 461).

[4]WP to J. Logan, 4 January 1701/02, in *ibid.*, pp. 455–456; WP to J. Logan, 4 February 1701/02 and 13 September 1703, in HSP, *Memoirs*, IX, 69, 241.

[5]Sophie Drinker, *Hannah Penn* (Philadelphia, 1958), p. 20; WP to J. Logan, 4 December 1702, in HSP, *Memoirs*, X, 251, and many subsequent letters.

1688. At that time he was apparently unaware of Ford's chicanery, a most telling commentary on the credulity of the kindly Quaker. When he finally did realize what was happening, he told no one; rather, he capitulated to Ford's threats of public exposure by further committing himself to debt. In 1697 he gave Ford the royal charter for Pennsylvania and the deeds of enfeoffment for the Three Lower Counties, in turn leasing the province and territories from his steward. When Ford died in 1701, his son, Philip, Jr. (who much more resembled his progenitor than William Penn, Jr., did his), came to Pennsylvania and threatened to publish the mortgage if Penn would not pay the rent due. Young Ford returned quietly to England after receiving a small amount of money. In 1702 Penn tried to refer this matter to an impartial judge, but the Fords resisted, holding him to account for over £11,000. There followed three years of fruitless negotiation.[6]

If the crisis in Penn's financial affairs was not enough cause for discouragement, 1702 also marked the beginning of his acrimonious debate, already described, with Robert Quary. Furthermore, there was a new and disheartening development on the English domestic scene, which suggested to Penn a drastic solution for all his problems. He wrote to James Logan:

The scene is much changed since the death of the king. The church party advances upon the whig, and yet I find good friends, though severely against some people's wills. I have had the advice of some of the wisest and greatest men in England, that wish me well, about bargaining with the crown for my government. They all say, "stay awhile, be not hasty;" yet some incline to a good bargain: and to let Quarry begone, and change him to another province, if we can do no better.[7]

[6]Shepherd, *Proprietary Government*, pp. 184–190.
[7]WP to J. Logan, 21 June 1702, cited in n. 2, above.

Penn had recently said that his colony could not be taken but must be bought; he had never previously mentioned a voluntary sale of his province. This represented a major policy change, as Penn himself, to judge from the uncertainty with which he stated his position, may have subconsciously recognized.

Hardly had he posted his letter when he received a surprisingly similar message from Logan. Penn's secretary expressed the belief, general in Pennsylvania, that war would oblige Parliament to annex the chartered colonies to the Crown, and he concluded: "Nor can I find any, even of our friends, desirous that it should be otherwise, provided thou canst make good terms for thyself and them; for they seem both weary and careless of government."[8]

Logan's advice encouraged Penn to sell, but his efforts were desultory for the better part of a year. Even when he opened negotiations with the Board of Trade, he refused to disclose the terms on which he would dispose of his government until the Board got the Privy Council's approval of the transaction in principle.[9] Penn was obviously and understandably reluctant to part with his colony, but his financial plight—and not the antiproprietary bent of the Board—forced him to negotiate.

If he was to sell, however, he determined to do so on his own terms.[10] He asked that "the Province of Pennsylvania and Territories continue to be the same distinct

[8]J. Logan to WP, 2 May 1702, in HSP, *Memoirs*, IX, 87.

[9]WP to J. Logan, 28 July 1702, in *PMHB*, XXXVI (1912), 303–308; J. Logan to WP, 1 December 1702, in HSP, *Memoirs*, IX, 147; WP to J. Logan, 20 February 1702/03, in *ibid.*, p. 163; *CSP, 1702–3*, secs. 684, 705.

[10]*CSP, 1702–03*, secs. 715, 728, 802, 803, 811, 823, 825, 837. These proposals were submitted on 18 June 1703.

Government under the Crown that it hath always been and now is"; that the "Laws and Constitutions thereof be confirmed by the Queen, except such few as I shall object against"; that he be issued a patent for the Three Lower Counties, "according to a grant begun by the late King James"; that he be awarded £30,000 for the transaction and one-half penny per pound on tobacco coming from the colony;[11] that he be allowed to nominate several persons from whom the Crown would choose the governor and vice admiral of the colony; that no appeals valued at less than £200 go to the Queen; that he retain all rights to the land, as distinct from the government. The Board, noting the second and fifth articles, objected that if Penn could nominate the governor, he was in effect retaining the government; and that his scheme for the confirmation of laws would diminish the Queen's power, rather than grant her a right she did not already possess.[12] The Board could have added that for Penn to have the right to nomi-

[11] In arriving at this figure, Penn claimed that his initial expenditure on Pennsylvania was £10,500 and that his government had since then cost him twice that sum—a total of approximately £30,000. He estimated the customs revenue at £10,000, a reasonable guess.

[12] *CSP, 1702–03,* sec. 864. The requirement in Pennsylvania's royal charter that all acts be laid before the King in Council did not prevent the proprietor from expressing assent or dissent. But in practice his opinion was superfluous and, therefore, worthless. If the Crown disapproved an act, that was the end of it; if the act were approved, it remained in force (Shepherd, *Proprietary Government,* pp. 475–476). The proprietor could try to influence legislation, but Penn had little success at this while in the province, and as to the effect of his opinion when he was in England, the Attorney General decided that "Mr. Penn or his deputy (who when appointed is as himself) must give the assent to the Laws in the place where the Assembly is, and cannot doe it in any other place" *(Journal of the Commissioners for Trade and Plantations from 1704 to 1782* [14 vols.; London, 1920–38], I, 166; *CSP, 1704–5,* secs. 1372, 1383, 1394, 1463, 1466).

nate the vice admiral would have augmented his privilege. Furthermore, to give Penn a clear title to the Three Lower Counties and to insure his hold on the land would be tantamount to underwriting his quitrents from that region. The £30,000 would allow him to pay off the Fords, whose claim on his province he never mentioned to the Board, and have a substantial sum left over. On the other hand, he would have been absolved of responsibility for the defense of his colony and, for that matter, for all the actions (not to mention the financing) of its legislature.[13]

Penn asked for too much, and the Board rejected his terms for that reason. This should not obscure the significance of his attempt to sell the government, however. In the past, he had often spoken of the unbreakable link between power and property, saying that without the former, the latter was of little worth. Now he was apparently forsaking this belief. In actuality, this change of mind was generated by a latent despair, the result of too many setbacks in his affairs. The spirit which impelled Penn to fight, no matter what the odds, for the continued life of the "holy experiment" was gradually being sapped. By accepting the Charter of Liberties in 1701, Penn had altered his original plan regarding the political institutions of the colony. Now he had taken a far more decisive step—he demonstrated his willingness to part with the government of the province altogether.

[13]That Penn was well aware of the magnitude of his request is evident in his confidence to Logan: "I am actually in treaty with the ministers for my government, and so soon as it bears, you shall be informed of it. I believe it repents some they began it, for now't is I that press it, upon pretty good terms, as well for the people as self, in the judgment of the wisest and best of my friends" (6 June 1703: HSP, *Memoirs,* IX, 188). The implication that someone other than Penn instigated the surrender is nowhere else borne out by the evidence.

Two issues in particular, military defense and the public administration of oaths, finally confirmed Penn in his desire to sell his government. But he tried first to find solutions to these problems which arose from the Quaker domination of Pennsylvania. Had he been able to deal with a monolithic community, he might have had some success. Instead, politics in Pennsylvania after the proprietor's departure in 1701 was characterized by an even greater amount of turmoil and party strife than previously.

Although Penn was gratified to see James Logan emerge as head of the proprietary party, which was composed mainly of substantial Quaker merchants from Philadelphia who dominated the provincial council, this group seldom held a majority in the assembly. Control of the lower house remained in the hands of David Lloyd and the popular party, mainly "country" Quakers, who emphasized liberty rather than property and continually attempted to usurp power from the proprietor and his wealthy urban backers. Robert Quary, on his return from England, reassumed leadership of the Anglican party; his lieutenant was John Moore. This group vociferously opposed the enactment of Quaker principles into Pennsylvania law. But it was also more anxious to subvert the proprietary than to show its distaste for democracy, which is to say that Quary was more apt to ally with Lloyd than with Logan.[14] Finally, there remained the Three Lower Counties, a distinct political interest. Now maintaining an assembly separate from Pennsylvania's, the inhabitants of this area petitioned to

[14]F. B. Tolles plays down the importance of the Anglican party at this time, picturing Pennsylvania politics as a contest between the two Quaker parties (see *Meeting House and Counting House* [Chapel Hill, 1948], pp. 14–19). Outside the legislature, however, the Anglicans played a very important role.

be attached to the Crown.[15] This action naturally attracted the interest of the Anglicans, and the non-Quaker composition of the Three Lower Counties strengthened the attraction. When Quary arrived in England in 1702, much of the evidence he had regarding the military unpreparedness of the Quaker province had come from the people in Delaware.

The political situation in Pennsylvania which resulted from the interplay of the proprietary, popular, and Anglican parties worked almost always to Penn's disadvantage. While the country Quakers found it possible to work with the Anglicans on occasion, the proprietary group was often isolated. This was a strange development in view of the community of interest Friends were expected to display. In fact, the assembly party remained true to Quaker principles and felt it necessary to translate some of these beliefs into law. The proprietary party, recognizing the Anglicans' hostility to this practice, was anxious to conciliate the royalists in the interest of the colony's continued autonomy. It was in this point of view that Penn's salvation lay, but he was unsuccessful in winning a majority of the colonists to it.

Just before he left Pennsylvania in 1701, for example, the proprietor recommended that an act concerning marriage be reconsidered by the assembly because it gave offense to some members of the Church of England. Instead, the lower house passed the law and the proprietor saw no course but to approve it. Immediately the minister and vestry of Christ Church warned the Board of Trade that the Quakers were working with Penn to keep "the Priests out of his Province, and the Magistracy and Gov-

[15]*BTPr.*, VII (1702–1704), L 20.

ernment in their hands." The marriage law itself became a *cause célèbre* for the Bishop of London.[16]

The most important issue over which the Quaker community divided, thereby giving the Anglicans an advantage, was that of defense. This had not been the case during King William's War, at the outset of which the Friends, with one voice, turned down the royal order that Pennsylvania prepare to defend itself. Nor would the colony recruit troops for the aid of New York. And Penn did not instruct the inhabitants of his province to obey the Crown's demands. As a result of this refusal to act, Pennsylvania became a royal plantation under the rule of the governor of New York, Benjamin Fletcher. After considerable effort, Fletcher was able to wring a small amount of money from the assembly, but only on the condition that it not be used for military purposes. Soon thereafter Penn regained control of his province, promising that he would go to America and see to it that the assembly received and acted upon imperial defense requirements. His personal attitude toward the fulfillment of this condition was ambiguous, however. In 1694 he intimated to the Pennsylvanians that they need not regard the stipulation too seriously, since it had been forced upon him. But when in 1695 the assembly turned down a request for troops or the monetary equivalent, the proprietor reprimanded the members of his government. The assembly was unmoved by Penn's apparent change of heart; in 1696 it again refused to satisfy the defense requirements placed before it. The termination of the war finally resolved the problem—temporarily.

[16]*Colonial Recs.*, II, 48, 56; *BTPr.*, VI² (1701–1702), 12; Bishop of London to Board of Trade, 29 December 1701, in *CSP, 1701*, sec. 1124.

Several years later, as England prepared to resume hostilities against France, Penn sought a way to avoid responsibility for assuming a military posture. In early 1701 he pointed out: "King Charles, King James, & King William knew that we are a Quaker colony, it was so intended; how be it rather than Loose our Govermt for that let the Govermt of New York be colonell of the forces here."[17] Yet when, later that year, the Board charged Pennsylvania to contribute £350 toward the erection of fortifications in northern New York, the proprietor took the demand before the assembly. His motion was flatly rejected by the dominant country Quakers, who were not only committed to pacifism but also unperturbed by the Board's recent attack on the private colonies.[18] Penn's primary aim, on the other hand, was the protection of his province. He was again placed in the ambiguous situation of having to forsake the principles of the "holy experiment" in order to preserve it as a physical reality.

The result of Penn's failure to win the support of the assembly substantiated his fears. Robert Quary, when he returned to England in 1702, made a great stir about this matter, pointing out that while the assembly could not afford £350 for New York, it had granted £2,000 to the proprietor. Penn could only reply weakly that he had offered to pay the £350 himself, only to be turned down by the governor of New York. To Quary's charge that the resistance of the royal plantation to the defense quotas was due to the example of the private colonies, Penn had no rejoinder.

[17]WP to William Penn, Jr., 2 February 1700/01, in Hazard *et al.*, *Pa. Archives*, ser. 2, VII, 11–12. An incident revealing Penn's ambiguous attitude toward pacifism is in F. B. Tolles, *James Logan and the Culture of Provincial America* (Boston and Toronto, 1957), p. 13.

[18]*Colonial Recs.*, II, 30–31, 35, 41.

War was declared in May, 1702, and again the Board of Trade ordered Penn to put his colony in a state of defense and prepare to assist New York. Again the assembly refused to act.[19] When Deputy Governor Andrew Hamilton, acting in the capacity of captain-general as allowed by the royal charter, attempted to raise troops without financial aid from the assembly, the greatest opposition came not from the country Quakers but the Anglicans. It was obviously their purpose to discredit the Pennsylvania government, and James Logan went so far as to put part of the blame for the defeat of the appropriations measure in the assembly on the members of the Church of England.[20] Both Robert Quary and the governor of New York, who was also a strong Church man, were recommending immediate royalization of the Quaker province as the cure for its waywardness.[21] The cry was familiar, but the action was not yet justified. Pennsylvania was not the only offender in the matter of defense at this time and, futhermore, military action was not centered in New York but farther north.

Nevertheless, Penn recognized the potential danger in the situation. The new deputy governor whom he sent to Pennsylvania in 1703, John Evans, was instructed to placate the Anglicans and ensure that "nothing may lye at my door in reference to the Defense of the Country." Evans was to

[19]*Ibid.*, pp. 78–81; *CSP, 1702*, sec. 957.

[20]J. Logan to WP, 29 July and 1 December 1702, in HSP, *Memoirs*, IX, 124–125, 152–154; A. Hamilton to WP, 19 September 1702, in *BTPr.*, VII (1702–1704), L 10. Hamilton noted, however, that "the Cavalier part of the Church despise these Mean devices & take Comicons."

[21]R. Quary to Board of Trade, 16 June 1703, in O'Callaghan and Fernow, *N.Y. Colonial Docs.*, IV, 1052–1053; Lord Cornbury to Board of Trade, 9 September 1703, in *ibid.*, p. 1070; Board of Trade to WP, 21 May 1703, in *CSP, 1702–3*, sec. 718.

raise money as well as a militia, but he was not to consent to a law which would penalize pacifists.[22] This qualification was added by the proprietor to salve his own conscience, because his instructions to Evans were clearly a violation of Quaker ethics regarding war and, consequently, a further breach of the "holy experiment."

From 1704 until he left the colony in 1709, Evans was continuously engaged with the assembly in a controversy over money for defense, while at the same time the Anglicans obstructed his efforts to raise a militia. With regard to the legislature, it became evident that the opposition of the country Quakers was not based only on pacifistic principles. The defense issue also provided leverage for the expansion of the assembly's power. When Evans urged that the lower house reconsider its rejection of his first plea for funds, he received in return an objection to a clause in his commission which allowed Penn the final assent or veto on bills already approved by the deputy governor. The council, seeking to break the impasse, agreed to nullify the clause.[23] Immediately the assembly resolved to vote £200 for defense (the Three Lower Counties were presumably expected to raise the remaining

[22]WP to J. Evans, 9 August 1703, in HSP, Granville Penn Book, p. 7. A similar letter was sent to members of the provincial council on 31 December 1703, in HSP, *Memoirs*, IX, 261–263. Penn hoped the new deputy governor would influence the chaplain of Christ Church, Evan Evans, since "Welshmen are mightily akin" (WP to J. Logan, 27 August 1703, in *ibid.*, p. 206).

[23]*Colonial Recs.*, II, 138, 140–142, 144–147, 149. Logan had disapproved of this clause from the start, writing to the proprietor on 15 February 1703/04: "In the governor's [commission] there is one clause that will much disgust, viz., saving to thyself a final assent to all bills, and which I think is too much in any but those relating to thy property" (HSP, *Memoirs*, IX, 268). The Attorney General in England agreed with the council's decision (see n. 12, above).

£150 of the delinquent £350). Both Evans and Quary were skeptical, however, and with just cause. The assembly reneged on its promise to pass an appropriations act.[24]

At the same time that the deputy governor was unsuccessfully pressing the legislature for a defense bill, he was actively promoting a militia—three companies in Philadelphia and seven in the Three Lower Counties.[25] Despite opposition from members of the Church of England, he met with limited success.[26] This served to underscore the obstinacy of the assembly, not only to Evans but also to the merchants of the proprietary party whose commerce was endangered by French and Spanish privateers.[27] The deputy governor's continued pressure on the lower house made him very unpopular with that body. Finally, he was openly insulted by one of the representatives. The deputy governor promptly jailed his assailant. If this were not enough to alienate many Pennsylvanians, Evans proceeded to spread a false alarm that a French fleet was coming up the Delaware. Philadelphia was thrown into a panic from which the inhabitants recovered with bitter feelings. The precariously existing militia disintegrated, since no one trusted to serve under the apparently irrational Evans. Furthermore, the false alarm made the defenseless condition of Pennsylvania painfully obvious.[28]

[24]Hazard et al., Pa. Archives, ser. 8, I, 414, 416, 428; Colonial Recs., II, 163; J. Logan to WP, 26 May and 14 July 1704, in HSP, Memoirs, IX, 286, 303; J. Evans to Board of Trade, 30 May 1704, in CSP, 1704–5, sec. 359; R. Quary to Board of Trade, 30 May 1704, in ibid., sec. 353. Evans' account of this situation is in ibid., sec. 599.

[25]Ibid., sec. 359i; J. Logan to WP, 25 and 26 May 1704, in HSP, Memoirs, IX, 285, 287.

[26]J. Logan to WP, 28 September 1704, in ibid., pp. 317–318.

[27]Root, Relations, p. 271.

[28]J. Logan to WP, 28 May, 12 June, 10 August 1707, in HSP, Memoirs, X, 122–136, 144–145.

Had this been the deputy governor's only error, Penn would have forgiven him. Evans became, however, more and more unpredictable. Nor did he attempt to justify his actions; on the contrary, he simply stopped writing to Penn. The proprietor had no choice but to discharge him.[29] To replace Evans, Penn appointed Charles Gookin, a man whose military background recalled to mind former Deputy Governor Blackwell. The difference was that Gookin had the positive backing of the proprietor, who wrote enthusiastically about him to James Logan. The provincial secretary replied honestly: "Were he a Solomon, he will certainly meet with enough to try his temper."[30]

Gookin arrived in Pennsylvania in early 1709, the same year in which the Crown decided, after a long period of inactivity, to mount an intensive campaign against the French in the North. The new deputy governor was put in

[29]As usual, Penn was very reluctant to act against one of his appointees. He gave the deputy governor fair chance to vindicate himself, but Evans disregarded the proprietor (WP to J. Evans, 15 May 1707, in *ibid.*, pp. 220–222; WP to J. Evans, 27 May 1708, in ACM, XLVI, 321–324; WP to J. Logan, 3 May 1708, in HSP, *Memoirs*, X, 267–268). The governor was successful elsewhere, as Logan pointed out: "Colonel Evans...is now entirely dead to all his former friends and acquaintances, and lies buried, I think, night and day in the fair Rebecca's arms, that was, but is now the equally fair Madame Evans, which name she assumed in church, the 28th of 8 br last, I hope much to her satisfaction" (J. Logan to ?, 8 November 1708, in *ibid.*, p. 300). Rebecca was John Moore's daughter, a fact which caused Logan some worry during the courtship, due to Moore's connection with the Anglican party (J. Logan to WP, 24 June 1708, in *ibid.*, p. 277).

[30]*CSP, 1706–8*, sec. 1495; *CSP, 1708–9*, sec. 37; WP to J. Logan, 11 September 1708, in HSP, *Memoirs*, X, 288–289; J. Logan to ?, 22 November 1708, in *ibid.*, p. 305; J. Logan to WP, 3, 17, and 24 February 1708/09, in *ibid.*, pp. 308, 312, 316; WP to Friends in Pennsylvania, 1708, in Janney, *Penn*, pp. 524–525; WP to J. Logan, 29 December 1708, in *ibid.*, pp. 523–524.

the awkward position of having to go before the assembly with a request for 150 men or £4,000 to be used for the invasion of Canada and the recapture of Newfoundland. The representatives refused to send men and proclaimed that they "could not in Conscience provide money to hire Men to kill each other." But they were willing to grant £500 to the Queen "as a Testimony of our unfeigned Loyalty, & thankful acknowledgements of Her Grace and Clemency towards us." Gookin tried, but without success, to have the assembly augment its grant. He had therefore to inform the commanders of the expedition to Canada and Newfoundland that he had failed to obtain the necessary supply, though he was "assisted by the Councill and most of the men of note in the Town, Quakers and others."[31]

What Gookin did not realize was that the proprietary forces had won the day. Although the deputy governor did not get the full amount of money he requested, he nevertheless received a great concession. The assembly's violation of the pacifist ideal was only thinly veiled. Yet the composition of the lower house in 1709 did not differ from that of its predecessors which had refused to grant military appropriations. (The grant of £2,000 without restrictions as to use in 1711 *can* be explained by the altered composition of the assembly.) The change of heart in 1709 was apparently due to the attack made by a French privateer on Lewes, Delaware, in May. Never before had the war been so close to home.[32] This was not, of course, Penn's reason

[31]Robert L. D. Davidson, *War Comes to Quaker Pennsylvania, 1682–1756* (New York, 1957), pp. 17–18; *Colonial Recs.,* II, 449–467; C. Gookin to Colonels Nicholson and Vetch, 17 June 1709, in *CSP, 1708–9,* sec. 580.

[32]On the composition of the 1709 assembly, see J. Logan to WP, 29 August 1709, in HSP, *Memoirs,* X, 357; on the 1711 assembly, see Isaac Norris to J. Logan, 28 August 1711, in *ibid.,* p. 436. A brief account of the attack on Lewes is in Tolles, *Logan,* pp. 48–49.

for disregarding pacifism. But the significant development was the gradual closing of the division in the Quaker community with regard to defense.[33]

There was no division among Friends concerning the public administration of oaths. All opposed this practice, including William Penn, who knew this issue was not so important to the home government as the problem of defense. But the proprietor underestimated the storm that would be created when the Anglicans and the Quakers clashed head on.

The trouble began when the Pennsylvania assembly passed a law in 1700—while Penn was in the province— which allowed anyone whose conscience prevented him from swearing to give an affirmation rather than take an oath.[34] This act conflicted with an English statute, passed in 1696, which forbid the use of an affirmation when evidence was given in criminal cases, when serving on juries and when qualifying for an official position in the government.[35] Furthermore, while the Pennsylvania legislation was not intended to force Quaker practice on anyone outside the denomination, it did just that. For, given the number of official positions held by Friends, who would no more administer than take an oath, it was often impossible for a person to swear even if he wanted to do so.

Immediately the vestry of Christ Church wrote to the

[33]Daniel J. Boorstin, in his provocative but ironically dogmatic book, *The Americans, The Colonial Experience* (New York, 1958), denigrates this (see p. 52) and other evidence of Quaker adaptation to the New World environment.

[34]Mitchell and Flanders, *Pa. Statutes,* II, 39–42.

[35]Root, *Relations,* p. 235. There is an accurate description of the problem of oaths in early eighteenth century Pennsylvania in *ibid.,* pp. 234–255, and in Shepherd, *Proprietary Government,* pp. 351–369.

Board of Trade, the Archbishop of Canterbury, and the Bishop of London in angry protest.[36] The Anglicans were sincere in expressing their doubts about the binding nature of the affirmation. But their portrayal of the Quaker province as a place where crime went unpunished, and the assertion that members of the Church of England had enjoyed free exercise of religion only until Penn's arrival, were distortions of the facts. The influence of Robert Quary could be seen in their claim that the only remedy was to royalize Pennsylvania.

Penn had given Anglicans positions in his provincial government. He viewed their protest as a greedy and unwarranted desire for more power, and he claimed that they were trying to "make us Dissenters in our own Countrey."[37] When the proprietor returned to England (closely followed by Quary, who brought the matter of oaths before the Board of Trade), he maintained that the laws of Pennsylvania had to conform to the views of Quakers, who had founded the colony with him. The Board did not find this position satisfactory, but its members informed Penn that "they were willing at present to acquiess with it."[38] This was not true, however. The Board had been unfriendly to Penn since Locke resigned, and it was particularly perturbed at the moment because the Quaker

[36]Vestrymen of Christ Church, Philadelphia, to Board of Trade, in *CSP, 1701,* sec. 101; see also *BTPr.,* VI[1] (1701–1702), G 13; VI[2] (1701–1702), I 2.

[37]WP to C. Lawton, 1700, in Hazard *et al., Pa. Archives,* ser. 1, I, 141; WP to R. Harley, [c. 1701], in HMC, *Portland,* IV, 30–32. Note that Penn suggested that Lawton use a similar argument in defense of Pennsylvania before Parliament (see Chapter VI, page 202).

[38]*CSP, 1702,* sec. 508, 1207, 1208; *CSP, 1702–3,* secs. 3, 9. For references to the dialogue between Quary and Penn, see Chapter VI, note 66.

proprietor had been able to get his deputy governor approved by the Queen against its recommendations.[39] In retaliation the Board requested that the Crown require all persons assuming public office in Pennsylvania to take an oath or an affirmation, as conformable to English law, and require also that all persons who "are obliged and are willing to take an oath in any public office or judicial proceeding, be admitted to do so by the proper officers and judges in Pennsylvania and the said Counties." On the same day, the approbation of Penn's deputy governor and the Board's request were issued as two Orders in Council.[40]

Penn protested against this Order on religious and constitutional grounds. In the first place, many positions now held by Quakers would no longer be open to them because of their aversion to administering oaths. Furthermore, the Crown had no right to extend a specifically English law to the plantations. This was a violation of the royal charter, which reserved to the proprietor and freemen the right to legislate. Penn concluded that only Parliament or the provincial assembly had the right to do what the Crown was now attempting by force of the prerogative, and he asked that the Order in Council be changed to an instruction. Penn argued carefully and persuasively; he was fighting for a religious and legal cause he truly believed in,

[39]Quary told the Board that the deputy governor in question, Andrew Hamilton, was a man of "good sense and parts," but had been "head of the Quakers' faction" in the Jerseys. Given the similar political situation in Pennsylvania, Hamilton was "the most unfittest person for that Government in the world." Edward Randolph accused Hamilton of fostering illegal trade with the Scots while governor of New Jersey (*CSP, 1702*, secs. 609, 611). Penn took his case directly to the Queen, who approved Hamilton, thus evoking a petulant message from the Board (*ibid.*, secs. 1019, 1115, 1141, 1142).

[40]21 January 1702/03 (*CSP, 1702–3*, secs. 218–220).

rather than deviously defending the irresponsible acts of the Pennsylvanians. But he lost the battle, even though it was unmistakably clear that the second part of the royal order was unrealistic in view of the preponderance of Quaker officeholders.[41]

The provincial council tried to convince Quary of this fact when he returned to Pennsylvania with the Order in Council. James Logan was pessimistic as to whether the courts of Bucks and Chester Counties could continue functioning. A few months later John Moore reported to Quary that in Philadelphia County the only remaining justices were Anglicans.[42] But the vice-admiralty judge was not concerned that the provincial courts function; he wanted the provincial government undermined. Logan informed Penn that Quary "boasts that he not only foiled thee before the Lords of Trade, but had gained his point before the Queen herself." At this, continued the secretary caustically, Quary's allies "hug themselves, and are over-grown with expectation of all becoming Dons, & c."[43] Logan was not exaggerating when he implied that the Anglican party was intent on discrediting the Quaker government.[44]

Penn thought that this problem could be resolved if Quary could be disposed of. In March, 1703, the proprietor was somehow able to obtain Quary's removal along with John Moore, who was serving as attorney general of the province.[45] Only a few months earlier the vice-admiralty

[41]*BTPr.*, VII (1702–4), L 18; *BTJ,* XV (1702–1703), 396.

[42]Root, *Relations,* pp. 240–241; J. Logan to WP, 7 and 11 September 1703, in HSP, *Memoirs,* IX, 236, 239; J. Moore to R. Quary, 7 September 1703, in *CSP, 1702–3,* sec. 1150 iii.

[43]J. Logan to WP, 1 December 1702, in HSP, *Memoirs,* IX, 144–145.

[44]For illustrations of this, see Root, *Relations,* pp. 241–243.

[45]*Ibid.,* p. 114; *CSP, 1702,* sec. 665; WP to J. Logan, 20 and 24

judge had reported to the Board of Trade that "Mr. Penn had filled the heads of all his friends with strange notions of his extraordinary great influence at Court.... The Quakers...endeavor to persuade all men that Mr. Penn is the chief steersman at the helm of Government in England." After his dismissal, Quary warned the Board that his successor was no more than Penn's puppet, which enhanced the proprietor's influence even more.[46]

Nothing could have moved the Board more quickly to Quary's defense, which was doubtless why he made this statement.[47] The Board's recommendation that Quary be reinstated was carried out within a few months.[48] Penn's alleged "influence at Court" was minimal.[49] In fact, the proprietor had lost touch with official circles. He repeated-

February 1702/03, in HSP, *Memoirs,* IX, 163, 170. How Penn accomplished Quary's dismissal is nowhere evident in the records. The temporary nature of Penn's victory suggests that the Board of Trade was caught off guard.

[46]R. Quary to Board of Trade, 7 December 1702 and 25 July 1703, in *CSP, 1702–3,* secs. 16, 950.

[47]*BTJ,* XVI (1703–1704), 239; *CSP, 1702–3,* sec. 1180.

[48]HSP, *Memoirs,* IX, 285; *CSP, 1702–3,* secs. 1133, 1136, 1140; *CSP, 1704–5,* sec. 118; Shaw, *Cal. Treas. Books,* XVIII (1703), 439.

[49]When Lord Cornbury, son of the Earl of Clarendon and nephew of the Earl of Rochester, was appointed governor of New York, Penn viewed him as a possible ally and suggested that the Quakers treat him as such, which they did. Cornbury, however, turned to the Anglicans, revived the issue of oaths and apparently hoped to attach Pennsylvania to New York. Penn finally admitted that he had influence neither with Clarendon nor Rochester (*DAB,* IV, 441–442; Tolles, *Logan,* p. 38; WP to J. Logan, 4 January 1701/02, in HSP, *Memoirs,* IX, 73–75; J. Logan to WP, 18, 23, and 25 April 1702, in *ibid.,* pp. 109–110; WP to J. Logan, 6 September 1702, in *ibid.,* p. 133; J. Logan to WP, 1 December 1702, 14 June, 9 July, and 2 September 1703, in *ibid.,* pp. 158, 191, 202, 221–225; WP to J. Logan, 27 August 1703, in *ibid.,* p. 205; Cornbury to Board of Trade, 29 May 1703, in *CSP, 1702–3,* sec. 761; see also *ibid.,* secs. 941, 962, 984).

ly assured Logan that he had reached an amicable relationship with the Board, and when Quary was reappointed,
he was sure that the Board would caution the vice-admiralty judge to act more moderately.[50] Instead, the Board
reinforced Quary's independence by obtaining for John
Moore the appointment as collector at the port of Philadelphia.[51] That Penn could so clearly misplace his confidence was evidence that the strain of affairs was taking
its toll on him.

While the proprietor attempted to carry on his business
in England, he was hopeful that his new deputy governor,
John Evans, would have a salutary effect on conditions in
Pennsylvania. He warned Evans to have "a close eye upon
Coll. Quarry and J. Moore" and to distrust their promises.
But Evans should not sidestep the main issue dividing
Quakers and Anglicans: he must ensure the functioning
of the courts and allow the affirmation, lest Friends be
excluded from government. Warned of the power of the
Anglican party, Evans acted accordingly. When he arrived
in Pennsylvania, he immediately called upon Quary and
Moore to administer the oath of office to him.[52] Further-

[50]WP to J. Logan, 4 December 1703, 10 March 1703/04, 10 July
1704, in HSP, *Memoirs,* IX, 247–248, 271, 294–295; *Jour. of B. of T.,*
I (April 1704–January 1708/09), 12; Board of Trade to R. Quary,
11 May 1704, in *CSP, 1704–5,* sec. 312. This letter from the Board to
Quary was very moderate, as James Logan was dismayed to find out
(J. Logan to WP, 5 April 1705, in HSP, *Memoirs,* X, 7).

[51]*CSP, 1702–3,* sec. 1045; J. Moore to Bishop of London, 24 July
1704, in HSP, *Memoirs,* IV, pt. 2, p. 350; Shaw, *Cal. Treas. Books,*
XIX (January 1704–March 1705), 417.

[52]Evans' instructions are cited above, in n. 22. The relevance of
having Quary and Moore administer the oath to the executive grew
out of the quarrel between the provincial council and the royal
commissioners in the interim between the terms of deputy governors
Hamilton and Evans (see above, n. 44).

more, only nine out of the sixteen men chosen to serve on the provincial council were Quakers, causing Logan to admire Evans' finesse in dealing with Anglicans: "[He] is inclinable to make as fair weather as he can in the government, which doubtless is not unadvisable."[53] Evans had been in Pennsylvania barely a month when he assured the Board of Trade that all the quarterly courts of the province were holding session.[54] It appeared that the proprietor's hopes for the new deputy governor were justified.

But Evans had not yet encountered the obstinate assembly. This body had drawn up and passed a "Bill for the Affirmation to pass instead of the Oath," which the deputy governor promised to send to England. Then he changed his mind, deciding that the assembly's action was counter to the recent Order in Council and suggesting that the lower house amend the bill to make its operation contingent on the Queen's affirmation. The assembly refused to act on this advice. The courts continued to function, but the fundamental problem remained unsolved.[55]

The lower house remained uncooperative. When it heard that the Board of Trade had recommended disallowance of the act passed in 1700 regarding oaths, it simply passed another act of almost identical nature.[56]

[53] J. Logan to WP, 15 February 1703/04, in HSP, *Memoirs*, IX 268.

[54] J. Evans to Board of Trade, 12 March 1703/04, in *CSP, 1704–5,* sec. 175. It has been asserted that Evans appointed "his Anglican friends to replace Quakers in the Supreme Provincial Court and in the Philadelphia County courts" (Lokken, *Lloyd,* p. 135). No evidence for this statement, nor for the implication that Evans appointed Anglicans to any posts because they were his friends, can be found.

[55] Hazard *et al., Pa. Archives,* ser. 8, I, 415, 426–430; *Colonial Recs.,* II, 225–230, 236.

[56] *CSP, 1704–5,* secs. 604, 1278, 1324, 1463, 1466; *CSP, 1706–8,* secs. 34, 40, 87; Mitchell and Flanders, *Pa. Statutes,* II, 266–272; J. Logan to WP, 29 January 1705/06, in HSP, *Memoirs,* X, 98.

Fortunately, the Attorney General in England, whose opinion of this second law was solicited by the Board, agreed with the Pennsylvania assembly and the position taken earlier by Penn: "as is stated, the greatest part of the inhabitants are Quakers, the Proprietor being also a Quaker, and Quakers by the laws there may have judicial places, I do not see but the Law, which is made with the Spirit of the Quakers, may be allow'd them." The English law allowing Quakers an affirmation rather than oath did not extend to the plantations, said the Attorney General (thus agreeing with Penn's constitutional argument against the Order in Council of 1702/03), and therefore the provincial assembly could frame its own bill for that purpose.[57]

But the Bishop of London, recently appointed a permanent member of the Board, labeled the act "a new instance of Mr. Pence insolence.... I presume the next fit of conscience will be not to allow the sight or conversation of any man upon their holy ground, that can take an oath." Adverse comments came also from the vestry of St. Paul's church in Chester, Pennsylvania, and from Robert Quary.[58] The Board used these and other arguments to put Penn on the defensive, even though he had the backing of the Attorney General. Finally, the Pennsylvania law was dis-

[57]A. G. to Board of Trade, 9 July 1706, in *CSP, 1706–8,* sec. 422. The English statute referred to was passed in 1689 (see Chapter III, note 1, above).

[58]Bishop of London to Board of Trade, 4 July 1706, in *ibid.,* sec. 415; *DNB,* IV, 902; R. Quary to Board of Trade, 28 June 1707, in O'Callaghan and Fernow, *N. Y. Colonial Docs.,* V, 17–20.

When the issue of oaths became hot, Penn noted that "the great blower-up of these coals [is] the Bishop of London" (WP to J. Logan, 8 April 1704, in HSP, *Memoirs,* IX, 278). But Penn's contention that the Bishop was then "under humiliations" is not borne out by Edward Carpenter's *The Protestant Bishop* (London, 1956), an account of the life of Henry Compton.

allowed.[59] In the 1680's Penn had been the beneficiary of the English government's capricious approach to decisions regarding the plantations, but he was no longer so fortunate.

It was unfortunate also that the matter of oaths was continually pertinent (unlike the military issue) and, consequently, continually an irritant in Penn's relations with the home government. Nor was there any real solution, as Isaac Norris, a prominent Quaker merchant, pointed out to the proprietor:

We say, our principles are not destructive or repugnant to Civil Government, and will admit of free liberty of conscience to all; yet to me it appears, according to the best scheme I can form, from the opinions of many Friends, to be concerned in Government and hold them, we must either be independent and entirely by ourselves; or, if mixed, partial to our own opinion, and not allow the liberty to others, who make conscience, they say, to have an oath, we desire from them; or be, as thou used to express it, 'Dissenters in our own country.'[60]

The political basis of the "holy experiment" had already been seriously weakened. Norris stated that the religious foundation had also proved unworkable.

The Quaker merchant did not suggest that the Friends' principles be compromised. Rather, he feared that "it must be a Governour immediately from the Crown that must set us to rights."[61] Penn, too, had several times despaired of salvaging the "holy experiment." He had unsuc-

---

[59]Root, *Relations,* p. 245; *Jour. of B. of T.,* I (April 1704–January 1708/09), 272–273, 396, 404; *CSP, 1706–8,* secs. 569, 628, 708, 1049, 1098, 1227, 1247, 1267; Isaac Norris to J. Logan, 14 July 1707, in HSP, *Memoirs,* X, 239; WP to J. Logan, 8 July 1707, in *ibid.,* p. 235.

[60]Isaac Norris to WP, 29 November 1710, in HSP, *Memoirs,* X, 431.

[61]Isaac Norris to Joseph Pike, 18 March 1709/10, in *ibid.,* p. 423.

cessfully negotiated for the sale of his government in 1703, had twice renewed negotiations (again without success) since that time, and had just brought up the matter for the fourth time when he received Norris' letter in 1710.[62]

Progressive disillusionment with the course of affairs in the province and the consequences of these developments in England had caused Penn to renew negotiations for the sale of Pennsylvania, but he had other reasons as well. His financial situation had deteriorated even further, until he was sometimes unable to pay for the processing of colonial business. Even worse, Hannah Penn and her children were forced to live in Bristol with her father.[63] William Penn, Jr., continued to be an economic liability, nor was this defect balanced by any virtues. It was almost inconceivable that he would some day assume the proprietary duties.[64] James Logan, whose judgment was highly

[62]One of the greatest discouragements was the assembly party, which carried its attack on the proprietor to the utmost limits in a "Remonstrance" prepared by David Lloyd. Penn was accused of being a tyrant who neither honored the frames of government nor looked after the colony's best interests in England. But he was charged not to surrender the government! The "Remonstrance" was sent to Friends in England who were to present it to the proprietor. But by a strange coincidence, Penn received it first. (J. Logan to WP, 28 September and 27 October 1704, in *ibid.*, IX, 317, 338–339; Logan paper, n. d., in *ibid.*, pp. 331–332; D. Lloyd to G. Whitehead *et al.*, 3 October 1704, in *ibid.*, p. 327; Lokken, *Lloyd*, p. 153. Lokken does not explain why Lloyd opposed royal government.)

[63]Peare, *Penn*, p. 391; J. Logan to WP, 26 May and 14 July 1704, in HSP, *Memoirs*, IX, 288, 299; H. Penn to J. Logan, 5 October 1704, in *ibid.*, p. 335 (postmarked Bristol); WP to J. Logan, 11 July 1704, in *ibid.*, p. 297.

[64]The young man wrote to his father from Pennsylvania: "I am Extreamly well Pleas'd wth the place now I am here. I have been at Pensbury & like itt well. believe If thee wouldst allow me a Good Gardiner I could make it one of the pleasantest places in the world. . . . I begg I may have some more hounds sent over for they

valued by Penn, encouraged the sale of Pennsylvania.[65]

But the proprietor had a stronger sentimental attachment to the colony than his provincial secretary did. He approached the prospect of surrendering his government with reluctance and circumspection. Negotiations which he began in October 1704 were carried on sporadically for over one year, until his desire for a guarantee of complete liberty of conscience and Quaker eligibility for any civil office could not be reconciled with the Board's demand for unconditional surrender. (He also requested that Bucks County be transformed into a palatinate—and this amounted to still another rejection of the "holy experiment.") Surrender negotiations were terminated for two years.[66]

During this interim period, Penn was deeply involved in litigation with the Fords. Meanwhile, Deputy Governor Evans was alienating the Pennsylvanians and, when hostility toward him was at its peak, he committed the supreme

---

will do mighty well over here. The stalion two that I spoke off. . . . The promest to Gett for me he is a fine horse and well worth sending" (William Penn, Jr., to WP, 15 February 1703/04, in ACM, LXXII, 191–192).

As a result of a tavern brawl and consequent court arraignment, William Penn, Jr., claimed he had been treated disrespectfully. He gave this as his reason for leaving both the Society of Friends and the province of Pennsylvania (Isaac Norris to Jonathan Dickinson, 27 September 1704, in HSP, *Memoirs*, IX, 315; J. Logan to WP, 28 September 1704, in *ibid.*, pp. 318, 320; Isaac Norris to WP, 11 October 1704, in *ibid.*, p. 337).

[65]Logan had urged a surrender in the summer of 1703. Now his suggestions in this regard were more circumspect and subtle as he tried to convince Penn that there was no reasonable alternative (see letters written in autumn of 1704, in *ibid.*, pp. 323, 340, 348–350).

[66]WP to Edward Southwell, 20 February 1704/05, in ACM, XLV, 107; *CSP, 1704–5*, secs. 786, 788, 809, 810, 945, 946, 1126, 1156, 1158; *BTPr.*, VIII[1] (1704–1705), N 32, N 43; *Jour. of B. of T.*, I (April 1704–January 1708/09), 77, 131, 143, 169, 181, 183–184.

folly of calling for the election of a new assembly. Logan called it "the worst that ever I knew in the Province." The legislature responded with an attempt to impeach the provincial secretary, who now pressed Penn to renew negotiations for surrender. But this time the proprietor made only a perfunctory attempt to sell, since his flagging energy was completely absorbed by the Ford affair.[67]

Yet when the Ford business was resolved more favorably than Penn had reason to expect, he found that provincial affairs were in as bad a state as ever. The Anglican party remained a source of endless trouble.[68] The assembly was becoming even more independent.[69] James Logan could well ask the proprietor: "Why shouldst thou contend for those who so little regard thee, or consider anything further than thy own interest, and the ease of such of thy Friends here who really deserve the title?"[70]

Penn responded as Logan had hoped he would. He was infuriated by the continued opposition of the assembly, and he wondered, rhetorically, how long the leaders of the antiproprietary Quakers would "have lived in England before they had been members of assembly and justices of peace? Have they forgot their low circumstances? I have not!"[71] This outburst by the proprietor was in direct con-

[67]Shepherd, *Proprietary Government,* pp. 190–198; HSP, *Memoirs,* X, 94–95; J. Logan to WP, 6 October and 26 November 1706, in *ibid.,* pp. 171, 180; *Colonial Recs.,* II, 262–271; HSP, Logan Papers, IV.

[68]"Colonel Quary has broke his word, by vile letters he sent against us," Penn wrote, "and I think Dr. Oates was a saint to him" (WP to J. Logan, 11 September 1708, in HSP, *Memoirs,* X, 289).

[69]The assembly met of its own will in March 1708/09, and when deputy governor Gookin challenged its ability to do this, the assembly replied that Gookin was listening to "evil council" (*Colonial Recs.,* II, 449–461).

[70]J. Logan to WP, 14 June 1709, in HSP, *Memoirs,* X, 350–351.

[71]WP to J. Logan, 14 October 1709, in ACM, XLVII, 186–194.

flict with his initial political program for Pennsylvania, which was to allow Quakers participation in government in America because they were denied this opportunity in England. When Penn got word that an assembly of the same nature was elected in October, 1709,[72] he sent to the inhabitants of Pennsylvania a long and deep-felt letter, reviewing his reasons for founding the colony, its subsequent history, and the many difficulties he had suffered on its account. Whereas in 1681 Penn had stressed the benefits to be had by prospective colonists in his "holy experiment," he now emphasized that he "had reason to expect a solid comfort from the services done to many hundreds of people; and...I have not been disappointed in seeing them prosper. . . . But, alas! as to my part, instead of reaping the like advantages, some of my greatest troubles have arisen from thence." He had granted political concessions; the colonists had only taken advantage of his good nature, and their disputes blackened the name of the province. They had refused him financial support. He concluded: "The opposition I have met from thence must at length force me to consider more closely of my own private and sinking circumstances in relation to that province."[73]

On considering more closely his own circumstances, Penn decided to renew negotiations for the sale of his government. When he had first attempted this in 1703, he had stipulated a number of conditions which had to be accepted if the transaction were to succeed. He had even expected to retain a veto on the "Laws and Constitutions" and to be able to nominate the "governor and Vice Ad-

[72]*Colonial Recs.,* II, 502; Hazard *et al., Pa. Archives,* ser. 8, II, 911.

[73]WP to Friends in Pennsylvania, 29 June 1710, in Janney, *Penn,* pp. 529–534.

miral" of the colony. In 1710 he asked only that his ownership of the soil of the Three Lower Counties be confirmed,
that the rights of the inhabitants of Pennsylvania be re-
spected, and that "some particular mark of respect to be
continued to his family, for distinguishing them above the
rank of those who have planted under him."[74] While this
latter request was an odd one for a Quaker to make, it
shows the direction Penn was traveling with regard to the
"holy experiment."

The Board of Trade presented Penn's offer to the
Queen, commenting only that "the revesting the Government of Pennsylvania in your Majesty will be a benefit"
to trade and obedience to the navigation acts, to royal
authority, the administration of justice, defense and "the
strengthening the British interest, upon the Northern Continent of America."[75] The proprietor could hope for good
treatment by the Crown without the Board's aid, however.
His close friend Robert Harley had been appointed Chancellor of the Exchequer a year earlier. More recently he
had been titled the first Earl of Oxford and designated
Lord High Treasurer.[76] And indeed, Oxford did take
charge of the matter, ordering the Attorney General to
study the Board's report, Charles II's original grant, and
other related documents. The Attorney General's only
reservation was the lack of "any provision made for the
support of the Govt. there by any Act of Assembly, or
otherwise, without wch. the Government will be a charge

[74]*CSP, 1710–1711,* sec. 326; *Jour. of B. of T.,* II (February 1708/
09–March 1714/15), p. 191.

[75]*CSP, 1710–11,* sec. 649; Lord Dartmouth to WP, 15 February
1710/11, in HSP, Penn-Forbes Collection, II, 42.

[76]Penn's correspondence with Harley at this time is in HMC,
Portland, V, 17–18, 125.

to H.M."[77] But Penn could now point to just such an appropriation. The assembly elected in October, 1710, was entirely sympathetic to him. Not one member from the previous body was returned! It voted £500 for the support of the government and £200 to Penn for negotiating the laws passed by the legislature.[78] Penn could honestly tell Oxford, who would decide on the price to be paid for the Pennsylvania government, that the assembly was reliable.

But as Penn's case became stronger, the proprietor himself was enfeebled by a stroke. He was weakened to the point of requesting that a conference with the Lord High Treasurer be at his home rather than at the office because he was "wearing a night gown still, wch makes an odd figure at the Treasury."[79] On March 12, 1712, Penn was paid £1,000, although the deed of surrender had not as yet been completed. A month later he was too ill to carry on his affairs. He recovered sufficiently to reach an agreement with Oxford and the Chancellor of the Exchequer, whereby he would receive £12,000 to be paid from the date of surrender over a period of four years.[80] In October

[77]Attorney General to Lord High Treasurer, 25 February 1712: *CSP, 1711–12*, sec. 331. The deed of surrender is in HSP, Penn-Forbes Collection, I, 13–14.

[78]*Colonial Recs.*, II, 538; Provincial Assembly to WP, 28 February 1710/11, in HSP, Pa. Misc. Papers, Penn & Baltimore, Penn Family, p. 75; Provincial Council to WP, April–May 1711, in HSP, Penn MSS, Official Correspondence, I, 45. In relation to the negotiation of laws, see *Jour. of B. of T.*, II (February 1708/09–March 1714/15), 297, 303, 314, 317; *CSP, 1711–12*, secs. 58, 203, 221. The laws themselves, with dates of confirmation or repeal, appear in Mitchell and Flanders, *Pa. Statutes*, II, 301–399.

[79]WP to Oxford, 28 February 1711/12, in Reddington, *Cal. Treas. Papers*, IV (1708–14), 362.

[80]*Ibid.*, pp. 360, 428; Shaw, *Cal. Treas. Books*, XXVI (1712), 17,

he again suffered a stroke, but this time it was more serious. He never recovered but lingered on pathetically for six more years.[81]

No official agreement had been reached on the terms of surrender before Penn's final seizure. In 1714 the Queen in Council tried to perfect the deed by act of Parliament. But the men to whom Penn had mortgaged the province in order to be rid of the Fords now opposed the Crown's move. No parliamentary bill was enacted.[82] It was quite fitting that Penn's illness should prevent the surrender of Pennsylvania, just as his early vigor had been responsible for its existence. He had put his best efforts into nurturing and protecting it through infancy, and now it had reached a hardy maturity. Like his eldest son and namesake, the province was inclined to waywardness, but his love for it had never faltered. Recovering from his first stroke in 1712, he wrote to his closest friends in Pennsylvania:

I purpose to see you, if God give me life, this fall, but I grow old and infirm, yet would gladly see you once more before I die, and my young sons and daughters also settled upon good tracts of land, for them and theirs after them, to clear and settle upon, as Jacob's sons did. I close when I tell you I desire fervent prayers to the Lord for continuing my life, that I may again see Pennsylvania once more before I die.[83]

54; G. Lawton to Oxford, 14 April 1712, in HMC, *Portland*, V, 163. Lawton was worried lest the negotiations not be successfully completed, partly because Penn's want of money made him too niggardly in his fees.

[81]Penn's last letter to Logan and an account of these final years is in Janney, *Penn*, pp. 538–547.

[82]Reddington, *Cal. Treas. Papers*, IV (1708–1714), 574; Chalmers, *Opinions*, I, 351–352.

[83]WP to S. Carpenter, E. Shippen, R. Hill, I. Norris, C. Pusey, S. Preston, T. Story, G. Owen, etc., 24 July 1712, in Janney, *Penn*, pp. 537–538.

But in noting the proprietor's love for his "holy experiment," it must not be forgotten that he moved further and further from the principles on which it was founded, and that the sale of his government was blocked only by the accident of his stroke.

At the end of his career, William Penn could look back on two great accomplishments. He had founded a colony in America which was distinguished by its autonomy at a time when the home government was bringing other plantations into a position of greater subservience and by the ideas embodied in the "holy experiment," which were so strikingly different from the religious and political practices of the Stuarts. Penn's second great accomplishment, more difficult but less obvious than the first, was the defense of his American province for three decades. During these thirty years the home government was more vigorous than at any other period before 1763, and the private colonies were under special scrutiny. Yet Pennsylvania managed to survive with its autonomy relatively unimpaired (though the same could not be said of its original principles), largely as a result of its proprietor's efforts.

As a youth, Penn publicly rejected the Anglican royalist tradition, embracing instead nonconformity and republicanism. The young Quaker used these new religious and political ideas as the basis for the "holy experiment." However, in order to get the land and powers of government needed to establish the experiment, Penn had to depend upon men of his father's persuasion. The "holy experiment" itself showed the proprietor at his creative best, and his reliance on influence at court was both necessary and restrained. But the dualism involved in the founding of Pennsylvania—high ideals and practical politics—was to characterize and complicate Penn's relations with his colonists and the home government over the next three decades.

No sooner had the "holy experiment" been established in Pennsylvania than the Quaker proprietor extended it to the Three Lower Counties. Not only were the inhabitants of this region outside the Society of Friends, but Penn's claim to the area was dubious. When Lord Baltimore challenged his title, Penn's career began to take on its defensive aspect. The Maryland proprietor had a stronger case for ownership of Delaware, but Penn won possession as a result of his court connections.

The Quaker leader's most important ally in the founding of Pennsylvania and the acquisition of the Three Lower Counties was James Stuart, and Penn moderated his stand on the religious and political situation in England as a result of his debt to the new monarch. But he wanted still more from James II—protection for Pennsylvania and the English dissenters. To achieve these goals, Penn exceeded the bounds of moderation. He did not speak his true feelings regarding abrogation of the Test Act, and he gave his silent assent to the policy of tampering with parliamentary elections. At the same time, the political situation in Pennsylvania was developing in a direction not anticipated by the proprietor. Exasperated by the tumultuous proceedings in his province, Penn finally sent a retired military man to take the situation in hand. In other words, he violated the "holy experiment" in America, but not so seriously as he had compromised himself in England.

The end of James II's reign marked a decisive point in Penn's career. From this time forward he was entirely on the defensive. In 1689 his influence at court was virtually nonexistent, while the increased power of Parliament made it necessary that he gain, rather than lose, allies. At the same time, the initiation of King William's War posed a direct challenge to Quaker pacifism. The unwillingness of the Pennsylvanians to compromise on this issue, supplemented by Penn's fall from royal favor, resulted in the annexation of the Quaker government to New York—a development the proprietor had been able to prevent during the reign of James II.

Nevertheless, as the war came to a close Penn was able to regain his government. Here again he was more fortunate than Lord Baltimore: Maryland remained a royal colony until 1715. The Quaker proprietor's re-established connections made the difference, but the situation was not the same as that of 1685. Penn was still on the defensive. He was powerless to prevent the passage and implementation of the Navigation Act of 1696. This was due not only to the advantage held by Edward Randolph and the executive agencies, but also to the problem posed by parliamentary participation in colonial policy-making.

If the new legislation was to be rigorously enforced, the Pennsylvanians would have to be held to its terms. On the other hand, Penn wanted to circumscribe the jurisdiction of the admiralty courts created by this Act. For these reasons, and because he had not been successful in guiding affairs in England, Penn sailed to America. But he found that he could not control affairs in Pennsylvania either. The proprietary interest was represented by only one of four parties. A less important faction represented the political desires of the Three Lower Counties, an area which had never been compatible with the dominant Quaker counties. The most powerful party in Pennsylvania controlled the provincial assembly and was able to get the proprietor's consent to the Charter of Liberties, an important alteration of the political ideas of the "holy experiment." This faction was also a great source of trouble to Penn in his relations with the home government, for the assembly was unwilling to assume the responsibilities assigned to the proprietor by the Crown. The fourth party in Pennsylvania represented the Anglican royalist tradition which Penn had rejected in principle but compromised with in practice.

Unable to regulate affairs in Pennsylvania, harassed by the Board of Trade at home, and realizing that his connections were too weak to be of service to him at a distance of 3,000 miles, Penn returned to England to protect his government against parliamentary attack. Under unfavorable conditions, the best he could hope to do was to maintain the *status quo* in colonial affairs. But this was impossible when the political demands of the home government were irreconcilable with the religious principles of the provincial Quakers, as was illustrated with the issues of defense and oaths.

When Penn convinced his colonists to contribute to the military effort, he was shielding Pennsylvania from the home government at the expense of the "holy experiment." With regard to oaths, the Pennsylvania Quakers could retain their principles only by forcing their views on others—a course which also violated the principles of the "holy experiment." But the greatest deviation from Penn's original ideals was his own effort to dispose of the experiment altogether. The attempts to sell his government were the consequence not only of his dire financial condition but also the frustration involved in reconciling imperial politics with religious principles. And the pressure of imperial politics was due, at least in part, to

Penn's inability to maintain a strong influence within the British government after 1689.

The Quaker leader's physical decline terminated the transaction which was leading to the sale of his government. With the death of Queen Anne began the atrophy of that vigorous colonial policy which had characterized the years of Pennsylvania's founding and early growth. William Penn had carried the colony safely through this period; it could now prosper without the proprietor's protection in the atmosphere of "salutary neglect."

Bibliography

Manuscript Sources

It is the good fortune of Penn scholars to have the manuscript materials concerning his life located in this country. Although the Albert Cook Myers Collection of William Penn Papers (ACM)—located in the Chester County Historical Society, West Chester, Pennsylvania—contains few holographs and autographs, it does have a wealth of accurately transcribed copies of letters from depositories here and in England. Most of these letters were written by Penn. The Historical Society of Pennsylvania (HSP) is the other major source for unpublished documents concerning William Penn.

Also in the Historical Society of Pennsylvania are three series of volumes transcribed from original manuscripts in the Public Records Office, London. The first series is the *Board of Trade, Journals* from 1675 to 1782 (*BTJ*), a ninety-volume record of the meetings and business conducted by the Lords of Trade and the Board of Trade. The second series, twenty-five volumes in length, is the *Board of Trade Papers, Proprietaries* from 1697 to 1776 (*BTPr.*), containing the letters, memorials, petitions, orders in council and such documents sent to the Board concerning the private colonies. The *Board of Trade*

Papers, Plantations General (BTPG), twenty-eight volumes covering the period 1689–1780, contains the same type of material for the royal colonies.

Primary Sources

An evaluation of the major primary sources may be found in Chapter I, notes 40 and 79. The following volumes all proved useful in the preparation of this book. The respective titles clearly indicate the content.

Browne, W. H., *et al.*, eds. *Archives of Maryland.* 65 vols. Baltimore, 1883–1952.

Browning, Andrew, ed. *Memoirs of Sir John Reresby.* Glasgow, 1936.

Chalmers, George. *Opinions of Eminent Lawyers, on various points of English jurisprudence, chiefly concerning the colonies, fisheries and commerce of Great Britain.* 2 vols. London, 1814.

Colonial Records of Pennsylvania, 1683–1790. 16 vols. Philadelphia, 1852–1853.

Dalrymple, John. *Memoirs of Great Britain and Ireland.* 3 vols. London, 1790.

Douglas, David C., ed. *English Historical Documents.* 7 vols. [series incomplete]. London and New York, 1953–1959.

Foxcroft, H. C. *The Life and Letters of George Savile, First Marquis of Halifax.* 2 vols. London and New York, 1898.

George, Staughton, *et al.*, eds. *Charter to William Penn, and Laws of the Province of Pennsylvania, Passed Between the Years 1682 and 1700 Preceded by the Duke of York's Laws.* Harrisburg, 1879.

Grant, W. L., and Munro, James, eds. *Acts of the Privy Council of England: Colonial Series.* 6 vols. London, 1912–1923.

Hazard, Samuel. *Annals of Pennsylvania, from the Discovery of Delaware, 1609–1682.* Philadelphia, 1850.

Hazard, Samuel, *et al.*, eds. *Pennsylvania Archives.* 9 ser., 138 vols. Philadelphia and Harrisburg, 1852–1949.

Historical Manuscripts Commission. *The Manuscripts of His Grace the Duke of Buccleuch and Queensbury, K. G., K. T.* 3 vols. London, 1899–1926.

————. *The Manuscripts of the Earl of Dartmouth.* 3 vols. London, 1887–1896.

————. *Report on the Manuscripts of the Marquess of Downshire.* 4 vols. London, 1924–1940.

————. *The Manuscripts of the Earl of Egmont.* 2 vols. London, Dublin, 1905–1909.

————. *Report on the Manuscripts of Allan George Finch, Esq.* 3 vols. London, 1913–1957.

————. *The Manuscripts of the House of Lords.* 13 vols. [1678–1714]. London, 1887–1953.

————. *The Manuscripts of S. H. LeFleming, Esq., of Rydal Hall.* London, 1890.

————. *The Manuscripts of the Earl of Lonsdale.* London, 1893.

————. *The Manuscripts of His Grace the Duke of Portland. . . .* 10 vols. London, 1891–1931.

————. *The Manuscripts of the Earl of Westmoreland, Captain Stewart, Lord Muncaster and Others.* London, 1885.

Historical Society of Pennsylvania. *Memoirs.* 14 vols. Philadelphia, 1826–1895.

Jennings, Samuel. *Truth Rescued from Forgery and Falsehood.* Philadelphia, 1699.

Journal of the Commissioners for Trade and Plantations from . . .1704 to . . . 1782. 14 vols. London, 1920–1938.

Journals of the House of Lords. 9 vols. [1660–1714]. London, c. 1767–1777.

Marquis of Lansdowne, ed. *The Petty-Southwell Correspondence, 1676–1687.* London, 1928.

Massachusetts Historical Society. *Collections.* 7 ser., 79 vols. Boston, 1792–.

————. *Proceedings.* 3 ser., 96 vols. Boston, 1791–.

Mitchell, J. T., and Flanders, Henry, eds. *Statutes at Large of Pennsylvania from 1682 to 1801*. 17 vols. Harrisburg, 1896–1915.

Myers, A. C., ed. *Narratives of Early Pennsylvania, West New Jersey and Delaware*. New York, 1912.

O'Callaghan, E. B., and Fernow, Berthold, eds. *Documents Relative to the Colonial History of the State of New York*. 15 vols. Albany, 1856–1887.

The Select Works of William Penn. 3d ed. 5 vols. London, 1782.

Reddington, Joseph, ed. *Calendar of Treasury Papers*. 6 vols. London, 1868–1889.

Sainsbury, W. N., *et al*. *Calendar of State Papers, Colonial Series, America and the West Indies*. 26 vols. [1574–1714] London, 1860–1926. (Abbreviated as *CSP*, and the year or years covered by the volume.)

Shaw, William A., ed. *Calendar of Treasury Books*. 27 vols. [1660–1718] London, 1904–1957.

Singer, S. W., ed. *The Correspondence of Henry Hyde...and Lawrence Hyde...with the Diary of Lord Clarendon...1687 to 1690*. 2 vols. London, 1828.

Stock, Leo F., ed. *Proceedings and Debates of the British Parliament respecting North America*. 5 vols. Washington, D.C., 1925–1941.

Thorpe, F. N. *The Federal and State Constitutions, Colonial Charters, and Other Organic Laws*. 7 vols. Washington, D.C., 1909.

Toppan, R. N., and Goodrick, A. T. S. *Edward Randolph: Including His Letters and Official Papers...1676–1703*. 7 vols. Boston, 1898–1909.

Votes and Proceedings of the House of Representatives of the Province of Pennsylvania, 1682–1776. 6 vols. Philadelphia, 1752–76.

Whitehead, W. A., *et al*., eds. *Archives of the State of New Jersey, 1631–1800*. 52 vols. Newark, etc., 1880–1949.

BIBLIOGRAPHY

Secondary Sources

William Penn wrote no autobiography, although he did put together "Fragments of an Apology for Himself" when he was in hiding in the early 1690's. His erstwhile agent in England, Charlewood Lawton, wrote an equally brief account, also with the intent of clearing Penn of the charges of complicity in the unpopular measures of James II. (Both are reproduced in the *Memoirs* of the Historical Society of Pennsylvania, Vol. III, pt. 2, pp. 213–243.) Since that time Penn has been the subject of numerous biographies. William I. Hull's *Eight First Biographies of William Penn in Seven Languages and Seven Lands* (Swarthmore, 1936) is a scholarly and interesting starting point. Professor Hull, who must have known more about Penn than any other man in this century, points out the materials available to and the peculiar emphasis of each of the early biographers. Included in Hull's study are the biographies by Joseph Besse (appended to the "Works" of William Penn), Mason L. Weems, Willem Sewel and Gerard Croese, among others. It is Hull's point of view that: "Full-length biographies of William Penn in England did not begin until Thomas Clarkson, a non-Quaker, wrote one in two volumes and published it in London in 1813. Since that time, numerous others have appeared; but they have all, including Clarkson's, been based on Joseph Besse's biographical sketch of 1726, which was largely autobiographical" (p. xiv).

This statement is undeniable. S. M. Janney's *The Life of William Penn* (Philadelphia, 1851) is usually singled out as the best nineteenth-century study, and it is still valuable. But it virtually reproduces Clarkson's organization and much of his account. Both authors pay particular attention to Penn's religious and political tracts and reproduce many of his letters. W. Hepworth Dixon's biography (London, 1851) relies more on narrative than documentation. Five-sixths of the book is devoted to the years before the Glorious Revolution.

At the turn of the century three biographies were issued,

all in the Besse mold and all especially fascinated by the apparent dichotomy in Penn's life. Sidney George Fisher states in *The True William Penn* (Philadelphia, 1900): "He was double. He was both a cavalier and a Quaker. . . . This double nature was at the same time his strength and his weakness" (pp. 104–105). Augustus C. Buell, whose biography was published in New York in 1904, disputed Fisher's opinion of Penn; "Sometimes he was a great statesman; at other times he was a great Quaker; but he was never both at the same time" (p. 364). Mrs. Colquhoun Grant put the conflict into the title of her book, but that is probably the only noteworthy fact about *Quaker and Courtier* (London, 1907). None of these three biographies discusses Penn's relations with the English government in more than a superficial manner.

Several decades passed before another spate of biographies appeared and, perhaps because of significant changes in the writing of history in the interim, a number of these studies broke from the traditional framework. In *The Making of William Penn* (London, New York, 1930) Mabel R. Brailsford treats only the early life of her subject (to 1681), putting considerable emphasis on childhood influences and Quakerism. She sees a striking parallel between the lives of Penn and his father, rejecting the idea that a great man is a freak of nature. "More perfectly, perhaps, than any other man of his time he [Penn] shared the multifarious life of England, . . . and gathered up into one consistent whole the jarring tendencies of his century" (p. xvii).

Two less successful attempts at reconsideration were made by Bonamy Dobrée in *William Penn, Quaker and Pioneer* (London, 1932) and C. E. Vulliamy in *William Penn* (New York, 1933). Dobrée, asserting that previous biographers had depicted Penn as "too perfect a figure," concludes that Penn was "a trifle too much addicted to the things of this world" to be a perfect Quaker (pp. v, 417). But worldliness made him a more complex and creative person, and consequently a greater man. On the other hand, Vulliamy states: "The true significance of Penn...is that of a broken idealist.... He was the last of the great Puritans. Penn is the Rousseau [about whom Vulliamy had also written a biography] of religious history" (p. 293). While the emphasis in both these books may be contrasted to earlier studies, neither Dobrée nor Vulliamy much altered the framework within which Penn had been treated.

William I. Hull, who pointed out in 1936 that all studies of Penn were based on Besse's model, published *William Penn. A Topical Biography* (London, New York, 1937). Although the book is original in approach and painstaking in research, the essence of Penn as a politician is missing. Hull would rather call his subject a mediator than a courtier because, "although he took a mansion in Hyde Park and was almost continuously calling on the king [James II] in one or another of the royal palaces, the business which he transacted with him...was in behalf of others" (p. 245). This was not the case.

Edward C. O. Beatty's *William Penn as Social Philosopher* (New York, 1939) is also novel in its approach, for it is a study of the mind rather than the life of Penn. The book is interesting and handy, but such practices as comparing Penn's views on monopoly to the theories underlying the National Industrial Recovery Act of 1933 (p. 238) seem farfetched. W. W. Comfort's *William Penn* (London, Philadelphia, 1944) is undistinguished but concise. Its emphasis is on Penn's religious activities.

In 1957 Catherine Owens Peare published *William Penn: A Biography* (Philadelphia, New York), which presents a good synthesis of recent scholarship in an engaging style. It also has the merit of including a complete bibliography of Penn's writings. But, like Hull, Miss Peare does not fully grasp the political implications of William Penn's role as a colonial proprietor.

Sophie Drinker's *Hannah Penn* (Philadelphia, 1958) and Frederick B. Tolles' concise *James Logan and the Culture of*

Provincial America (Boston, Toronto, 1957) give interesting accounts of the two people closest to Penn in his later life. Roy N. Lokken, *David Lloyd, Colonial Lawmaker* (Seattle, 1959), advances the case for Logan's chief antagonist; useful for bits of information, it has real stylistic defects. Information on some of the lesser known colonial governors whose careers affected Pennsylvania can be found in Allen Johnson and Dumas Malone, *Dictionary of American Biography* (22 vols.; New York, 1928–1944), which appears in the footnotes as *DAB*.

The English statesmen and civil servants with whom Penn had close contact have fared well at the hands of their biographers. J. P. Kenyon's *Robert Spencer, Earl of Sunderland, 1641–1702* (London, New York, Toronto, 1958) is excellent. Not far below this work in quality are Maurice Cranston's *John Locke: A Biography* (London, New York, 1957); H. C. Foxcroft's study of George Savile, Marquis of Halifax, entitled *A Character of the Trimmer* (Cambridge, 1946); and F. C. Turner's *James II* (London, 1948). There is a brief sketch of Lawrence Hyde, Earl of Rochester, in John Biggs-Davison, *Tory Lives* (London, 1952); Penn does not appear in it. Other biographies of statesmen with whom Penn had limited association are: Andrew Browning, *Thomas Osborne, Earl of Danby and Duke of Leeds, 1632–1712* (3 vols.; Glasgow, 1944); Edward Carpenter's study of Henry Compton, *The Protestant Bishop* (London, New York, 1956); and Tresham Lever, *Godolphin. His Life and Times* (London, 1952).

With regard to civil servants, Michael G. Hall has written a first-rate account of *Edward Randolph and the American Colonies, 1676–1703* (Chapel Hill, 1960). Less impressive but often useful is Gertrude A. Jacobsen's *William Blathwayt* (New Haven, 1932). Leslie Stephen and Sidney Lee, eds., *Dictionary of National Biography* (63 vols.; London, 1885–1901), which appears in the footnotes as *DNB*, is often of great aid in establishing relationships among English politicians.

David Ogg's *England in the Reign of Charles II* (2nd ed., 2 vols.; Oxford, 1955–1956) and *England in the Reigns of James II and William III* (2nd ed.; Oxford, 1957) provide a most comprehensive and interesting portrait of an age, along with penetrating analyses of some of its main actors. While Ogg's approach is traditional, Robert Walcott, in his *English Politics in the Early Eighteenth Century* (Cambridge, Mass., 1956), applies the Namier thesis in the time of Queen Anne. The role of the Friends in Stuart England is well described in Arnold Lloyd's *Quaker Social History, 1669–1738* (London, New York, 1950).

The development of English imperial policy is clearly shown in the fourth volume of C. M. Andrews, *The Colonial Period of American History* (4 vols.; New Haven, 1934–1938). R. P. Bieber's *The Lords of Trade, 1675–1696* (Allentown, Pa., 1919) is longer than but not so analytical as W. T. Root's "The Lords of Trade and Plantations, 1675–1696," *American Historical Review,* XXIII (1917–1918), 20–41. Philip S. Haffenden's article, "The Crown and the Colonial Charters, 1675–1688," *William and Mary Quarterly,* XV (1958), 297–311, 452–466, is a masterful piece of work. The same topic may be followed into a later period in L. P. Kellogg's "The American Colonial Charter," American Historical Association, *Annual Report for 1903* (Washington, 1904), pt. 1, pp. 185–341.

General problems of imperial administration are treated in E. B. Russell, *The Review of Colonial Legislation by the King in Council* (New York, 1915); J. H. Smith, *Appeals to the Privy Council from the American Plantations* (New York, 1950); C. M. Andrews' introduction to D. S. Towle, ed., *Records of the Vice-Admiralty Court of Rhode Island, 1716–1752* (Washington, D.C., 1936); and G. A. Washburne, *Imperial Control of the Administration of Justice in the Thirteen American Colonies, 1684–1776* (New York, 1923).

The imperial question as it touched the Quaker colony is treated in W. T. Root's *The Relations of Pennsylvania with the British Government, 1696–1765* (New York, 1912). Each point at issue is handled separately so that little attention can be paid to developing trends. Penn's role as an imperial politician is recognized in Alison G. Olson's "William Penn, Parliament and Proprietary Government," *William and Mary Quarterly,* XVIII (1961), 176–195.

W. R. Shepherd's *Proprietary Government in Pennsylvania* (New York, 1896) is a storehouse of useful knowledge, but it should be supplemented by Frederick B. Tolles' *Meeting House and Counting House* (Chapel Hill, 1948) and Edwin B. Bronner's *William Penn's "Holy Experiment." The Founding of Pennsylvania, 1681–1701* (London, New York, 1962). The best source for the boundary controversy between Maryland and Pennsylvania is Edward B. Mathews *et al., Report on the Resurvey of the Maryland–Pennsylvania Boundary Part of the Mason Dixon Line* (Harrisburg, 1909). On the Three Lower Counties see B. A. Konkle, "Delaware: A Grant yet not a Grant," *Pennsylvania Magazine of History and Biography (PMHB),* LIV (1930), 241–254, and R. S. Rodney, "Early Relations of Delaware and Pennsylvania," *ibid.,* pp. 209–240. William H. Loyd's *The Early Courts of Pennsylvania* (Boston, 1910) contains some valuable information, as does C. H. Smith's "Why Pennsylvania Never Became a Royal Province," *PMHB,* LIII (1929), 141–158.

This is not a complete list of the secondary sources I have used in the preparation of this book, but only an acknowledgment of the most useful and significant. Other works are cited in the footnotes.

Index

261